$\leq l$

W9-BDQ-718

WITHDRAWN

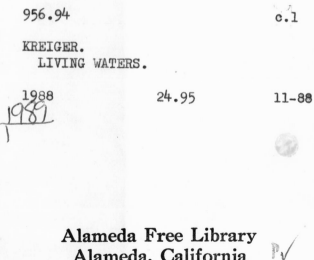

LIVING WATERS

LIVING WATERS

Myth, History, and Politics
of The Dead Sea

Barbara Kreiger

Foreword by Noel Perrin

c. 1

CONTINUUM · NEW YORK

1988

The Continuum Publishing Company
370 Lexington Avenue
New York, NY 10017

Printed in the United States of America

A Seth Press Book

Library of Congress Cataloging-in-Publication Data

Kreiger, Barbara.
    Living waters : myth, history, and politics of the Dead Sea /
Barbara Kreiger ; foreword by Noel Perrin.
        p.   cm.
    Includes index.
    ISBN 0-8264-0406-5
    1. Dead Sea Region (Israel and Jordan)—History.   2. Dead Sea
(Israel and Jordan)—History.   I. Title.
DS110.D38K73 1988
956.94—dc19   88-10924
                                                                               CIP

For Alan and Saul

Contents

Photograph gallery follows p. 128.

Foreword

For so small a country—it's less than one percent the size of the United States—Israel contains a truly astonishing number of famous sites. There are small towns whose names almost every Christian knows, and has sung a thousand times, such as Bethlehem and Nazareth and Jericho. There are ancient fortress sites such as Masada, known to even the most secular Jew; there are remnants of crusader cities like Acre. There is Jerusalem itself, the city that shares with Rome and perhaps Athens the honor of being the very archetype of what people in the West have meant by a city. There's the river Jordan, more famous than the Mississippi or the Amazon, though infinitely smaller than either. There's that fairly large lake (about two-thirds of one percent the size of Lake Erie) known as the Sea of Galilee. And there is also the lowest and saltiest body of water in the world, the Dead Sea.

Like most people who have never visited Israel, I've tended to have a comic-strip view of all these places. Well, not exactly comic strip: more like the illuminations in a medieval manuscript. If I think of Bethlehem, of course I see the manger, the ox and ass, the shepherds and the wise men. What I don't see is the motor traffic of 1988, the restaurants and hotels in Manger Square, the people in jeans and sweatshirts pouring into Siniora's Butcher Shop to pick up six pork chops or a pound of bacon. If I think of the Sea of Galilee, I see St. Peter walking on the waves, and I see on the shore about ten thousand people in archaic clothes eating loaves and fishes for dinner. I do not see the high-rise Tiberias Plaza Hotel, much less the Vered Ha Galil Dude Ranch.

As for the Dead Sea, my image has been even more vague and romantic, deriving less from the Bible than from that dramatic and resonant name. In my mind's eye I have seen something large and somber and almost unearthly: a remote place of silence and strangeness.

I have not been alone in this. For two thousand years, at least, the

Dead Sea has been the object of romantic speculation. Many people have believed strange things about it. Some of these beliefs do derive from the Bible, such as that under its dark surface lie hidden the destroyed cities of Sodom and Gomorrah. Some are pure medieval superstition, such as the story that iron will float on the surface, while light things like feathers sink. Or that other story, still current when the European explorer Ulrich Seetzen arrived in 1807, that if a flock of birds were rash enough to fly out over the Dead Sea, they would suddenly all crash lifeless down, and then vanish into the depths. Some are based on natural phenomena, such as the report by a fourteenth-century pilgrim that during storms the Dead Sea casts up beautiful pebbles—and if later you run down to the shore and pick one up, your hand will smell horrible for three days.

The sea casts up no such pebbles. But it *does* send lumps of natural asphalt floating up, and not only pebble-sized ones, but pieces as big as a school bus. The Bedouin used to go out in boats, and cut them up to sell. Pick up a lump of fresh asphalt, and your hand might indeed get dirty. Add that there are sulphur springs in places along the shore, springs sending up enough fumes so that one of the old Arab names for the Dead Sea was the Stinking Lake, and you see how the pilgrim's story might get started.

To read Barbara Krieger's *Living Waters* is to turn this vague picture into sharp reality. The motionless sea of the illuminated manuscript suddenly develops waves, and a two-lane paved road along the shore, and factories, and health resorts. But it does not lose its strangeness or its beauty. On the contrary, these get emphasized, as the background is filled in, and one begins to hear the crash of waterfalls in the wild mountain gorges by the Dead Sea, and to see the mists rising, and the ever-changing colors of the low waves, perhaps to notice fresh leopard tracks near the shore.

About this remarkable place Barbara Kreiger has written a remarkable book. It does at least four things at once. In the first place, it gives a natural history of the Dead Sea, from its really rather recent beginning 12,000 years ago up to the present. One learns how it came to be the lowest place on earth, and where that asphalt floats up from, and what happens to fish who get washed down from the river Jordan.

The book also gives the human history of the Dead Sea. It's a history approximately the same age as the sea itself, since, as Ms. Kreiger points out, civilization seems to have begun at Jericho, some ten or twelve millennia back. That is, civilization probably began—and the first city was probably built—about five miles from the Dead Sea.

The human history of the sea is both complex and fascinating.

Though no life, or almost none, can exist in the sea itself, much life has come from it, or been healed by it. Two thousand years ago rich Romans were importing Dead Sea water for use in their hot tubs, at the same time that religious Jews were freely bathing in the sea itself, and shipping jars of its water up to Jerusalem. They could do these things even on the Sabbath because a special exemption had been made on health grounds.

Today it is the sun more than the water that enjoys a curative reputation (though Dead Sea salts can be bought in pharmacies in and out of Israel). Because this is the lowest place on earth—four times as far below sea level as its puny American rival, Death Valley—the air is thicker than anywhere else on earth. One consequence of *that* is that most of the ultraviolet rays are filtered out. Sunshine is thus safer here than anywhere else on earth. Psoriasis patients, for example, who need sunshine for their cures, can and do sunbathe on the shores for six or seven hours a day, with no fear of getting burnt.

The Dead Sea has also yielded salt (and, of course, asphalt) throughout its long history, though neither now emerges in commercial quantity. Instead, potash does. Millions of tons annually. On the Israeli side, the giant Dead Sea Works produces for a European market, and on the Jordanian side the almost-as-large Arab Potash Company ships mainly to Japan. The two companies quietly cooperate in ways that may prefigure a more general cooperation between Israel and Jordan. The book is both thrilling and convincing on that possibility.

A third thing that Barbara Kreiger does in *Living Waters,* and does with great authority, is to write what amounts to a travel book about the Dead Sea. Here she extends her scope both in time and space. In space, she includes an account of much of the land bordering the Dead Sea, and especially some of the oases and wadis on the Israeli side. This is territory that she herself has often explored. I like her best of all on the oases Ein Feshkhah and Ein Gedi, both nature reserves.

In time, she goes back to give the story of the European rediscovery and reexploration of the Dead Sea, which took place mostly in the nineteenth century, often under the auspices of the Palestine Exploration Fund. European and American, to be accurate. The most famous of those expeditions arrived in 1848, and it was led by Lt. William Lynch, a Virginian on leave from the United States Navy, and composed of ten young American seamen, picked by him. There were the ones who first took accurate depth readings. Lynch was probing the Dead Sea at much the same time that Thoreau was probing Walden Pond—and, of course, under much more difficult conditions. Lynch's two immediate predecessors both died of malaria. And Lynch had 340 square miles to deal with, as compared to Thoreau's 90 acres.

Finally, the book gives the political history of the sea and its shores. There has been a lot. Once the Dead Sea basin was the private estate of King Herod. Cleopatra of Egypt owed the palm groves of Jericho for a time—one of many gifts she wheedled out of Mark Antony. In modern times ownership has been divided between Israel and Jordan— only today ownership means more than who collects the taxes and checks passports. The rising power of technology now enables the owners to determine the fate of the sea itself.

The Dead Sea is currently eighteen miles shorter than it used to be. The principal source of its water has always been the river Jordan, flowing down from the Sea of Galilee. The river is also the principal source of irrigation water for both Israel and the Kingdom of Jordan— and over the last thirty years the diversion canals of the two countries have reduced the river's flow to a mere trickle in the summer. One result: the southern basin of the Dead Sea no longer exists as a natural phenomenon, but only as a giant pump works for the two potash companies. There are those who fear that the northern basin, though so much deeper, must eventually dry up, too, and the Dead Sea cease to exist. Barbara Kreiger shows in this book why that is unlikely.

But she also shows how fragile the ecosystem of this ancient valley is, and how much the survival of the sea depends on the will and the cooperation of its human owners. "One is struck not by the sea's immutability but by its vulnerability," she writes at the end of this book. One is struck indeed. Something of the magic once attributed to the Dead Sea itself is to be found in this book about it, and it is a fair hope that the existence of *Living Waters* will do something to ensure the existence of the sea.

Noel Perrin
Thetford Center, Vermont

11

Acknowledgments

M ANY PEOPLE have devoted years to the study of the Dead Sea and its environs, and to them I am indebted. Many also gave me of their time, as I traipsed up and down the wadis and along the lake's shore, stowed away on a boat going out to study the water and sediment, and worked my way from library to library—all along accosting anyone who might take a few minutes to answer my questions or provide me with a new lead. Unfortunately some of them remain unnamed, but I thank them for their help.

I was greatly aided in my research by the generous assistance of the staffs of two libraries in particular. I thank Wanda Aftergood and Giovanna Barouch at the library of the Rockefeller Archaeological Museum in Jerusalem, and Patricia Carter, in the inter-library loan department of the Baker Library at Dartmouth College. I also thank my patient typist, Elaine Vigneault.

Moshe Shamir, of the Tamar Regional Council, discussed with me plans for development on the Israeli side of the lake in a long conversation graciously translated by Rina Na'aman Nicholson and Ḥa'im Goldgraber; I further thank Ḥa'im for providing me with material I would otherwise have overlooked. Ze'ev Vilnay told me the stories of his discovery, and recovery, of certain Dead Sea relics; Joseph Shadur, of the Society for the Protection of Nature in Israel, offered advice regarding photographic collections.

I am grateful to David Shalita and Elimeleḥ Mor, of Ein Gedi Films, for their hospitality at Kibbutz Ein Gedi, where I went to look at their photo archive, and to David for his continued assistance as I gathered photographs for the book. Thanks also to Arthur Kreiger, for the hours he spent at the Library of Congress with an important photographic collection there.

I was aided in my work by several institutions and individuals in Jerusalem: Sima Selig, director of the photo archive of Keren Kayemet (the Jewish National Fund); Reuven Koffler, director of the photo archive of the Central Zionist Archives; the staff of the photography department of the Israel Government Press Office; Gilad Livneh, research advisor at the Israel State Archives; the staff of the manuscript room of the National and University Library; and Shoshana Klein, head of the cartography department there.

A number of people had conversations with me about their work: Eli Raz, who at that time was head of the Field School at Ein Gedi; Uzi Plitmann, a botanist who opened the world of desert flora to me. I thank Aharon Oren, a microbiologist who shared with me the results of his work on the microorganisms of the Dead Sea; and Len Aronson, a zoologist who spent eleven years at the Dead Sea, and whose conversation, as well as the manuscript he invited me to read, gave me a special understanding of the wildlife of the region. It was also my pleasure to meet and talk with Professor Leo Picard, the "father of geology" in Israel.

David Neev, one of the foremost figures connected with contemporary scientific investigation at the Dead Sea, shared his thoughts about the lake's future and gave me an insight into the environmental dangers it faces today. David Anati, an oceanographer who has concentrated in the last few years on studying the physical properties of the Dead Sea, was forthcoming and helpful in clarifying certain important points. Cippora Klein, tireless in her pursuit of evidence that would shed light on the Dead Sea's lifecycle, was most generous with her time as she explained her work on the fluctuations of the lake's level.

There are others whose lives have been bound up with the Dead Sea in one way or another: Rudolph Bloch, though ailing, spent a long morning relating to me the genesis of the idea that led to the solar electric ponds now situated by the Dead Sea (I am sorry to say he has since died); Hannah Leszynsky introduced me to Professor Bloch, and I am further grateful to Hannah for her careful reading of my manuscript. Eli Nevo, a former member of the first kibbutz established at the Dead Sea, talked with me about the farm's early days; and Moshe Langotzki related to me with boyish exuberance his fascinating story. (I am sorry to add that he too has recently died.)

It was Shlomo Drori, until recently Director of Information at the Dead Sea Works, who made my meeting with Mr. Langotzki possible. I am indebted to Shlomo for much more than that, for he was always ready to share with me his recollections of individuals and events. Three decades at the Dead Sea has not dampened his enthusiasm for the area; he is, if anything, more idealistic than ever, and optimistic about what the lake can mean both to Israel and to relations between Israel and Jordan.

I am grateful to Nazeeh Samawi and Marwan Khoury, of the Arab Potash Company, who welcomed me to their office in Amman and discussed with me their projections for the future of the Jordanian industrial enterprise.

I would also like to thank the Jordan Information Bureau in Washington, D.C. for supplying me with articles, photographs, and additional material pertaining to the many questions I had concerning Dead Sea-related issues in Jordan.

I thank Professor Walter E. Rast, editor of the *Bulletin of the American Schools of Oriental Research*, for his correspondence with me. As co-leader of the excavations at Bab edh-Dhra and other nearby sites over the course of a number of years, he was able to give me an important perspective on archaeological thought concerning those Early Bronze Age towns.

I could not have written parts of this book without the patient help of Raeli Saraf, who guided me through the labyrinth of geological history, made it all real to me through our field trips, and introduced me to the workings of the solar ponds.

I also especially thank Gila Yudkin, professional tour guide, who was my hiking companion and personal guide in the Dead Sea wadis along the western shore, and whose careful reading of my manuscript was most valuable.

Page Stegner and Ronald Steele were early supporters of my work. I am also grateful to Martin Sherwin, Mary Catherine Bateson, and Annabelle Melzer for their support and much needed readings.

Finally, a thank you to my husband, Alan Lelchuk. He knows what his encouragement and faith have meant these past years.

Jerusalem/Canaan, N.H.
Spring — Fall 1987

Preface

FEW BODIES of water can lay claim to geographical and chemical uniqueness, and few can be said to have provoked the curiosity, even passion, of historians, travellers, and scientists for not mere centuries but for two millennia. The Dead Sea is such a place. One finds descriptions of its peculiar properties in the works of ancient writers; one hears it reviled in the travel accounts of medieval pilgrims; and one sees it eagerly and carefully studied by enlightened explorers of the post-Napoleonic age.

What was the attraction of this salty reservoir? What secrets did it hold that two centuries of serious investigation would be required to fathom them? This book, in part, will trace the course of Dead Sea exploration in modern times. As we will see, that course was no routine one, for the Dead Sea had the unusual fate to have been subjected for many prior centuries to discussion that was more hyperbolic than factual, and the first of its serious explorers were confronted with a body of information that was at times more impediment than tool. Those nineteenth-century explorers who investigated the Dead Sea region constitute an important yet only partially told chapter in the history of the Holy Land, and it would be difficult to exaggerate the wealth of information contained in their travel accounts. Yet for all their erudition, they are highly readable—indeed often beautifully written—and these narratives strike the contemporary reader as authentic records of deeply felt experiences.

The Dead Sea is not merely the lowest place on the face of the earth; at minus 1,332 feet it is the lowest by far. (The second lowest is variously given as Lake Assal in Djibouti, or the Turfan

15

Depression in northwest China, both at minus approximately 490 feet. The lowest place in the western hemisphere is Death Valley, in California, at minus 280 feet.) The question invariably asked by the modern traveller is how it got to be that way. I will try here to make some sense of the world of stones and strata in order to piece together that strange geological tale. The readjustment of one's inner clock to accommodate time spans of millions of years results in a new way of looking at the lake and its environs. The valley comes to life; rocks are no longer mere rocks, but details of something akin to facial characteristics. As the cliffs speak, the Dead Sea itself comes to life, and one understands why so many travellers fell into the habit of personifying it in one way or another. There is something decidedly human about the story of the Dead Sea, perhaps because such a large part of our early collective life was played out along its shores and along the banks of the Jordan River; perhaps also because its unique environment, uncommon beauty, and potential wealth charge us with the responsibility of defining our relationship with the natural world.

That relationship has far-reaching implications, for it happens that the Dead Sea's fate is inextricably bound up with the social, political, and technological lives of the two nations who share it. Monumental demands have been placed on it to give, to produce, to defy the name "Dead." But that very act of defiance may be extremely costly, and this is a subject to be explored here. Nevertheless, there are those in Israel, and likely in Jordan too, who staunchly maintain that one day the Dead Sea might serve as an instrument of peace between the two countries. That view has been dismissed as quixotic and naive, and perhaps it is, given the fact that going back to ancient days, the lake has been frequently contested and a source of hostility. But to deny the possibility is to give in all too readily to the obvious, and if there is one thing we can say about the story of the Dead Sea, it is that it is anything but obvious.

When one stands on the western shore of the Dead Sea and looks out toward its center, where both Arab and Jewish waves casually wash over the imaginary international boundary that looks so convincing on a map; and one looks beyond, a mere ten miles or so to the eastern coast—one cannot help but feel that the prospect for peaceful cooperation is reasonable indeed. Reason suggests that it is not harmony between neighbors that is incongruous, but discord;

16

not cooperation that violates the valley's wholeness, but antagonism.

In this century the Dead Sea has been characterized, because of its vast store of mineral wealth, as a life-giver. It would be a fitting chapter in its history, the circle closed, for this salty basin to help bring neighbors together. For what greater life can be offered than peace between nations? And if the experts proclaim such to be unlikely, let it be said that we quickly grow accustomed to the unexpected at the Dead Sea. Cooperation between neighbors? Stranger things have happened on these shores.

A Note on Usage

VIRTUALLY EVERY place I have reason to mention has two names, Hebrew and Arabic, and sometimes a very different English equivalent—as in the very name of the Dead Sea itself. Where it is important, I give both the Hebrew and Arabic; otherwise I have tried to use the name by which the place is more commonly known to an English reader. One will also notice that spelling varies, since current transliteration practice is often different from what it was at other times. My purpose throughout has been clarity, and respect for both Arab and Jewish usage, which reflects their long histories in the vicinity of the Dead Sea.

All Biblical quotations are taken from the Standard Jewish Version (Jewish Publication Society, 1917).

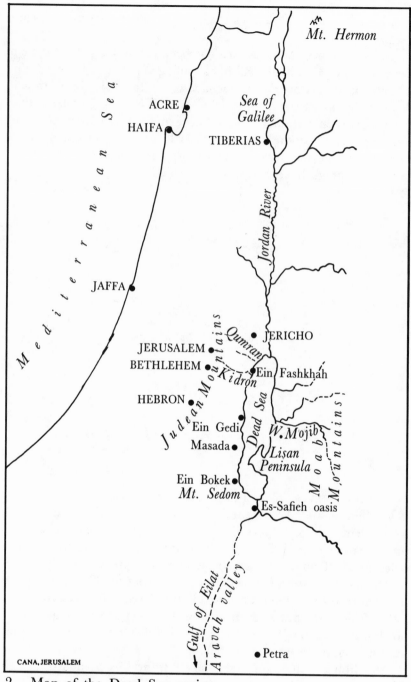

2. Map of the Dead Sea region.

18

PART I

This Strange Water

In graceful lines the hills advance,
The valley's sweep repays the glance,
And wavy curves of winding beach;
But all is charred or crunched or riven,
Scarce seems of earth whereon we dwell;
Though framed within the lines of heaven
The picture intimates a hell.

Herman Melville
*Clarel, A Poem and Pilgrimage
in the Holy Land*
(**II**, xxix, ll.13-19), 1876

1

Some Early History,
Travellers, Myths

THE DRIVE DOWN to the Dead Sea from Jerusalem is a plunge of more than 4,000 feet in the space of twenty miles, and the sensation it creates is that of landing in an airplane, ears stopped and voices muffled. If one can reach the bottom of the valley before the sun shows itself over the eastern Moab Mountains, one will catch the pink wash that is thrown briefly on the western side. One drives south along the shore, with the lake stretching out on the left and separated from the road by bare, rocky beach, a few scrappy bushes scattered among the stones. Immediately to the right is the line of cliffs whose contours the road will follow most of the length of the sea.

The Moab Mountains, just a few miles across the lake, are veiled by a dusty haze, and the entire southern portion of the sea is barely distinguishable from the sky. The shore is outlined by a line of froth created by little waves stirring the edge of the water. The two-lane asphalt road winds as the coast does, a black ribbon imitating the thread of white foam.

It is still early, this late winter day, yet the sun is high enough for the morning to feel full. As the road swings up, the shape of the shoreline becomes apparent, and one can also see whitecaps on the now active sea. Breezes pick up at either end of the day, with the heating or cooling of the air, and the the waves may increase, then die down, only to resume in the evening. The lake seems to breathe with a life of its own, and one comes to feel its rhythms, often agitated in the morning, placid in mid-afternoon.

The haze begins to lift, but even on clear days it may hang for some hours over the sea. From lake level, one notices that it is not resting on the water but is suspended over it. Beneath it the lake is cobalt, perhaps gray, later turquoise with patches of green and purple. From earliest times, observers have remarked on the ever-changing colors of the Dead Sea. Nineteen centuries ago, the Jewish historian Josephus digressed from his account of the Jewish war against the Romans to describe the lake, saying that "thrice daily it alters its appearance and reflects the sun's rays with varying tints."

As the sun climbs, the blue of the water intensifies, and the surface of the lake is flecked with points of light, as though tiny diamonds had been strewn and remain afloat to catch the light. It is no wonder that over the centuries for every traveller who disparaged the sea, there were others who found its beauty unsurpassed. What one found "dreary and dismal," another described as "a shining lake, whose immense and silvery surface reflects the rays of light like a mirror." The Dead Sea, rich in historical and legendary associations, had power to impress beyond that of even more spectacular natural phenomena. Almost without exception, travellers projected their moods onto the sea, often investing it with the spectres conjured up by their imaginations.

The shores of the Dead Sea are regions of contrasts. One has simultaneous impressions of disparate qualities, and at times it is difficult to draw those perceptions into line to define time and place. Coming down to the valley from the west, one is aware of extraordinary depth and fantastic height. The lakeshore itself is arid and infertile, but it is interrupted by spring-fed expanses of reeds and rushes. There is one place where pools of spring water rest next to the lake, separated only by a yard-wide stretch of beach. Where the shore is barren, the fields of a kibbutz relieve the monotony. The green expanse lies with the royal blue of the sea, with multi-toned brown cliffs behind and purplish mountains across. A visitor may squint from the sheer intensity of this multiple juxtaposition of colors.

Then there are the wadis: the dry river beds which have carved their way down to the lake with winter floods, inviting a wealth of plant and animal life. And water, the fresh, cool waterfalls of some of the gorges, splashing into clear pools not half a mile from the sea. This shore, lifeless and gloomy one has heard, is vitalized by overwhelming beauty and irrepressible life. The saltiest water in the world, and some of the sweetest; naked beach and rich canyons;

22

plants, animals, birds winging their way between steep walls; colors running the length of the spectrum. Opposites mingling, as they always have here, in a lasting symbiosis.

By late afternoon there is not a ripple on the sea, and soon the entire western side is in shadows. The sun is so bright that the glare turns the lake and eastern mountains into a pastel rendition of the midday landscape. The whole scene is muted, suffused in light, the brilliance of a few hours ago attenuated as the sun sinks. But once it has settled behind the mountains, the day clears again, as though having shaken off a late afternoon lethargy. The Moab Mountains are rose in the setting sun, their shade spilled into the sea in pools of pink and purple light that seem to float on the slate blue water. The hiker who has spent some time here knows that this unexpected visual delight is just one more surprise of beauty from the valley's store.

In the days of the Exodus of the Israelites from Egypt, given roughly as the thirteenth century B.C.E., the western side of the Dead Sea was in the province of Canaan. At around the same time the eastern side became settled by the kingdoms of Moab and Edom. When the Israelites entered Canaan, the tribe of Reuben and the Moabites both occupied the lake's east bank, while the west belonged first to the tribe, then to the kingdom, of Judah. Such was the status of the Dead Sea environs for the next several centuries. In the sixth century B.C.E., the Jews were exiled to Babylonia, and around that time the eastern shore was conquered by the Nabateans, a people from southern Arabia. The western side was divided between Judah and, to the south, Idumea, settled by the Edomites when they were pushed from the east to the west side of the valley.

Given the long history that has been enacted on its shores by many nations, it is not surprising that the Dead Sea has had various names. Its oldest is *Yam Ha-Melaḥ*, the Salt Sea, that name first appearing in the Bible, in the books of Genesis, Numbers, Deuteronomy, and Joshua, where it usually serves as a geographical landmark. To the Greeks it was Lake Asphaltites because of the lumps of asphalt that were periodically thrown up from its depths, and that name persisted in the texts of medieval writers. Christians of the Middle Ages also knew it as the Devil's Sea, and their Arab contemporaries referred occasionally to the Stinking Lake, presum-

23

ably because of the smell of sulphur emitted from several places along the shore. But the names which appear most frequently in Arab texts are commemorative of the cataclysm that engulfed Sodom and Gomorrah. They called it simply The Overwhelmed, "from the cities of Lot that were overwhelmed in its depths," or the Sea of Zughar (i.e. Zoar), after the town that had escaped destruction and flourished in the Middle Ages. Likewise the Jews, who sometimes referred to it as the East Sea, to distinguish it from the Mediterranean, or the Sea of the Aravah, referring to the valley in which it lies, but more often called it the Sea of Sodom. Except for the little used Arab name *Al Buḥairah al Miyyatah*, the Dead Lake, the notion of lifelessness is not reflected in Arab and Jewish names, though *Mare Mortuum*, the Dead Sea, had appeared in early Roman texts. (In Tacitus' *History* we also find it called the Jewish Sea.) Today the Arabs call it *Baḥr el-Lut*, the Sea of Lot. To the Israelis it is still *Yam Ha-Melaḥ*.

As early as Hellenistic times, and through the days of the Roman empire, geographers and historians wrote about the peculiar nature of the Dead Sea. In the Middle Ages, however, religious attitudes overtook scientific curiosity, and the medieval attraction to the fantastic found a natural subject in the strange lake. Christian pilgrims sometimes stopped at the Dead Sea, either en route from Mt. Sinai to Jerusalem or as an excursion from the holy city. But many were also discouraged from undertaking the dangerous trip, warned off by tales of deadly beasts and poisonous reptiles lurking about on the shore and in the water. "In this country the serpent tyrus is found," wrote a fourteenth-century German pilgrim. "When it is angry it puts out its tongue like a flame of fire, and one would think that it was fire indeed, save that it does not burn the creature... Were it not blind, I believe that no man could escape from it, for I have heard... that if they bit a man's horse, they would kill the rider."

The Dead Sea itself had a reputation that was dreadful and frightening, its vapors thought to be fetid and noxious. "In storms it casts up many beauteous pebbles," this pilgrim went on, "but if anyone picks them up his hand will stink for three days so foully that he will not be able to bear himself." Those who did descend approached timidly, not taking lightly this sea which had opened to swallow the evil cities of Sodom and Gomorrah as brimstone and fire raged out of an angry heaven. As one pilgrim explained, "It is

24

plain that here is a mouth of hell, according to us Christians, because we believe that hell is in the midst of the earth, and that the Holy City standeth on the mountains above it."

For centuries the Dead Sea had inspired this kind of curiosity, awe, and even contempt. As they journeyed to the remote valley, travellers had absorbed the myths of the region, and if they did not add their own to the accumulation, others more sedentary did. The collection of fantastic tales was reinforced by the quite real dangers of the region, and by modern times the lake had become shrouded in superstition. In an attempt to break the intellectual quarantine which had been imposed, one of the first Dead Sea explorers, travelling in 1810, refuted, first of all, the notion "that iron swims upon it, and light bodies sink to the bottom—that birds, in their passage over it, fall dead into the sea." And several decades later, a Frenchman approached the Dead Sea and demanded with temerity, "Where then are those poisonous vapours, which carry death to all who venture to approach them? Where? In the writings of the poets who have emphatically described what they have never seen. We are not yet five minutes treading the shores of the Dead Sea, and already, all that has been said of it appears as mere creations of fancy. Let us proceed fearlessly forward, for if anything is to be dreaded here, certainly it is not the pestilential influence of the finest and most imposing lake in the world." A Dutch contemporary concurred: "In vain my eye sought for the terrific representations which some writers... have given of the Dead Sea. I expected a scene of unequalled horror, instead of which I found a lake, calm and glassy, blue and transparent, with an unclouded heaven, with a smooth beach, and surrounded by mountains whose blue tints were of rare beauty."

Some of the many explorers who journeyed to the Dead Sea in the last century were adventurers, others were driven by religious fervor. But the largest number were scientists and geographers, and their combined efforts over the course of the century yielded important finds in the fields of Biblical geography and the natural sciences. The Dead Sea, they would come to discover, is hundreds of feet below sea level and is part of the great Syrian-African Rift. They would discover that it is nearly one third solid; that its salt-encrusted shores had been cultivated by centuries of Jews, Romans, and Byzantines. They did not know that in the caves of Qumran, on the northwest side of the lake, the Essenes stored the

25

manuscripts that twenty centuries later would be found and become known as the Dead Sea Scrolls. But they did identify Masada, thirty miles south, where the Jewish zealots made their last stand against the Romans in 73 C.E. The puzzle would be slowly pieced together, and the image that emerged would be rich in detail.

A great deal of attention has been paid to the exploration of the Nile River, where European efforts were more glamorously concentrated in the nineteenth century. The Nile was wrapped in the mystery of a region that had never been seen by westerners, and the race to locate its source was intense and at times bitter. This was not the case with the Dead Sea. There was no compulsion to be the first. No Burton-like expeditions were ever mounted to discover where its strange water came from; it had one major and well-known source, and no issue, thus containing its own mystery in a basin just forty-seven miles long and eleven wide.

Why did so many travellers—dozens in each decade of the last century—make their way down to what according to some accounts was not just a mouth of Hell, but a fair approximation of the place itself? Why are the pages of the geographic journals filled with reports and articles ranging from the most carefully analytical to the vastly speculative, all concerning this one small lake? What was the attraction? There are probably almost as many answers to these questions as there were explorers. Certainly the Dead Sea's uniqueness and strangeness had a lot to do with it. Many travellers, especially early on, were prompted to verify for themselves the strange phenomena about which they had heard. No doubt also the Dead Sea's connection to the Biblical Cities of the Plain served to attract. More than a few, and they not eccentrics, searched assiduously for the ruins of the ancient towns, and an occasional claim was made that Sodom or Gomorrah had been discovered.

That impulse to bring to light evidence of the Bible's authenticity suggests another reason. One of the most striking shared traits of those who explored the Dead Sea region was their familiarity with the Bible. Having read it all their lives, they felt they knew the territory, were somehow at home there. The routes these modern explorers took had been walked by their spiritual ancestors; the places they visited had been named by them; the events they recalled as they trudged up and down the cliffsides were some of those that defined western civilization. How familiar it all must have seemed. And yet it wasn't. The events and figures that made the Dead Sea and its environs familiar were two thousand years past, and the familiar had receded into shadow. Exploring in the Dead Sea valley was like cutting one's way through thick underbrush to get to a path marked on the map. No one, not even the most coolly scientific, doubted that the path was there, or questioned that hard work would reveal it.

A well-worn copy of the Bible would be found among the gear of any serious expedition, along with the compasses, thermometers, barometers. Early in the century one traveller observed that "the manners and customs of the natives of these countries remain unchanged since the days of the passage of the Children of Israel from Egypt into the Land of Promise," and he went on to say that "the Bible is, beyond all comparison, the most interesting and the most instructive guide that can be consulted by the traveller in the East." Such was the universal opinion, and so strongly felt that the author of a popular guide, having devoted years to its compilation, opened by agreeing that "the Bible is the best Handbook for Palestine; the present work is only intended to be a companion to it." No fear of heresy prompted his modesty; all the travel accounts of his day, teeming with Biblical allusions, express the same opinion. So while nineteenth-century explorers of Africa were stepping into darkness, those of the Dead Sea region were walking in a hazy light thrown by antiquity—oblique, but nonetheless considerable.

In the early part of the nineteenth century, it required no small amount of courage to travel to Palestine, let alone to such a remote place as the Dead Sea. The Ottoman empire was fast coming apart—Palestine was in fact seized by Mohammad Ali, the ruler of Egypt, in 1831 and held for nine years—and the Bedouin tribes who lived in the desert around the lake recognized no outside ruler. The Turks had sole authority to issue firmans (a kind of visa) to those wishing to enter their territory, but Constantinople was far from the Dead Sea valley, and the Turks exercised virtually no control there. The land was divided among the Bedouin much as in Biblical days it had been divided among the tribes of Israel, and the Bedouin did as they pleased, from exacting tribute of European travellers to plundering the villages and farmlands of sedentary Arabs. From time to time the Turks would engage in a bloody show of force, in retribution or capriciously. But for the most part the Bedouin were left to themselves, and their relationships with one another, more than any external influence, determined their lot until late in the century.

Westerners were easy prey, so many studied Arabic and Moslem customs before setting out disguised as Arabs. No explorer travelled unarmed or unguarded, and no account concludes without some pages having been devoted to the skirmishes that were fought, or the care taken to avoid them. Aside from being dangerous, travel was extremely arduous. The most famous Dead Sea explorer, the American William F. Lynch, described what it was like near mid-century to convey his boats overland in order to reach the lake: "The word road means, in that country, a mule-track. Wheel carriages have never crossed it before. In their invasion of Syria [during the Napoleonic wars], the French transported their guns and gun-carriages (taken apart) on the backs of camels, over the lofty ridges, and mounted them again on the plain." Without the help of their Bedouin guides, who knew the terrain most intimately, knew which regions were impassable, and always knew where at least a little stagnant pool of water could be found, very few Europeans would have been able to make the trip—their Bibles notwithstanding.

By the second half of the century, a trip to the northern, more accessible, end of the Dead Sea took no special courage and had in fact become standard fare for a new kind of traveller—not explorer but tourist. They came in increasing numbers—French, English, Dutch, German, American—often travelling in sizeable groups, their objective usually being a quick glimpse of the lake and a chance to scoop up a jar of water from the Jordan River to take home.

The travel guide book so familiar to modern tourists is no recent innovation; many travellers carried one for help in identifying sites. A particularly popular one was John Porter's *Handbook for Travellers in Syria and Palestine*, first published in 1858. Porter's "route 10" sent tourists on a three-day excursion which took in Jericho, the Jordan River and the Dead Sea, the monastery of Mar Saba, and Bethlehem—a journey more than enough for most. One of these tourists was Mark Twain, whose account of his trip is contained in *The Innocents Abroad*. He was not very appreciative of eastern life or people and evinced, at best, disappointment in what he encountered in the Holy Land. But for insight into the collective frame of mind of

28

one of these tourist-pilgrim groups, his narrative is singular. He described the reluctance with which his group, having heard rumors of tribal war in the Dead Sea valley, undertook the journey. Tempted to remain in Jerusalem, they found, to their chagrin, that a little caravan had already been assembled and was waiting for them. "[W]ith the horses at the door and every body aware of what they were there for, what would *you* have done?... You would have done as we did: said you were not afraid of a million Bedouins—and made your will and proposed quietly to yourself to take up an unostentatious position in the rear of the procession.

"I think we must all have determined upon that same line of tactics, for it did seem as if we never would get to Jericho. I had a notoriously slow horse, but somehow I could not keep him in the rear... He was forever turning up in the lead. In such cases I trembled a little, and got down to fix my saddle. But it was not of any use. The others all got down to fix their saddles, too. I never saw such a time with saddles. It was the first time any of them had got out of order in three weeks, and now they had all broken down at once. I tried walking, for exercise—I had not had enough in Jerusalem searching for holy places. But it was a failure. The whole mob were suffering for exercise, and it was not fifteen minutes till they were all on foot and I had the lead again. It was very discouraging."

Jericho was a welcome destination. It was the only town in the vicinity of the lake, it was the point from which pilgrims went to the Jordan River for immersion in the holy water, and, as an oasis, it offered year around relief to weary travellers. Jericho is the lowest, and probably the oldest, city in the world. By virtue of its location, climate (tropical in summer and mild in winter), and fertility, it first attracted settlers some 12,000 years ago. The very beginnings of civilization are revealed in its strata, and evidence indicates it witnessed the transition early man made from a nomadic to a sedentary way of life. As early as the eighth millennium B.C.E., the settlement was organized into an urban unit. Archaeologists believe that some 2,000 people lived in the town, which suggests a dependence on agriculture that brought with it advances in irrigation and the need for communal fortifications.

Josephus, writing nineteen centuries ago, referred to one section of the town as Old Jericho. According to the Bible, it was the first town conquered by Joshua and the Israelites on their entry into the

Promised Land in the late Bronze Age, Joshua instructing his spies:
"'Go view the land, and Jericho.'" (Joshua 2:1) Yet archaeological
evidence suggests that Jericho was destroyed in the second half of
the fourteenth century B.C.E.—a century before the Israelites
appeared—and had not yet been rebuilt.

For centuries, kings and queens had their winter palaces there,
and Jericho was one of the most coveted sites in all the surrounding
lands in ancient days. The palm trees and sugar-cane which
flourished into the Middle Ages were gone by the nineteenth
century, but Mark Twain still found it "one of the very best
locations for a town we have seen in all Palestine." Of the old city he
observed: "Ancient Jericho is not very picturesque as a ruin. When
Joshua marched around it seven times, some three thousand years
ago, and blew it down with his trumpet, he did the work so well and
so completely that he hardly left enough of the city to cast a
shadow."

3. The conquest of Jericho. From *Yosifon*, 1743, a Yiddish
translation of *Josippon*, tenth century.

Starting out the next morning—very early, advised the *Handbook*, to the dismay of the group—they crossed the plain to the Jordan River. Again, Mark Twain described the less exalted aspect of this milestone in the lives of Christians: "With the first suspicion of dawn, every pilgrim took off his clothes and waded into the dark torrent, singing... But they did not sing long. The water was so fearfully cold that they were obliged to stop singing and scamper out again. Then they stood on the bank shivering, and so chagrined and so grieved, that they merited honest compassion... They had promised themselves all along that they would cross the Jordan where the Israelites crossed it when they entered Canaan from their long pilgrimage in the desert... They were at the goal of their hopes at last, but the current was too swift, the water was too cold!"

From there it was an hour's ride to the Dead Sea. "Here we feel the oppressive atmosphere of this desolate region," notes the *Handbook*. "The air becomes close and hazy as the sun ascends, giving a wavy motion to the parched soil and a strange indistinctness of outline to distant objects. After an hour's weary ride we reach the shore of the Dead Sea, with its unwholesome swamps and slimy margin, and ridges of *drift* wood, all incrusted with salt." Those inclined would take a quick dip, expressing general disappointment at the dreariness of the setting while picking up bits of sulphur commonly supposed to have been left by the raining down of brimstone described in Genesis.

One can understand the determination of pilgrims to bathe in the revered water of the Jordan River, but one hardly knows why many of them agreed to go any further on a journey which, though but two days longer, was stressful and taxing by any estimation. Even Mark Twain's humor evaporated under the midday sun: "I can not describe the hideous afternoon's ride from the Dead Sea to Mars [sic] Saba. It oppresses me yet, to think of it. The sun so pelted us that the tears ran down our cheeks once or twice. The ghastly, treeless, grassless, breathless canons [i.e., canyons] smothered us as if we had been in an oven. The sun had positive *weight* to it, I think. Not a man could sit erect under it. All drooped low in the saddles."

On their approach to Mar Saba, tourists who referred to their *Handbook* were warned of the rule that holds even today: "Ladies will remember that they cannot under any circumstances obtain admission" to the monastery. But the men were treated to a tour of

4. A view of the monastery Mar Saba and the Dead Sea, by David
Roberts. From *The Holy Land*, vol. II, 1843.

"the most extraordinary building in Palestine." In the fifth century, St. Saba retreated to the desert, drawing thousands of followers to the site on which they would construct the magnificent, jewelled monastery which in its prime (until plundered by the Persians in the seventh century) would be home to 5,000 Greek Orthodox monks. It was built over the course of many years, and its treasures were hauled all the way from Greece.

"By God's grace," wrote the twelfth-century Abbot Daniel, "the situation of the Laura of St. Sabbas is a marvellous and indescribable one. A dry torrent bed, terrible to behold, and very deep, is shut in by high walls of rock, to which the cells are fixed and kept in place by the hand of God in a surprising and fearful manner. These cells, fastened to the precipices flanking this frightful torrent, are attached to the rocks like the stars to the firmament." The blue-domed monastery is stitched to the walls of Wadi Kidron, and today a handful of monks studiously maintains the complex while performing the same isolated devotions that St. Saba observed fifteen centuries ago.

The Dead Sea was as much a catalyst to the literary imagination as it had earlier been to the religious one. Half a century before Mark Twain travelled there, Sir Walter Scott had found in the Dead Sea region (which he never visited) the setting he required for his novel *The Talisman, A Tale of the Crusaders*. As his knight crossed the desert of the Dead Sea in the book's opening page, he forgot all his privations as he recalled "the fearful catastrophe which had converted into an arid waste and dismal wilderness the fair and fertile valley of Siddim, once well watered, even as the garden of the Lord, now a parched and blighted waste, condemned to eternal sterility.

"Crossing himself as he viewed the dark mass of rolling waters, in colour as in quality unlike those of every other lake, the traveller shuddered as he remembered that beneath these sluggish waves lay the once proud cities of the plain, whose grave was dug by the thunder of the heavens, or the eruption of subterraneous fire, and whose remains were hid, even by that sea which holds no living fish in its bosom, bears no skiff on its surface, and, as if its own dreadful bed were the only fit receptacle for its sullen waters, sends not, like other lakes, a tribute to the ocean."

Benjamin Disraeli's hero Tancred wandered in the desert east of the lake, and Gustav Flaubert made the journey himself. But in no literary imagination did the Dead Sea burn so keenly as in Herman Melville's. The lure of the East extended as far back as his childhood. In his autobiographical *Redburn*, he recalled having seen a man who had just returned from Egypt and the Dead Sea: "I very well remembered staring at a man... who was pointed out to me by my aunt one Sunday in Church, as the person who had been in Stony Arabia, and passed through strange adventures there, all of which with my own eyes I had read in the book which he wrote, an arid-looking book in a pale yellow cover.

"'See what big eyes he has,' whispered my aunt, 'they got so big, because when he was almost dead with famishing in the desert, he all at once caught sight of a date tree, with the ripe fruit hanging on it.'

"...I never saw this wonderful Arabian traveller again. But he long haunted me."

Melville travelled to the Holy Land some years later, in 1856, a few years after *Moby Dick* was published and lambasted. Suffering still from the depression brought on by his novel's reception, he found in the East something quite different from what his boyhood fantasies had taught him to expect. His despondency found a focus in the Dead Sea, which provoked him to the melancholic reflection recorded in his journal: "Ride over mouldy plain to Dead Sea—... smarting bitter of the water,—carried the bitter in my mouth all day—bitterness of life—thought of all bitter things—Bitter is it to be poor & bitter, to be reviled, & Oh bitter are those waters of Death, thought I." But his experience provided him with the material for a major literary effort, the 18,000 line poem *Clarel*, large portions of which are set either in Jerusalem or at the Dead Sea. There was the holy city on high, overlooking the dry sunken valley 4,000 feet below. The geographical arrangement could not have been better devised by Dante himself, and Melville made full use of it.

.   .   .

Since the Middle Ages, not a century has passed during which some European traveller, motivated by religious fervor, scientific curiosity, or personal eccentricity, hasn't made his way to the Holy Land and descended to the lowest place on earth—its reputation established by the sinners of Sodom and Gomorrah and nurtured by superstitions of later ages—and identified it as a facsimile of Hell. The accounts of those early travellers are enlightening, though the light they shed is often not so much on the nature of the Dead Sea as on the preconceptions of those who eagerly awaited the latest report on the desolate chasm from the brave ones who, it seems, did not always in fact make the descent, but fashioned their accounts to coincide with the fantastic expectations of their readers. Thus, for instance, the much-quoted thirteenth-century description of the sea as "always smoking, and dark like Hell's chimney." Passed on in a text for pilgrims, the hyperbolic expression was perhaps intended to discourage Christians from venturing too near the presumably still contagious seat of ancient sin.

There were voices, too, which sought from the earliest stage of western encounter with the lake to dispel superstition and lift the cloud of ignorance which hung over this most strange body of water, whose peculiarity had been recognized and remarked on throughout historical times. The Dead Sea first attracted the notice of the ancient Greeks and Romans: Aristotle referred to it in his *Meteorology*, Pliny discussed it in his *Natural History*, and Strabo in his *Geography*—all by the end of the first century C.E. Medieval reports were frequently less informed, though not because their authors were less serious. On the contrary, if seriousness is a measure, texts of the Middle Ages hold up with any. "Much has been written and said about this sea by divers [sic] people," wrote Burchard with thirteenth-century solemnity; "you must know that I fear not to tell what I have seen with my own eyes... which is, that the whole of the valley which used rightly to be called the Illustrious Valley... is made barren by the smoke of this sea... This is indeed a dreadful judgment of God, who for so many centuries so punished the sins of the Sodomites, that even the land itself pays the penalty thereof after so many thousands of years." As the passage suggests, the works were intended not as natural history but, as stated in the introduction to a popular thirteenth-century compendium, "to explain the allusions to natural objects met with in the Scriptures." Faithful reporting was not the foremost goal, though at times an accurate chord was struck. In this latter book, the English

Franciscan Bartholomew described a lake called the Dead Sea because "it breedeth, ne receiveth, no thing that hath life."

Two hundred years saw virtually no alteration in approach, and we read in another pilgrims' text about a lake known as the Dead Sea "because it does not run, but is ever motionless." Yet another two centuries did witness a change; travellers who claimed to have seen the lake were more likely to have done so, and among those who did see it, there was a growing inclination to report soberly. The basic pedagogical approach lingered, however, nowhere more unabashedly manifested than in Thomas Fuller's 1650 *A Pisgah-sight of Palestine*. This lake, he explained, is sometimes called the Dead Sea "either because the charnel-house of so many dead carcasses then destroyed therein; or because it kills all creatures coming into it; or lastly, because dull and dead, not enlivened with a tide, or quickened with any visible motion, one main cause of the offensive favour there, laziness disposing men to lewdness, and waters to putrefaction."

Explorers were generally familiar with the accounts of travellers who preceded them, and two early works which they admired were Henry Maundrell's 1697 *A Journey from Aleppo to Jerusalem* and Richard Pococke's lengthy 1740 account, *A Description of the East, and Some Other Countries*. Given its early date, Maundrell's book is notable for its author's attitude: "I am sensible of two general Defects... running through this whole paper," he wrote in a preface addressed to his uncle. "One is, frequent Errours; the other, Tediousness... But... I profess with a clear Conscience, that whatever Mistakes there may be, yet there are no Lies." Maundrell's and Pococke's works were used by numerous later explorers for the purpose of comparison.

Despite the currency of certain myths, there were those even before the turn of the nineteenth century who attempted to dig for truths about the lake over or on which, it was said, no living thing could pass without being affected by its vapors. The more we read, the more we realize that the achievements of those early travellers were not just quaint but truly significant. One of the lake's greatest mysteries had to do with its level: how did the Dead Sea, which received the abundant water of the Jordan River and other smaller tributaries—and which had no apparent issue—maintain a constant level? Diodorus had observed in the first century B.C.E. that "although great rivers of remarkable sweetness empty into it, the lake gets the better of them by reason of its evil smell..." Thirteen centuries later, the Arab geographer Dimashki summarized the various views then current about how the lake maintained its level: "The people have many opinions concerning the disappearance of the waters (of the Dead Sea). Some say that its waters have an exit into a country afar off, whose lands they irrigate and fertilize, and here the waters may be drunk... Others say that the soil all round the lake being extremely hot, and having beds of sulphur beneath, there never cease to rise vapours, and there, causing the water to evaporate, keep it to a certain level. Others again say there is an exit through the earth whereby its waters join those of the Red Sea; and others again affirm it has no bottom, but that there is a passage leading down to the Behemoth (who supports the earth)." Charming, and on the whole farfetched—yet the second, for all its elaborateness in suggesting evaporation as the cause, approached the truth.

Whether or not later western science read medieval Arab geography is unclear, but it would be six more centuries before Europe came to some agreement about the phenomenon. Thomas Fuller filled the gap. While his less pedantic successors would struggle with the question, Fuller displayed singular equanimity: this sea, he asserted, "hath but one good quality, namely, that it entertains intercourse with no other seas; which may be imputed to the providence of nature, debarring it from communion with the ocean, lest otherwise it should infect other waters with its malignity." A century later, Pococke puzzled over the phenomenon, wondering whether so much water could indeed be lost to evaporation, and he leaned toward the theory that there must be some secret outlet: "It is very extraordinary that no outlet of this lake has been discovered, but it is supposed that there must be some subterraneous passage into the Mediterranean." Apparently his was the prevailing view of the eighteenth century, and it took another half century or so for that view to shift. According to a book published in the first years of the 1800s, it had until recently been a prominent view that the Dead Sea "discharges its superfluous waters by subterraneous channels," but it was by then commonly believed that evaporation was in fact the cause of the disappearance of all the excess water.

Many early explorers regarded as untenable the notion that nothing could live in the Dead Sea—for of what use is a body of water, if not to support God's creatures? (The famous sixth-century Madaba map depicting a startled fish turning back up the Jordan before entering the lake was not uncovered until the 1880s.) Early on, rumors of the extraordinary phenomenon were accepted with aplomb not found in later, more sophisticated, investigators. Again the inimitable Fuller: "This *Salt-Sea* was sullen and churlish, differing from all other in the conditions thereof... [The] most sportful fish dare not jest with the edged tools of this Dead-Sea; which if unwillingly hurried therein by the force of the stream of *Jordan*, they presently expire."

Pococke, for one, found it particularly hard to accept, especially as he heard that a monk had seen fish caught in the lake, but he agreed to reserve judgment until all the evidence was gathered. Early in the 1800s the Frenchman François de Chateaubriand, camping by the Dead Sea one night, was startled by a sound upon the water and was told by his Bedouin guides that the noise was caused by "legions of small fish which come and leap about on the shore." An editor compiling such anecdotes some twenty years later was amused by Chateaubriand's gullibility and smirked that the fish were "doubtless seeking to be delivered from the pestilential waters." He chuckled that this was "nothing more than a hoax upon the learned Frenchman." Though Chateaubriand had disavowed any scientific intentions and insisted his book be read simply as memoir, he was subjected to criticism throughout the century for his impressionability. As for the editor, his smugness was made possible by a report which had come out around the same time as Chateaubriand's book, in which a highly respected scientist, having collected the snail shells which to many had been proof of life in the sea, identified them as a land species. (Actually they are freshwater snails, either washed down by the winter floods or coming from springs.)

There are probably few natural phenomena in the world which have so perplexed and enchanted travellers of all ages as the buoyancy of the Dead Sea. In the fourth century B.C.E., Aristotle had mused about a fabled lake in Palestine, "such that if you bind a man or beast and throw it in it floats and does not sink." Three hundred years later, Strabo turned his attention to the same subject: "The water is exceedingly heavy, so that no person can dive into it; if anyone wades into it up to the waist, and attempts to move forward, he is immediately lifted out of the water." Diodorus explained that "this liquid by its nature supports heavy bodies that have the power of growth or of breathing," and Tacitus wrote that "its sluggish waters support their freight as if on solid ground, and trained swimmers as well as those ignorant of the art are equally buoyant upon its surface."

Josephus observed that it "is not easy to go down into the depths even by deliberate effort," and he recounted that Vespasian, later to become Roman emperor, came to examine the water. Ordering some slaves to be thrown in with their hands tied behind them, he "found that they all came to the surface as if blown upwards by a strong wind." Finally among the ancient writers, Pliny described how "the bodies of animals will not sink in its waters, and even those of bulls and camels float there," but a nineteenth-century editor of his work assures us he exaggerated, that error itself an illustration of the uneven progress of Dead Sea investigation even in modern times.

In the thirteenth century, Bartholomew wrote that "whensoever thou wouldst have drowned therein anything that hath life with any craft or gin, then anon it plungeth and cometh again up; though it be strongly thrust downward, it is anon smitten upward." His Arab contemporary, the geographer Yakût, wrote that anyone who falls into the lake "cannot sink, but remains floating about til he dies." A century later, an Englishman known as Maundeville—about whom there is doubt he ever lived, let alone travelled to the Dead Sea—disagreed: "Neither man, beast, or anything that hath life, may die in that sea; and that hath been proved many times by men that have been condemned to death, who have been cast therein, and left therein for three or four days, and they might never die therein, for it receiveth nothing within him that breatheth life... And if a man cast iron therein, it will float on the surface; but if men cast a feather therein, it will sink to the bottom; and these are things contrary to nature." Recent geographers believe Maundeville's book to have been plagiarized from various sources, but consider it important anyway, as George H.T. Kimble noted, as an illustration of the layman's idea of the world in the fourteenth century. If the appeal of the fantastic was as great as Kimble explains it was in that age of supreme faith, one need have no fear that the medieval imagination went unexercised. With regard to the lake's buoyancy, the opportunities for invention were endless. A burning lantern will float, but an extinguished one will sink; try to immerse a living creature, and it will immediately leap out; no ship may sail on it, "for all things that hath no life sinketh down to the ground."

The attraction of the Dead Sea by virtue of this singular phenomenon did not end when it was explained. Early in the nineteenth century one explorer observed that "those of our party who could not swim, floated on its surface like corks," and a contemporary complained of the embarrassing posture forced on the would-be swimmer, whose stroke was rendered useless as his behind bobbed high out of the water. Another was positive he could have slept, "and it would have been a much easier bed than the bushes at Jericho."

Less pleased was the traveller who evidently had not taken to heart what he had heard about the effects of the water: "I think we were all good swimmers, but when I dashed in and threw myself forward to get out of my depth, there was enough to do without observing my friends. The unusual degree of buoyancy in the briny liquid threw me off balance, the salt stung my eyes, ears, and every abrasion of my skin, and I could scarcely tell in what direction I was striking out." Yet another put it most succinctly, saying simply that "the trial of skill is not to *swim*, but to *sink*." Finally Mark Twain, whose encounter with the waters of the lake occupies a full two pages in *The Innocents Abroad*: "No, the water did not blister us; it did not cover us with a slimy ooze and confer upon us an atrocious fragrance... It was a funny bath. We could not sink... No position can be retained long; you lose your balance and whirl over... If you swim on your face, you kick up the water like a stern-wheel boat... A horse is so top-heavy that he can neither swim nor stand up in the Dead Sea. He turns over on his side at once. Some of us bathed for more than an hour, and then came out coated with salt till we shone like icicles."

This strange water is as capable of supporting life *on* it as it is incapable of supporting life *in* it—both attributable to its chemical make-up. The Dead Sea is close to one third solid—more than Utah's Great Salt Lake (which is one quarter) and ten times more saline than the Mediterranean. While the salt content of most seas

40

and lakes is largely sodium chloride, the Dead Sea's largest concentration is magnesium chloride, which accounts for approximately one half its mineral content. Sodium chloride makes up another quarter; the last fourth consists primarily of calcium chloride, with potassium chloride, magnesium bromide, and several other minerals in relatively small concentrations. Roughly accurate analyses had been done since the end of the eighteenth century, and so confident was one traveller that he announced (prematurely) in 1837 that "modern science has solved all the mystery of this water."

As noted, one of the major attractions of the Dead Sea was its connection to the Cities of the Plain, whose arrogance and evil ways were dealt with by God in the days of Abraham and Lot, and whose fate is recorded in the Book of Genesis: "Then the Lord rained upon Sodom and Gomorrah brimstone and fire from the Lord out of heaven; and He overthrew those cities, and all the plain, and all the inhabitants of the cities, and that which grew upon the ground." Many hundreds of years later, Josephus reflected on the conflagration when describing the region: "The country of Sodom borders upon... [the lake], which was of old a happy land, both for the fruits it bore and the riches of its cities, although it is now all burnt up by lightning for the impiety of its inhabitants."

The possibility that the remains of the punished cities might be found was enough to prod on certain travellers who might otherwise have lacked the courage to descend to the mysterious valley. One such was Maundrell, who badly wanted to see the remains of those ancient towns "made so dreadful an example of the divine vengeance," and he looked hard for some sign. "[B]ut neither could I discern any heaps of ruins, nor any smoak [sic] ascending above the surface of the water; as is usually described in the writings and maps of geographers." (It has been suggested that Maundrell was possibly encouraged by a map such as the fifteenth-century one which illustrated William Wey's *Itineraries*, in which one can distinguish the outlines of the Cities of the Plain lying beneath the transparent blue water of the Dead Sea.)

In the nineteenth century, numerous travellers eagerly sought the ruins commonly thought to be located in the lake's depths. "Lying between the barren mountains of Arabia and Judea," considered one, "was that mysterious sea which rolled its dark waters over the guilty cities of Sodom and Gomorrah." Another referred to the

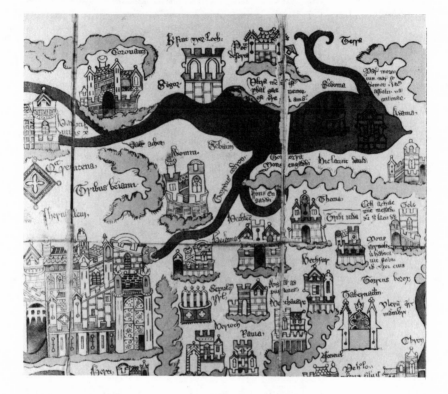

5. Map of the Dead Sea, showing four of the Cities of the Plain submerged beneath its water, and the spared town of Zoar (upper left). From an 1867 facsimile of the original map (located at the Bodleian Library) which accompanied *The Itineraries of William Wey*, 1458 and 1462.

damned Cities of the Plain "seething below the [Dead Sea's] waters," and a third observed that "to the north was the calm and motionless sea... while many fathoms deep in the slimy mud beneath it lay embedded the ruins of the ill-fated cities." At mid-century, the Dutchman C.W.M. Van de Velde described most evocatively the feeling that was shared by many who walked on the Dead Sea's shores in those days of greater spiritual certainty: "Solemn ride along this briny strand!... The burning and vanishing ground, with its doomed cities, comes up vividly before the mind. What a tract of country! What a terrible witness to the righteous vengeance of God's justice!"

Jewish, Moslem, and Christian tradition all placed the Cities of the Plain at the southern end of the Dead Sea, though some nineteenth-century investigators were convinced that a combination of geographical and Biblical evidence proved that they had been situated on the northern shore. Throughout the Middle Ages, the Arab town of Zughar flourished at the southern part of the lake. But whether the site it occupied was indeed the one that had been occupied by the ancient town of Zoar was a matter for the most tentative conjecture. (In the early 1920s, the eminent archaeologist William Foxwell Albright determined that it was not.)

Theories about the cataclysm—some based on observable, if wrongly interpreted, evidence, others just fantasy—were frequently put forth, and debate was widespread. One speculator departed from the widely held theory of volcanic destruction, suggesting instead that the cities had unfortunately been built upon a mine of bitumen which was kindled by lightning, causing them to sink "in the subterraneous conflagration." Another collected lumps of nitrate and small bits of sulphur, hypothesizing that they could have been left from the raining down of brimstone. The Frenchman Louis Félicien de Saulcy caused a commotion in 1850 by announcing that he had identified as Sodom the remains of a small stone building. His precipitous claim provoked indignation in one Reverend Albert Isaacs, who devoted an entire book to disproving it and discrediting de Saulcy in a caustic reprimand. The matter was put into perspective by someone less excitable, who simply responded that de Saulcy had gotten the answers he wanted from the local Arabs by asking leading questions.

But de Saulcy was not alone in hoping, even believing, that the ruins of the cities might be unearthed. "It is not perhaps impossible," wrote one, "that the wrecks of the guilty cities may still be found: we have even heard it asserted with confidence, that broken columns and other architectural ruins are visible at certain seasons, when the water is much retired below its usual level." And an American traveller named John Lloyd Stephens, usually modest in his expectations, was bent on searching in the deadly waters of the lake "for the ruins of the doomed and blasted cities." Stephens was the most vocal—and the most persuasive—of them all: "I had a longing desire to... search for the ruins of the guilty cities. And why not? If we believe our Bible...[the Dead Sea] covers the once fertile Vale of Siddim and the ruins of Sodom and Gomorrah; and why may we not see them? The ruins of Thebes still cover for miles the banks of the Nile; the pyramids stand towering as when they were built... Besides, that water [of the Dead Sea] does not destroy; it preserves all that it touches... and I can see no good reason why it should hide forever from man's eyes the monuments of that fearful anger which the crimes of the guilty had so righteously provoked."

By 1831, so much information had been gathered about the Dead Sea that one Josiah Conder compiled a summary of the West's geographical knowledge of "this celebrated lake, which the prevailing passion for the marvellous long invested with imaginary horrors, and of which the natives themselves still speak with a degree of terror." In *The Modern Traveller—Palestine*, Conder entered the Sodom and Gomorrah fray, though on the other side. He directed his respectful scepticism toward Strabo, who in the first century had even given the dimensions of the ruins of Sodom. Conder concluded with some regret that such a legend must be classed "with the dreams of imagination." Reluctant but dutiful, he cited travellers who had observed that the sea itself can throw up heaps of stones, and that many have mistaken them for the ruins of the ancient cities.

Still, all the speculation stirred him: "The bare possibility, that any wreck of the guilty cities should be brought to light, is sufficient to excite an intense curiosity to explore this mysterious flood, which, so far as appears from any records, no bark has ever ploughed, no plummet ever sounded." Actually, as Conder's book was being read, preparations were already being made to sound the lake's depths. And though for centuries the only barks to plow its waters

6.   Section of the sixth-century Madaba map, the earliest known of
the Dead Sea, showing the Dead Sea, with two boats, and a fish
fleeing up the Jordan River. Map reproduced by the Survey of
Israel and the Israel Exploration Society, from Palmer and Guthe's
reproduction, 1906.

45

were Arab rafts, there were times, in Roman days, in the Byzantine period, and during the Middle Ages, when navigation was common. Vespasian's ships had pursued Jews who were fleeing by way of the sea during the Jewish war, from 66 to 73 C.E., and documents from the time of the second Jewish rebellion against the Romans sixty-five years later suggest that Ein Gedi, on the western shore, was a major supply port. Part of the mosaic floor discovered in the Byzantine church at Madaba, on the east side of the Dead Sea, depicts a map of the lake (the earliest known) and shows two ships, one carrying salt, the other laden, it appears, with wheat or corn. And the Arab geographer Idrisi, writing in the twelfth century, described trade on the Dead Sea: "There ply on the lake small ships which make the voyage of these parts, and carry over corn and various sorts of dates from Zughar [at the southern end]... to Ariha [Jericho, at the north]." Before the nineteenth century was half over, navigation on the sea would resume, as science began to probe the lake's depths.

PART II

Nineteenth-Century Exploration

The clouds lifted just as we reached the crest, and we looked down on the grand panorama of the sea, and the line of the Moab Mountains beyond... At the risk of being accused of suffering from "Holy Land on the brain" ...I must confess that few landscapes have impressed me more than the sudden unfolding of the Dead Sea basin and its eastern wall from the top of this pass.

Henry Baker Tristram
The Land of Moab, 1874

2

Three Sailors, and a River

EXPLORATION OF the Dead Sea, most of which took place in the nineteenth century, may be roughly divided into two periods—from the end of the 1700s to 1848, and from 1865 through the early years of the 1900s, with the intervening years attached in different ways to both periods. Two hallmarks of the century were the Lynch expedition of 1848, in which the first half-century of exploration culminated, and the founding of the Palestine Exploration Fund, a society established in London in 1865 for the purpose of "investigating the Holy Land by employing competent persons to examine... archaeology, manners and customs, topography, geology, [and] natural science." It might be said that the first half of the century saw the transition from individual exploration to organized expeditions, and that the second half systematized, organized, and refined the methods of inquiry. If the secrets of the Dead Sea were by then less mysterious, the attraction of the awesome valley was not less compelling, and more and more names—English, French, German, American—became associated with research efforts there.

The first explorer to travel to the Dead Sea in the last century was the German Ulrich Jasper Seetzen, a naturalist and physician who was drawn to the East. The "indefatigable Seetzen," as he was later called, prepared carefully for his dangerous journey, studying Arabic as well as geography before setting out, and he travelled disguised as an Arab. At the end of 1806, he left Jerusalem for the Dead Sea, and by the early part of 1807 had become the first European on record to travel completely around the lake. He died mysteriously in southern Arabia three years later—poisoned, it is

thought, by Arabs suspicious of the specimens he was collecting—
and so his major work (untranslated) is a compilation done years
later. But he did write a short account of part of his trip in the form
of a letter addressed to the Palestine Association in London. It is
very brief, and Seetzen jumps miles in the space of a paragraph; but
a great deal of information is compressed into those fifty pages, and
his observations served as the measuring stick against which dozens
of future travellers gauged the accuracy of their own findings.
Throughout the century, the notes he took and the map of the lake
he drew were among the references most often cited by explorers.

Seetzen was soon followed by the Swiss expatriate John Lewis
Burckhardt, known principally for his rediscovery in 1812 of the
ancient Nabatean capital of Petra, southeast of the Dead Sea.
(Burckhardt was also an important figure in the exploration of
Africa, as Alan Moorehead relates in *The Blue Nile*, spending four
years there before dying, probably of dysentery, in Cairo in 1817.)
Although he didn't concentrate on the Dead Sea itself, Burkhardt
did study the Aravah, or Wadi Arabah, the region to the south
which is part of the same valley in which the lake lies. His work
there was crucial in leading other investigators to suspect a
structural link between the Dead Sea and the Red Sea—a theory
which not only turned out to be accurate, but which was also of
central importance in future scientific research on the rift that
stretched even further south into Africa. The significance of his
observations will become clear in a later chapter.

In 1817, two officers in the Royal Navy set out for a brief tour of
Europe and the Middle East. But curiosity soon turned into "an
increasing admiration of antiquities," and the tour became a
four-year journey. They had no intention of publishing an account
of their travels, but friends later prevailed on them to consent to a
limited edition of the letters they had written to their families. Their
book was praised by one explorer as "the most unpretending, and
one of the most accurate narratives" he had ever read.

Armed with muskets, pistols, sabres, and a rifle-like blunderbuss,
these two travellers, Charles Irby and James Mangles, came down
to the Dead Sea at the neglected southern end, where they intended
to concentrate their efforts. It was neglected for good reason, being
a kind of no-man's land where both climate and hostile tribes
discouraged travel. In the tenth century, the Arab geographer
Mukaddasi had written about Zughar, located in this district: the

"people of the two neighboring districts call the town Sakar (that is, Hell); and a native of Jerusalem was wont to write from here to his friends, addressing, *From the lower Sakar* (hell) *unto those in the upper Firdus* (Paradise). And verily this is a country that is deadly to the stranger for its water is execrable; and he who should find that the Angel of Death delays for him, let him come here, for in all Islam I know not of any place to equal it in evil climate." As if this weren't sufficient warning, the geographer Yakût took up the theme three centuries later. The valley in which Zughar lies "is most unhealthy, and its people only continue to dwell there because it is their native place. They are afflicted in most years with the plague, and it kills the greater number of them."

European travellers may not have been acquainted with the Arab texts, but the dangers of the region were no secret, and the prophecy of Jeremiah, though referring to Babylon, rang in their ears as they plodded along: "Her cities are become a desolation,/A dry land and a desert,/A land wherin no man dwelleth,/Neither doth any son of man pass thereby." (Jer. 51:43) The area was taken to be "one of the wildest and most dangerous divisions of Arabia," a reputation it would not soon lose. Two decades after Irby and Mangles' trip, a Frenchman exclaimed: "Here is desolation on the grandest scale, and beyond what the imagination of man could conceive: it must be seen—to describe it is impossible. In this striking and solemn waste, where nature is alike destitute of vegetation and inhabitants, man appears but an atom:—all around is enveloped in the silence of death—not a bird, not even an insect is seen!... The sun concealed itself by thick clouds, and seemed unwilling to shine upon the land cursed by the Almighty." And another report admonished in a manner that seems informed more by imagination than observation: "If any one has a doubt that this whole district is undermined by craters and fire passages, let him only come and spend the night here."

Still, Irby and Mangles paid no heed even to the pleas of their Arab guides, who begged them not to set up camp there. They passed an uneventful first night, but a chilly and sleepless one. Chilly because the wood that the sea had thrown up was too salt-saturated to permit kindling. (Instead of baking their bread, they drank the flour and water mixture "which, though not very palatable, served to appease our hunger.") Sleepless because their guides kept them awake all night with their cries of fear and warnings of attack, false alarms which cancelled sleep.

The next day they arrived at what had appeared to be a sand hill, but which on closer inspection was revealed to be a mountain of salt, spindles of which hung from its sides like icicles. As they examined Mt. Sedom—Usdum, the Arabs called it—they recalled Strabo, who had written that south of the Dead Sea were towns and cities built entirely of salt. "Although such an account seems strange," they commented, "yet when we contemplated the scene before us, it did not seem very improbable."

Crossing the salt marshes at the end of the lake, Irby and Mangles found themselves in a lovely wooded area of acacia, mimosa, tamarisk, osher, and a mustard-tasting plum-like fruit. Nearby, they met a tribe of Arabs who became their hosts for the night. These Goahrnays, they explained, were very different from both city Arabs and Bedouin, for they were farmers who cultivated corn and lived in carefully-planned villages of reed, rush, and cane huts. They were wild-looking, according to the Englishmen's account, but treated their guests well and complained to them of oppression at the hands of the Bedouin. (A century later, Albright would describe the "Ghawârneh" as the descendants of black slaves brought by the Arabs centuries before to tend the sugar and indigo plantations for which the fertile region, the southern Ghor, was renowned, and from which their appellation was derived.)

The letters that Irby and Mangles wrote as they travelled are especially important for the information they supply about the southern extremity of the lake. They referred to the woods there as jungle separated from the water by just a narrow strip of pebbly beach, and they noted the frequent tracks of wild boar in the marshes. They also drew the first map of the southern end of the lake, claiming that the lack of definition of the backwater accounted for discrepancies in reports of the lake's length.

As sometimes happens, most of Irby and Mangles' careful notes received less attention than did an observation casually made as they were returning along the eastern shore. When they approached the Lisan (or Lashon, both the Arabic and Hebrew meaning tongue) Peninsula—the broad extension of land that juts out of the eastern shore and nearly severs the Dead Sea two thirds of the way down—they met a small caravan of horses and mules en route to Jerusalem. The two parties travelled together for a while, then the Englishmen went on as the caravan rested. Later, after rounding the southern tip and heading north along the western shore, they were surprised to see what they took to be the same caravan up ahead of them. The distance between them may have been too great for positive identification to be possible, but they concluded that the caravan had forded the straits. It so happened that other investigators were engaged in a search for evidence that the straits were at times fordable, and had been so throughout history, and Irby and Mangles unwittingly threw themselves into a debate and subjected themselves to criticism from some who questioned their reliability. Nonetheless, they were probably correct in their observation. Over the next years a great deal of supporting evidence would be accumulated, and it would come to be accepted that until climatic changes in the nineteenth century brought about a rise in the lake, the straits were easily crossed.

"Should the Turks ever give permission," mused Chateaubriand, "and should it be found practicable to convey a vessel from Jaffa to the Dead Sea, some curious discoveries would certainly be made in this lake." In truth it was highly impractical, but a young Irishman, a student of theology, attempted it anyway. No traveller to the Dead Sea evokes as much sympathy as Christopher Costigan, who in 1835 became the first modern traveller to sail on the lake, and whose story of endless frustration and suffering came to epitomize the century.

It is likely that the details of Costigan's story would never have been assembled were it not for the determined efforts of the American lawyer John Lloyd Stephens, and it may be worth reintroducing him here. A New Yorker, Stephens undertook his own journey to the East, not long after Costigan, on the recommendation of his physician as treatment for a nagging throat infection. But once he set out from Egypt to the Holy Land, disguised as a merchant from Cairo, he became immersed in his adventure sometimes to the point of foolhardiness (as for example, when he insisted on trekking across the desert to Petra, becoming the first American to enter the ancient city). It was Stephens, according to his biographer, whom Melville saw in church that day; Stephens' intelligent and enlightened *Incidents of Travel in Egypt, Arabia Petræa, and the Holy Land* which had so stirred the boy (and which was reviewed admiringly on its publication in 1837 by the young Edgar Allan Poe, who described it as being written "with a freedom, a frankness, and an utter absence of pretension"). Stephens discovered Costigan's small boat in Jericho, where it was serving as a wall of the hut in which he was staying. He was so moved by the little bit he was able to learn that he committed himself to reconstructing the "melancholy tale" the hapless vessel told.

Costigan was twenty-five years old when he embarked on his journey to Palestine. Though he had been before to the East, he made a fatal error—choosing to travel in July and August, when the heat is greatest and the Jordan River lowest. Costigan and the Maltese servant who accompanied him had bought their boat in Beirut, transported it south to the town of Acre, and from there had conveyed it overland by camel to the Sea of Galilee. They explored the Galilee, then exited via the Jordan River, which they planned to follow down to the Dead Sea. But the rocks were so numerous and the rapids so fierce that after three days of being constantly overturned, they gave up and abandoned the route, fortunate to escape the river with their lives. Hiring camels and guards, they sent their baggage to Jerusalem while they made the arduous trek south on foot. They finally reached Jericho, in rags, and Costigan went up to Jerusalem to fetch the luggage. A few days later, the two men squeezed into the little boat and set sail on the Dead Sea.

So intent was Stephens on learning what had happened to the Irishman that he eventually tracked down the servant in Beirut and plied him for details. It seems they did the entire tour of the lake in eight days, sleeping on shore every night but one, when they stayed at sea for fear of a band of Arabs camped nearby. The servant recalled their having zigzagged the lake several times, sounding as they went with a line over a thousand feet long. They found the bottom to be rocky and of very uneven depths, ranging in places from 180 feet to 240 to 480 in the space of a few boat lengths. (Stephens, like Chateaubriand before him, believed that this alone contradicted the view that Sodom and Gomorrah were destroyed by volcanic eruption and that the sea now sits in the crater thus formed. Having seen both Vesuvius and Etna, Stephens assured his readers that no other crater shows such irregularities as are found in the floor of the Dead Sea. Actually, the Dead Sea's floor is not at all as then described. In an extensive geophysical examination in 1974, the lake was shown to be somewhat shallower than earlier believed, and nearly flat-bottomed over almost half its area.) In four different places they spotted ruins on the shore and could distinguish large hewn stones of the sort used for buildings. Costigan identified one of the sites as the ruins of Gomorrah—a claim which the ever-solicitous Stephens called "the most intensely interesting illusion that any man ever had" (an especially interesting comment when we recall that no one was more ardent than Stephens in searching for the ruins of the ancient cities).

Costigan also identified what he at first took to be an island at the southern end of the lake, but in falling victim to that visual deception he was not alone. Seetzen thought he had seen one, too, and his report prompted Irby and Mangles to search for it. Early on, however, they were able to verify the illusory source of Seetzen's report: "This evening, about sun-set, we were deceived by a dark shade on the sea, which assumed so exactly the appearance of an island, that we entertained no doubt regarding it, even after looking through a telescope. It is not the only time that such a phenomenon has presented itself to us... We were unable to account for these appearances, but felt little doubt that they are the same that deceived Mr. Seetzen into the supposition that he had discovered an island of some extent, which we have had the opportunity of ascertaining, beyond all doubt, does not exist." According to his servant, Costigan explained the optical illusion, satisfactorily for Stephens, as being a tongue of high land protruding straight up the center of the lake. The Lisan Peninsula does have a northern extension, and it was probably this raised horn that was responsible for the illusion.

Working his memory for details of their ill-fated voyage, the servant elaborated on the weather conditions. One detail, banal as it may seem, was the subject of some lively discussion among both ancient and modern writers. Every night, he recalled, a north wind blew, bringing with it great waves. That observation ran contrary to what many believed—namely, that the water of the Dead Sea was too heavy for waves to be raised. Tacitus was perhaps the first to suggest that the sea does not yield "to the action of winds." The medieval view was in accord: the Dead Sea "moveth not with the wind, for glue withstandeth wind and storms, by which glue all [the] water is stint." A few hundred years later, Thomas Fuller aired an objection to the waves which decorated his map of the Dead Sea: "Would not it affright one to see a dead man walk? And will not he in like manner be amazed to see the *Dead-Sea* moving?

Why have you made the surface of the waters thereof *waving*, as if like other seas it were acted with any *tyde*, which all Authors avouch, and your selfe confesseth to be a *standing stinking* lake?"

Chateaubriand came away believing that "the most impetuous winds can scarcely ruffle" the sea. But he was contradicted by one Thomas Jolliffe, who declared that in fact "a light breeze is more than sufficient to ruffle the surface." Jolliffe went on to claim, incorrectly, that the protection afforded by the mountains, not the density of the water, was responsible for the infrequency of waves. The water's density does not by any means prevent waves from occurring—as this would-be sailor can attest—but apparently it does hold them down somewhat. Once they are raised, they can achieve a height of three feet, and since they are forty per cent heavier than waves in the sea, one can understand why they were described as pounding like "the sledge-hammers of the Titans."

7. View of the Dead Sea. From *Picturesque Palestine*, vol. 2, edited by Charles Wilson, 1881.

For the first five days Costigan had shared the rowing, but on the sixth their water ran out and with it his strength. It was dreadfully hot, and on the seventh day they were compelled to drink the sea water—a dangerous thing to do, as the chemical make-up of the lake can fatally disrupt one's electrolyte balance. By the eighth, as they were nearing the head of the lake, the servant himself could no longer lift an oar, and they raised sail. They then made coffee from sea water, and at long last a favorable wind sprang up, enabling them to reach the shore in a few hours. Leaving his deathly ill companion on the beach, the servant went looking for help. In the meantime, Costigan was found by a group of Arabs who brought him to Jericho, where he was sheltered and nursed by an old woman.

Here Stephens halts in his narrative, as though snapping out of a reverie brought on by thoughts of the young man so close to him in age and adventurous spirit. He apologizes for detaining his reader with stories of the Dead Sea which could not possibly be of interest to anyone else as they are to him, and resumes the tale of his own journey up through the Kidron Valley. Arriving that night at the monastery of Mar Saba, he is given a divan and covers, crawls in, "and in a few moments the Dead Sea and the Holy Land, and every other land and sea were nothing to me."

So ends his account of Costigan's fate. But as Stephens lay deep in dreams on the divan at Mar Saba, Costigan lay where he left him, deep in fever in the old woman's hut. And there he lay, so to speak, until 1911, when Edward G. Masterman (whom we will meet later in another connection with the Dead Sea) did some further digging and was able to complete the story.

The servant, himself on the verge of collapse, his skin blistered from having poured sea water over his body to cool himself, finally reached Jericho, just a few miles away. He had water and horses sent back for his master, unaware he had been found. From Jericho, Costigan sent the servant to Jerusalem with instructions to send back a camel outfitted with mattresses and cushions "so as to admit of his lying should he not be able to ride his horse." But no camel was sent, and Costigan was too feeble to make the nineteen-mile trip without it. The story grows increasingly moving, as it turns into a tale of helplessness and frustration, the young man growing weaker, and his attempts to reach Jerusalem still futile.

Meanwhile, in Jerusalem, a certain Rev. Mr. Nicolaisen, whom

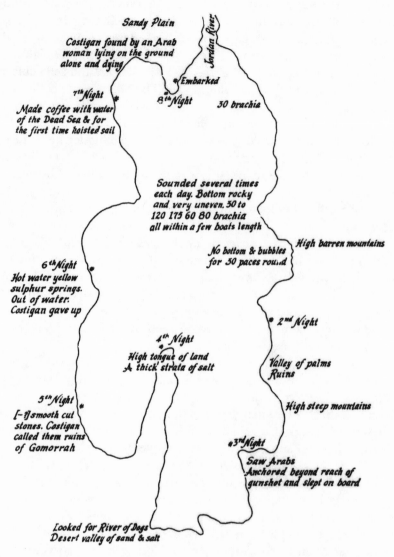

Sandy Plain

Costigan found by an Arab
woman lying on the ground
alone and dying

Jordan River

*Embarked

7th Night

8th Night

30 brachia

Made coffee with water
of the Dead Sea & for
the first time hoisted sail

Sounded several times
each day. Bottom rocky
and very uneven. 30 to
120 175 60 80 brachia
all within a few boats length

High barren mountains

No bottom & bubbles
for 30 paces round

6th Night
Hot water yellow
sulphur springs.
Out of water.
Costigan gave up

2nd Night

4th Night
High tongue of land
A thick strata of salt

Valley of palms
Ruins

5th Night
[–?] smooth cut
stones. Costigan
called them ruins
of Gomorrah

High steep mountains

3rd Night
Saw Arabs
Anchored beyond reach of
gunshot and slept on board

Looked for River of Dogs
Desert valley of sand & salt

8.   Map of the Dead Sea, showing Costigan's route, as drawn
by John L. Stephens, based on the account of Costigan's servant
and originally appearing in Stephens' *Incidents of Travel in Egypt,
Arabia Petraea and the Holy Land,* 1837. Redrawn for the University of Oklahoma edition of Stephens' book, edited by Victor
W. von Hagen, 1970.

58

Stephens had referred to as "the English missionary to the Jews," happened to hear the story and, there being no doctor in town just then, went himself to Jericho. He found Costigan at two in the morning lying outside the hut, utterly debilitated and running a high fever. He immediately began contriving a way to convey him to Jerusalem, but the Arabs were unresponsive to his requests for help. The heat grew more oppressive, a strong wind blew, and Costigan continued to suffer. Finally, a plan was devised by which just three men could do the job required; with Costigan balanced on a straw bed on a horse's back, a man on each side holding his legs and another in front guiding the animal, they set out after dark the next day. It was a long, painful trip up to Jerusalem, the sick man having to stop frequently and rest; the journey that now takes twenty-five minutes took them the entire night. They arrived Saturday morning, three days after Costigan had been found by the edge of the lake, and Nicolaisen was finally able to make him comfortable in a bed at the Casa Nuova in the Old City. There he was attended by a European doctor, and for a time his condition improved. But when the fever (probably malaria) returned that night, he had no strength to repel the attack, and gradually he lost use of his senses. He died quietly Monday morning and was buried the same day in the cemetery of the Latin Convent, which stands on Mt. Zion, on the southern slope of Jerusalem, from which the Judean Mountains roll down to the Dead Sea. No notes from his expedition were found among his papers.

Masterman mentioned that he was able to locate Costigan's gravestone, but by then—1911—it was upside down and obviously no longer marking the young man's grave. Today, because of the efforts of the Israeli geographer Ze'ev Vilnay, the memorial can once again be found in the Franciscan cemetery on Mt. Zion. For a long time, Vilnay had wanted to locate the marker, which he knew was in East Jerusalem; but the city had been divided since 1948 and part of Mt. Zion was under Jordanian rule. When the 1967 Arab–Israeli war left the entire city in Israeli hands, he began to look. The problem was that the Franciscan cemetery had been part of the no-man's land that ran along the border between Jewish and Arab Jerusalem, and it was dotted with mines that made entry impossible. Vilnay brought along a reconaissance unit, had the soldiers clear the mines, and succeeded in finding and reerecting the large but long forgotten tombstone. As for the Casa Nuova, in the

Christian Quarter of the Old City, it is still a hostel; the proprietor, not surprisingly, has never heard of the explorer who died there nearly a century and a half ago.

Two years after Costigan's death, G.H. Moore and W.G. Beke (sometimes spelled Beek) went down to the Dead Sea to do a trigonometrical survey of the lake. Setting out in March of 1837, the two Englishmen sailed from Beirut to Jaffa, then carried their boat overland to Jerusalem and down to Jericho. They managed to survey a good part of the shore but were soon forced to abandon the project when their fearful guards and guides refused to continue. As a result, they accomplished much less than they had hoped. They confirmed the lake's width as between ten and eleven miles, and they determined that it was shorter than had been supposed. Like Irby and Mangles, they realized that its length was subject to variation because an increase in water caused not a rise in the southern end but a flooding of the shore flats. Since their time, and until recently, the length was given as about forty-seven miles.

The significance of Moore and Beke's contribution would slowly be revealed, helped along by the findings of others who were also at work trying to determine the elevation of various sites in the Holy Land. At the time, though, their most important discovery was put to the public in a cautious understatement. In the report of their progress which was printed in the *Journal of the Royal Geographic Society*, the editor conveyed Moore and Beke's finding that from various observations they had made on the temperature of boiling water, the level of the Dead Sea "appears to be considerably lower than the ocean." One would have expected more fanfare to attend this momentous revelation, but the editor's hesitation was appropriate when we consider that determining a location's elevation was not a simple matter in those days. One method, the one which Moore and Beke used, was the observation of relative boiling points (the lower the place, the greater the air pressure, which in turn means that a higher temperature is needed to bring water to a boil). By their time, the 1830s, the barometer was widely in use and was accepted as a more precise method. It is unlikely, however, that Moore and Beke would have been able to convey so large and fragile an instrument as a mercury barometer with them on such a rough trip. (A decade later, an American explorer brought several, and halfway into his journey bemoaned the loss of the last one, broken when a strong wind blew down his tent.) Thus their use of boiling water, a method which could offer fairly precise readings. But not in their case, it seems, for their estimate of five hundred feet below sea level was considerably shy, and the sudden curtailment of their work prevented them from taking further measurements.

It might be worth pausing for a moment to reflect on the degree to which explorers were hampered in their efforts at exactitude by the physical inconveniences they had to bear, for it is a problem epitomized in the subject of barometers. Around the same time that Moore and Beke were at the Dead Sea, a Lt. Col. Sykes observed that good barometers were extremely costly and subject to breakage, beyond which, that to give accurate readings, they had to be checked regularly for certain variables. Seven years later, Mr. Roderick M. Murchison, a senior officer of the Royal Geographic Society, reiterated Sykes' misgivings about barometers but emphasized that the boiling water method likewise demanded many careful corrections. Modern science, he remarked hopefully, "could not offer a greater boon to the traveller, than a really portable instrument for the correct measurement of heights, an instrument neither fragile nor susceptible of derangement."

That boon might have been the recently introduced aneroid barometer, a non-liquid alternative. In 1851, the *Journal of the Royal Geographic Society* printed an article where it was observed that the aneroid's portability had indeed lately induced occasional travellers to employ it. But in comparing readings of mercurial and aneroid barometers, the author determined that it was ill-advised to substitute the latter, since it needed frequent calibration and could not be relied upon for any length of time—a judgment which left travellers back where they had begun (though it might be noted that a few years later, one explorer did obtain an accurate aneroid reading for the Dead Sea).

The drama of the scientific community's awareness of the depression of the Dead Sea, first recorded in the 1837 volume, unfolded in the pages of the *Journal of the Royal Geographic Society* over the next several years. Moore and Beke's own report was expected in the near future, but inexplicably, nothing of theirs appeared. In 1839 Mr. William Hamilton, a senior officer, delivered the Society's eighth anniversary address and reminded his fellow geographers that the "exact level of the surface of the Dead Sea is a point of increasing interest not yet satisfactorily cleared up."

Mr. Hamilton's remarks were occasioned by the reports of several other travellers, all within two years of Moore and Beke's visit. Gotthilf von Schubert's barometrical reading came to roughly minus six hundred feet, a tolerable discrepancy perhaps. But soon after, the Austrian Joseph Russegger offered the results of his barometric measurements: minus fourteen hundred feet; and around the same time, the Count Jules de Bertou arrived at a figure of approximately minus 1,330. Clearly something was amiss, but Mr. Hamilton was optimistic that the problem of the apparent depression of the Dead Sea, "one of the most remarkable features in the physical geography of the globe," would soon be solved. For the Society had recently "placed an excellent barometer, made by Newman... in the hands of two young Englishmen about to visit Palestine, with a special request that they would endeavour to settle the point in question."

Who these young men were we never find out, but their efforts must have been thwarted, for two years later we read with some sympathy: "We have not yet been able satisfactorily to ascertain the truth of the reported depression of the level of the Dead Sea below the Mediterranean, and we still hope for the account of some careful observer, who may carry thither a good mountain barometer."

By the following year, Mr. Hamilton did have news to report to the Society. Because of the enormous discrepancies that arose with temperature and barometrical readings, it seemed, as it had been suggested the previous year, that what was required was a detailed survey of the country so that the relative levels of the two seas (the Sea of Galilee and the Dead Sea) could be trigonometrically ascertained. In 1841, Lt. J.F.A. Symonds of the Royal Engineers set out to accomplish that task. Working alone for ten weeks, he "carried a line of levels across from Jaffa to the Dead Sea by two different routes," and obtained nearly the same results for the Dead Sea's level, approximately minus 1,311 feet, very close to de Bertou's calculation three years earlier. His method of triangulation, with "an excellent seven-inch theodolite," was reported in detail in the *Journal*, and it seemed quite beyond reproach. (Yet his calculation for the Sea of Galilee by the same method was about minus 330 feet—an error of some 300 feet, the significance of which would soon become apparent.)

Lt. Symond's work was obviously well-appreciated, for the

following year his father accepted on his behalf (he was still abroad) the Society's Gold Medal, awarded annually "to those who have distinguished themselves in advancing the cause of geographical science." In thanking the Society, the elder Symonds acknowledged that his son's success was made possible by his devotion to his profession, and by his having been entrusted with so fine an instrument as he was able to use—the last comment again emphasizing to the modern reader the limitations imposed when sturdy and accurate equipment was not available.

Mr. Hamilton, pronouncing Symond's findings as "the final settlement of the long-disputed point" regarding the comparative levels of the Mediterranean, the Dead Sea, and the Sea of Galilee, then asked geographers to turn their attention to the next pressing question: how to account for the alleged 1,000 foot difference in depth between the Sea of Galilee and the Dead Sea—a difference which means that the Jordan River, "not being a meandering stream," falls more than sixteen feet every mile of its course.

Drawn into the exchange was one of the most eminent explorers of the Holy Land, the American Edward Robinson, whose 1841 *Biblical Researches in Palestine, Mount Sinai, and Arabia Petræa* is regarded as a cornerstone of Biblical geography and as one of the nineteenth century's most significant works on Palestine. In 1847 he read a paper to the Royal Geographic Society in which he expressed his amazement not so much at the depth of the depression but at what it meant about the Jordan River, which figured as large in the mythology of the Holy Land as did the Dead Sea, and whose influence upon man's imagination, according to the Biblical geographer George Adam Smith, was matched only by the Nile.

The Jordan was the river of quintessential purity, made holy by John and Jesus and further glorified for its location next to the lake which abided no life and guarded the ruins of the cities that loved and practiced evil, while the Dead Sea was vilified for receiving into its "greedy bosom" the "whole body" of the Jordan River—the suggestion of carniverousness no doubt intentional. It might have been Pliny who first expressed what was taken to be the natural antipathy between the river and the lake: "With the greatest reluctance, as it were," the Jordan "moves onward towards Asphaltites [the Dead Sea], a lake of gloomy and unpropitious nature, by which it is at last swallowed up, and its bepraised waters are lost sight of on being mingled with the pestilential streams of the lake." His theme was sounded for the next eighteen centuries by generations of believers whose sensibilities were offended by the Dead Sea. Early in the 1800s, it took a rare and generous mind to proclaim that in fact the contamination worked the other way— that the yellow-brown Jordan dumped its muddy water into the clear blue of the lake, discoloring it in an unsightly stream. It is unfortunate that George Adam Smith's counsel came too late in the century to help disillusioned travellers, for it might have spared them some heartache: "Remember that [the Jordan] is... [in] a ditch as deep below the level of the ocean as some of our coal-mines, and you will be prepared for the uncouthness of the scene."

For centuries Christian pilgrims braved the desert in order to immerse themselves in the water where their saviour had been baptized—though if the medieval Russian pilgrim Daniel is to be believed, the site was not exactly the same. According to him, the precise place where Jesus had been baptized was a stone's throw from where the river ran in Daniel's time. The Jordan, he explained, "seeing its Creator approach for baptism... left its bed, and then affrighted turned back. Formerly the Sea of Sodom [the Dead Sea] came right up to the place of baptism... It was then that the sea, seeing the Deity naked in the midst of the waters of the Jordan, fled in terror, and the Jordan turned back, as the prophet saith, 'Why, O sea! have you fled? and you, O Jordan! why have you turned back?' (Psalm cxiv. 5)."

One nineteenth-century explorer observed about the place where the pilgrims gathered: "If not the true spot connected with reminiscences of high religious import, it is well chosen for the devout observance of the crowds of pilgrims who flock here to bathe, though sometimes the incautious or the over-faithful are carried away by the stream." Indeed, the over-zealous had been carried away for as long as pilgrims had journeyed to the Jordan. The fifteenth-century Felix Fabri described in detail the travails of his companions as they attempted to swim across the river, and another pilgrim speculated about the cause of so great a danger, surmising that "unnatural and hellish beasts" from the Dead Sea snatched their victims from below, or that the poison of the Dead Sea itself caused swimmers to be dragged down, while admitting also that "strong imagination" might have a part in it. Drownings were actually rare, but a nineteenth-century explorer-turned-lifeguard stopped by the river until a group of pilgrims had safely left the water in case any needed rescuing. Others, like the Irishman Eliot Warburton, had no worry of drowning because they could not even enter. Warburton was hopeful on approaching the river, "but sank up to my knees in its tenacious mud, and with great difficulty extricated myself."

As this suggests, the Jordan's character depended on the season. One March, a traveller found it "deep and rapid, rolling a considerable volume of waters," but in October, another found it decidedly sluggish. A much chargrined Mark Twain explained his disappointment in the reality of the Holy Land's lakes and rivers: "When I was a boy I somehow got the impression that the river Jordan was four thousand miles long and thirty-five miles wide. It is only ninety miles long... [and] not any wider than Broadway in New York. There is the Sea of Galilee and this Dead Sea—neither of them twenty miles long or thirteen wide. And yet when I was in Sunday School I thought they were sixty thousand miles in diameter.

9.   Pilgrims at the Jordan River. From *Landscape Illustrations of the Bible*, by T.H. Horne, 1836.

"Travel and experience mar the grandest pictures and rob us of the most cherished traditions of our boyhood. Well, let them go. I have already seen the Empire of King Solomon diminish to the size of the State of Pennsylvania; I suppose I can bear the reduction of the seas and the river."

As we saw earlier, the river's mystery arose in part from the question of what happened to it after it entered the Dead Sea. In an authoritative voice summoned to persuade, the fifteenth-century Maundeville had declared: "And you shall understand that the river Jordan runs into the Dead Sea, and there it dies, for it runs no further..." A Frenchman visiting Palestine two hundred years later was more corrective of nature in his explanation, describing "this beautiful Jordan, which becomes lost in the Dead Sea and after passing underground flows out into the Red Sea and thence into the Great Sea. This was proved by an incident which happened to a pilgrim who dropped a curiously wrought wooden cup into the Jordan River. He arrived at Messina [in Sicily], having completely forgotten the cup, and discovered it in the hands of those who had found it on the seashore."

The old opinion, which persisted through approximately the first third of the nineteenth century, was that the Jordan River had once passed through the valley of the Dead Sea. The esteemed Burckhardt, who would be admired as "one of the most careful of travelers," surmised that in ancient days the river continued to the Gulf of Eilat (Akabah), until the catastrophe which simultaneously destroyed the Cities of the Plain and plugged up the valley, creating for it a new terminus, the Dead Sea. That view, that the Dead Sea was only as old as the Biblical cataclysm, was widely held. One writer was hard-pressed to account for the incredible difference between Jordan River and Dead Sea waters "on any other principle than that which refers the origin of the lake to the convulsion recorded in the Scripture narrative." And as late as 1848, the respected William Lynch, describing his difficult survey of the Dead Sea, exclaimed: "At times it seemed as if the Dread Almighty frowned upon our efforts to navigate a sea, the creation of his wrath."

The creation of his wrath it may have been, but to Robinson at least it was very clear that "a lake must have existed in this place, into which the Jordan poured its waters, long before the catastrophe of Sodom." And in a provocatively titled book, *The Dead Sea: A New*

Route to India, William Allen commented on what he perceived to be a general reluctance to address the question of how the Dead Sea came to be so low, and speculated that many people were hesitant because they felt they had to connect the phenomenon with the disaster recorded in Genesis, in keeping with Jewish, Christian, and Moslem tradition. Allen himself insisted on the importance of unlinking the two, not because he doubted the Biblical account, but because he was interested in both scientific and Biblical veracity, and was convinced that the two events had occurred independently of one another. (Allen was not the first who presented the view. Aside from Robinson, Chateaubriand had mentioned a certain Professor Michaelis and "the learned Busching," who half a century before proposed that "physics may be admitted in the catastrophe of the guilty cities, without offence to religion.") Allen opposed the view that fire, followed by an inundation of the plain, destroyed the cities and led to the creation of the lake. The destruction of Sodom and Gomorrah was "the swift and sudden effect of the wrath of God upon the depraved nations seated in [the] neighborhood," he asserted, advising that we not look in that event for ordinary natural causes which, in the case of the Dead Sea, probably had been going on for many ages before the historical period.

It was also believed that despite the stopping up of the valley, the incline itself continued to the open sea. It had escaped Burckhardt that the Aravah Valley tilted upwards from the southern tip of the Dead Sea to the Gulf of Eilat, but he was far from alone in supposing that the slope which began at the very source of the Jordan should naturally continue to the sea. The progress made regarding this problem constitutes yet another fascinating moment in the history of science.

One of those who stand out with respect to the problem was the Frenchman Jules de Bertou. Of the Wadi Arabah (the explorers used the Arabic) de Bertou wrote: "We entered this celebrated valley, which at first had the appearance of the bed of a great river; and, if its slope were not visible towards the Dead Sea, one would exclaim on seeing it, 'this is really the bed of the Jordan;' it is, however, the bed of a torrent which flows in an opposite direction, viz., from S. to N., and falls into El Ghór." De Bertou was the first European in modern times to travel its whole length, from the Dead Sea to the Red Sea, and he demonstrated (though the instruments with which he made his elevation readings were unreliable) that "in the present state of things, the river Jordan never could have flowed into the Ætlantic Gulf [i.e., the Red Sea]."

De Bertou pre-empted Robinson, who had long planned to follow that very route in the hope of answering the same question. He had wanted to be the first, but even as he was preparing to leave Jerusalem, he met de Bertou, who had just returned. Robinson would soon write, in concurrence: "The nature of the country shows, without measurement, that the surface of the Dead Sea must be lower than that of the Red Sea or the Mediterranean." (For Robinson to agree with anything de Bertou claimed is noteworthy, since he criticized the Frenchman mercilessly for errors, carelessness, and downright ignorance.)

The issue would appear to have been resolved, but in 1849, a senior officer of the Royal Geographic Society warned that the matter of the Jordan's once having flowed to the Red Sea was not closed, for, as the well-respected Russegger suggested, the depression of the Dead Sea and the Jordan Valley may have been caused by volcanic action which opened up the fissure, stopped the Jordan's course, and altered the topography of the Wadi Arabah. This cautionary note notwithstanding, it does appear that investigators pretty much agreed by then that the Jordan never did flow to the Red Sea. (The actual configuration of the Aravah Valley is as follows: It extends for 103 miles from the Gulf of Eilat to the Dead Sea and is divided into three major sections. Its first part, forty-eight miles long, rises from Eilat and Akabah to 755 feet above sea level at the watershed between the Red Sea and the Dead Sea. The forty-six mile long central portion slopes towards the Dead Sea, and the nine-mile long northern section, the salt swamps, drops precipitously—460 feet in two miles—to the Dead Sea.)

As for the possibility of volcanic action, mentioned by several researchers, it seems to have been thought a possibility that at some time not so very long before the events recorded in Genesis took place (i.e., the second millennium B.C.E.)—or coinciding with those events—the region did experience eruptions. One of the principal questions Lynch directed his geologist to look into was the "volcanic phenomena of the Dead Sea." And to Lynch, the evidence of such activity was so clear that he assumed Mt. Sedom consisted "entirely of a volcanic product." He also noted characteristics of volcanic action in the Jordan Valley and on the Dead Sea's eastern shore, and what he hoped to do was gather specimens so as to compare that ancient volcanic evidence with specimens from Vesuvius or "some modern active volcano." Robinson was more sceptical, inquiring of a certain distinguished geologist if he thought, given Robinson's observations, that either a conflagration or volcanic action could have been the agent of particular alterations in the region. Today it is known with virtual certainty that there has been no volcanic action in the Dead Sea valley for many millennia (though there was in the northern Jordan Valley), and, as we will see in a later chapter, speculation as to the cause and nature of the massive destruction visited on the Cities of the Plain developed in this century along different lines.

Back to 1847, then, and Robinson's paper, which stands as a marvelous document of incredulity, and reflects the persisting misconception about the river. It was almost universally agreed that the Jordan's course was straight, with perhaps a curve here or there. Pliny had described it as "a delightful stream, and, so far as the situation of the localities will allow of, winds along its course and lingers among the dwellers upon its banks," but a nineteenth-century editor contradicted him in a patient footnote: "On the contrary... the Jordan runs in a straight line almost into the Dead Sea." Oddly enough, in his 1745 account, Pococke had referred to what he called the little turns of the Jordan; Seetzen's early map showed the river as twisting a bit as it flowed down the valley, and Irby and Mangles had noted that it "winds extremely" (at least just south of Tiberias). But for some reason, by the 1830s or so, it had come to be taken for granted that the river was more or less straight.

Robinson recalled that since the lineal distance from the Sea of Galilee to the Dead Sea was sixty miles, and the difference in depth between the two lakes had been given as roughly 1,000 feet, the river dropped sixteen feet every mile. It has, he continued, neither cataracts nor rapids, and he doubted that any would be discovered in the uncharted sections. "Yet in the 984 feet of its descent in 60 geographical miles, *there is room for* THREE CATARACTS, *each equal in height to* NIAGARA, and still to leave to the river an average fall equal to the swiftest portion of the Rhine, including the cataract of Schaffhausen!" Pronouncing such a rate to be "a very remarkable phenomenon," he went on to chastise "scholars and learned societies" of western Europe—that the Holy Land was but a few days journey and no effort had been made to arrive at a solution to

69

this impossible problem since attention was called to it four years earlier.

With all due respect, he wondered if Lieutenant Symonds might not have erred, for the information was inadequate to account for the depression of the Dead Sea, and, further, did little to shed light on "the great descent of the Jordan." Recapping Symonds' method, he doubted its reliability and suggested that the task of checking his figures would be a worthy one. It would be quite a small thing, he concluded, for England, France, or Prussia to send out an expedition to address the problem, "and it may be hoped that the Geographic Societies, which adorn the capitals of those countries, will not let the matter rest until it shall be fully accomplished."

Such fervor would not go unnoticed. Picking up the gauntlet which Robinson in his zeal had flung on the floor of the Royal Geographic Society, the now little known Augustus Petermann, reading his own paper before the assembly three months later, advised Robinson, in not so many words, to calm down. He himself was unruffled by Symonds' figure for the Sea of Galilee, and simply assumed that the generally reliable trigonometrical procedure had failed him there, so far out of line was his reading with barometrical ones. He also questioned Robinson's calculations and suggested that the rate of fall was not as great as his colleague determined, while also assuring him that such a phenomenon was not the anomaly Robinson took it to be anyway, even if the Jordan were shown to have no cataracts. Petermann agreed that the river was straight, except for a few bends; but those bends, he suggested, were sufficient to lengthen its course from sixty to eighty miles, thus reducing the rate of fall. And he insightfully added that he had no doubt that once the course were more fully explored, the rate of fall would be found to be even less.

The drama was fast approaching a climax. Even as Robinson and Petermann were going at it in London, an English sailor named Thomas Molyneux had already flushed out the river's great secret (though his findings had not yet been made public). Molyneux, whose name has come to be associated, along with Costigan's, with the perils of the Dead Sea valley, was serving aboard Symonds' ship docked at Beirut and in the summer of 1847 volunteered to head a small mission to the Dead Sea with the purpose of examining the course of the Jordan and the valley through which it runs, and to sound the lake. Taking with him three seamen and a dinghy,

Molyneux sailed to Acre, where they acquired four good camels for boat and baggage and set out the last week in August. Two days later, from Tiberias, they entered the Jordan River.

At first they found the river to be about a hundred feet across and four or five feet deep, but the water soon became so shallow that they were unable to keep the dinghy afloat, and from that point their difficulties multiplied. Molyneux's account of the journey, though often preoccupied with details of their troubles, is filled with careful observations about the Jordan River Valley. We read that the river in many places was subdivided into a number of small streams, each one unnavigable; that the valley is actually quite hilly, and can only properly be called a valley when compared with the mountains that enclose it; that the river usually passes between cliffs, but when the valley widens, and the plain becomes two miles broad, it is "so full of the most rank and luxuriant vegetation, like a jungle, that in a few spots only can anything approach its banks." And in the observation that was most pertinent to the day's wranglings, Molyneux described the river as winding in the most tortuous manner, adding: "It would be quite impossible to give any account of the various turnings of the Jordan in its way from the Lake of Tiberias to the Dead Sea." (Mark Twain would describe the Jordan's course more than thirty years later as "so crooked that a man does not know which side of it he is on half the time.")

Molyneux delighted in the magnificent scenery, but was also plagued by threats of skirmishes with tribes in whose territory he trespassed, and he, lacking the diplomatic touch of some of his successors, antagonized the Bedouin by scoffing at their offers to protect him. At the very outset of their trip on the river, they were stopped and tribute was demanded. Displaying their impressive array of weapons, Molyneux offered the sheikh a fraction of what he had demanded and continued on his way. But it soon became clear to the stubborn Englishman that it would be impossible to protect both their land-conveyed baggage and the boat, and he increased his offer to an acceptable figure. When the river became impassable—looking "like a giant serpent twisting down the valley"—and the boat could no longer bear the punishment of being flung over rocks, they abandoned it temporarily and went as a single group overland. Observing how populated the valley was, Molyneux realized that he could never have succeeded in making the trip without the bargain he struck with the local sheikh.

71

But authority was not constant, nor were the pacts recognized by each tribe, and he found himself without the patience to bargain anew at every juncture. The tribute was exorbitant, but the naive lieutenant courted disaster with his arrogance, always brandishing his weapons and choosing to go it alone. The trip was beginning to wear him down and he complained for the first time of the heat. He had hoped to reach the Dead Sea in four or five days, but this part of the journey, he wrote, was similar to advancing an army through enemy territory—one had not only to look out for food, but also to find defensible positions each time the party stopped. His nerves were strained; every time they spotted a band of men they were forced to prepare for battle, and though most of the alarms were false, they were taxing. Finally, he pushed his luck too far, and tried to avoid another payment by hiring extra guards. They were by then in extremely hostile territory, and refusing to pay was foolhardy and provocative. With the dinghy once more afloat and frequently out of sight in the water below the high banks, self-protection was all the more impossible.

When the boat failed to appear for a rendezvous, Molyneux sent out men to search for it. But meanwhile, they themselves were being reconnoitred, and they settled into position for an attack which never materialized. Finally, one of the scouts, having made his way upstream, returned to the anxious lieutenant with the news that he had found the boat, empty, their two Arab guides half-naked but unharmed—victims of what Stephens had called the "Arab mode of robbery"—and no sign of the English crew. Apparently forty or fifty men had gathered at the river's edge and begun pelting the boat with stones and firing near it into the water, until the crew was thoroughly frightened and easily subdued. The Arabs robbed the men of their arms and ammunition and let them go, in a "battle" that could have been bloody, considering the insult Molyneux had inflicted by refusing to pay tribute.

Molyneux turned his efforts towards searching for the missing men. In the jungle by the river, beating the bushes under cover of the dark as yet moonless night, he called out in loud whispers for his comrades, all along suffering greatly in the sweltering heat and fearful of being discovered. When the moon rose, Molyneux reluctantly gave up the search and began the thirty-mile trek to Jericho, hoping to find safety and assistance there. He arrived ten hours later, half dead with thirst, exhaustion, and anxiety. He persuaded the governor to send out a search party, pessimistic about ever being able to carry on his project.

From Jericho he made his way up to Jerusalem, where he assembled an armed guard and another search party and set out immediately to continue the vain hunt for the lost sailors. Feeling defeated, he went down to the Dead Sea and at long last the boat was put in place at the water's edge, Molyneux prodding himself on, despite the loss of all three sailors, only because he knew he would never forgive himself for the wasted opportunity. Assembling his "crew"—a guide from Tiberias and the Greek whom he had brought from Jerusalem—he shoved off from the "vile place, just as it was falling dark, with only two oars, and with no one who had much idea of using them, except myself, or any notion of boat-sailing." The enervated Molyneux was without heart, and he could not help but feel that he was embarking "in a silly if not a perilous undertaking."

Exhaustion and strain undoubtedly played on Molyneux's nerves, for his description of the Dead Sea is ill-tempered and impatient. No one would disagree that the water produces a greasy feeling on the skin, and that it is destructive to everything it touches, especially metals. But his assertion that the water throughout the lake was a dirty, sandy color, like the Jordan, and moreover that it had a disagreeable smell, would find little agreement among even the most prejudiced travellers.

In all fairness, though, the claim concerning the foul odor of the Dead Sea may have been derived from an old bias that originated in classical writings. Diodorus described the region surrounding the Dead Sea as "very torrid and ill smelling, which makes the inhabitants sickly in body and exceedingly short-lived." Much later, Yakût was even more explicit: "The foul odor of the lake is extremely noxious, and in certain years the miasma is blown across the land, and causes destruction to all living creatures, human and others. By this all the neighborhood villages are depopulated for a time; then other people come there who do not have a care for their lives, and these settle in the lands once more." Five hundred years later, the monks at Mar Saba pleaded with Pococke not to risk asphyxiation by going down to the lake, swearing to him that the air below was poisonous. Characteristically circumspect, Pococke allowed that it was possible, but doubted it could be so at all seasons. The modern traveller recognizes that the sulphur springs which encircle the lake do emit a strong and unpleasant odor, but unless one is in their immediate vicinity, the smell is not noticeable. No odor at all comes from the sea itself, not even the salt air smell we associate with the ocean.

After just two nights at sea, Molyneux concluded that he would be unable to reach the Lisan Peninsula, and he started to return to their embarkation point. But it was no easy task for men who could barely pull an oar and whose time was spent bailing out their severely leaking boat. He despaired of reaching safety, as he doled out brandy to treat his guide's chills. One wonders why they did not row to the nearest shore to rest, especially since Molyneux assumed he could find freshwater at Ein Gedi. All he says about it is that they made no attempt at landing because the heat was intolerable and they had been strongly recommended not to, for reasons of safety. They began rowing straight for the northern coast at three in the afternoon, and arrived at noon the next day.

Molyneux's account ends with their landing and learning of the safe arrival of their lost comrades at the mother ship, where Molyneux joined them the following week. The task of filling in the missing details was again left to Edward Masterman, who passed on the report of James Finn, the British consul who had helped Molyneux get down to the lake. Finn wrote this eerie description of the Englishman's embarkation: "There was a strong misty steam over the water concealing distant objects, well according with the uncertainty always connected with the place, and with the approaching events." Where Molyneux was reticent about his suffering, Finn was not; he recalled that on his return to meet Molyneux after the voyage, just three days later, he found him near Jericho "in an atmosphere of steam, producing drowsiness and depression of spirits." Molyneux went on to the coast for a reunion with his ship. The crew was sobbing and shouting joyously at the return of their officer, "skipping round the dingey and vowing she should never be washed from the slime of the Dead Sea." But Molyneux had suffered irremediably since leaving Tiberias just three weeks before, and he soon exhibited symptoms of the dreaded fever which had vanquished Costigan. He died, either in Tripoli or Beirut, in November of 1847.

There is no mention of Costigan's boat since John Stephens saw it in Jericho, but Molyneux's craft had a story longer than its captain's, one which was also brought to light by Ze'ev Vilnay.

Molyneux's commander, Captain Symonds, became a distinguished officer in the Royal Navy, and on his retirement was
awarded an estate in the English countryside. For reasons
unknown—guilt perhaps, or remorse over his lieutenant's death
years before—he requested the boat as a keepsake. Vilnay began to
track it down and was led to Symonds' estate in Devonshire by a
non-Jewish Zionist whose aid he had enlisted. There they met an
elderly woman who had been a maid on the estate, and she
conveyed her vague recollection of something called a boat-house.
Tramping through the woods, Vilnay and his companion discovered a little house overgrown with vines, its roof an overturned
dinghy. They cut away the tangle that hid it, and exposed the clear
lettering on the boat's side: "This boat was built in 1836, visited
Acre, Cana of Galilee, Lake of Tiberias, Jordan, Dead Sea,
Jerusalem Joppa—1847." Vilnay bought the craft for eighty
English pounds and brought it back to Israel, where it is on display
now at the Dead Sea museum at Shefekh Zohar, on the southwest
shore of the lake.

Though Molyneux is remembered as one of the early and
important explorers of the Dead Sea, his most distinct contribution
was to the solution of the mystery of the Jordan River. His
observations about its meandering course, which would be confirmed and elaborated on just a year later, were a fulfillment of
Petermann's expectations—that the rate of fall of the Jordan would
be reduced considerably once its course were fully expolored. We
now know that the Jordan, between the Sea of Galilee and the Dead
Sea, covers a linear distance of about sixty-five miles—but winds
through more than 130 to do so. This doubling of its length occurs
while it is dropping precipitously—but not the 1,000 feet Symonds'
figures suggested; for the Sea of Galilee is not 330 feet below sea
level, but twice that, hence the Jordan falls from minus 660 feet to
minus 1,300 feet at the Dead Sea. What Robinson figured to be a
fall of over 980 feet in sixty miles is actually one of about 640 feet in
130 miles—or approximately five feet per mile, not sixteen. All the
confusion meant, however, that there was still a need for an
expedition whose results could be taken as definitive. Circumstance
and force of personality created a small place in history for the
American who would spend a full year providing the world with
those conclusions.

Both Costigan and Molyneux were seriously thwarted in their efforts at doing an extensive survey of the Dead Sea by three things. They chose to travel at the worst time of year, when the temperature can be over a hundred and the river is at its lowest point; they failed to secure adequate guards, and they either had no knowledge of freshwater springs at various places around the lake or chose not to take advantage of them. But their attempts paved the way for the most ambitious and famous expedition, led by the American William Francis Lynch in 1848.

Born in 1801, "a motherless child" whose father was occupied by property management, Lynch left school at age sixteen and, as he described it, "embraced the roving, stirring, homeless, comfortless, but attractive life of a sailor." He sailed around the world, was engaged in the suppression of the slave trade on the African coast (about which he later wrote a brief but moving account), and hunted pirates in the West Indies.

He was promoted to lieutenant in 1828 and fought in the Mexican–American War in 1846, after which he received permission to undertake an expedition to the Holy Land. On his return a year later he was promoted to Commander. A few years afterwards he requested leave to explore the West African coast, but he failed to win the necessary backing, though not on the grounds of personal merit, we can suppose, since by 1856 he had been promoted once again, to Captain.

At the outbreak of the American Civil War, Lynch, a Virginian, resigned his commission in the U.S. Navy and was appointed Captain, first in the Virginia Navy, and later in the Confederate States Navy. He was described then as a cultivated man who showed special regard for the well-being of his officers and crew—traits that are clearly manifested in his book about the Dead Sea expedition. He was on active duty throughout the Civil War, and died six months after its conclusion, in October of 1865.

Lynch was a fervent Christian, at once humble and arrogant in his devotion, and a lover of adventure. He was capable of passion and eloquence, but more commonly practiced the reserve befitting his station. Care, patience, and diplomacy—these seemed to be the cornerstones in the nineteenth century on which successful journeys were built, and Lynch had the good fortune to possess all three. He was familiar with the trials endured by both Costigan and Molyneux (though he could not have known of Molyneux's death in

November of 1847, the very month he himself was setting out), and he methodically arranged not to commit any obvious errors in planning, timing, or judgment.

Through the U.S. Resident Minister at Constantinople, Lynch applied for permission from the Turkish government to explore the Jordan River and the Dead Sea. He then ordered two boats, a copper and an iron one, to be constructed, and selected ten seamen for his crew, being "very particular in selecting young, muscular, native-born Americans, of sober habits." Finally, he assembled his instruments, gear, and arms and awaited orders to proceed with his ship, the Supply, to the Mediterranean.

He followed up his application for a firman with a request for an audience with the Sultan, Abdul-Medjid I, in Constantinople. Not that he believed the Sultan could really help him—"for Eastern travellers well know that, ten miles east of a line drawn from Jerusalem to Nablus, the tribes roam uncontrolled"—but because not to have done so would have been a breach of good manners. So it comes as a surprise, until one realizes that above all Lynch was an intensely principled man, that he was willing to be denied the audience over what seems a trifling bit of protocol. Court etiquette required that Lynch remove his sword in the presence of the Sultan, but the American firmly declined, proclaiming it part of his uniform and deciding privately: "no sword, no audience." The requirement was suspended, and the audience, a brief exchange of pleasantries, was held without further delay.

By the end of March, Lynch was in Beirut to see the Pasha, who confessed with some embarrassment that he did not know if the east side of the Jordan River were within his jurisdiction or within that of the Pasha of Damascus. While in Beirut, he met with the Reverend Eli Smith, Edward Robinson's companion, who arranged an interpreter for Lynch. He also engaged a New Yorker, a Dr. Henry Anderson, as geologist and physician.

Reluctant though he was to leave the lovely city, Lynch deemed it "indispensably necessary" to reach the Jordan before its seasonal flood subsided. Sailing south, he anchored at the foot of Mount Carmel, "before the walled village of Haifa." Over the next several days he sent to Acre for horses, launched his two "Fannies"—the Fanny Mason and the Fanny Skinner, as he had named the metal vessels—for a trial run, and raised the American flag—perhaps the first time it had been raised outside the consul walls, he noted.

77

("May it be the harbinger of regeneration to a now hapless people!")

On the first of April, the much anticipated horses arrived, but the sight of them hardly cheered Lynch, for "our Arab steeds were most miserable galled jades... It was ludicrous to see how loosely the harness we had brought hung about their meagre frames." Later, at his meeting with the Governor of Acre, he complained and requested oxen instead, but when it became apparent to him that the Governor expected to be bribed, Lynch backed off, "determined to disappoint him." Finally Lynch proposed the novelty of attempting to harness camels to pull the trailers on which the boats were mounted, for unless they could be pulled by animals, they would have to be taken apart. (The boats had been built in sections to make transport more convenient, and Lynch had engaged a trained mechanic as part of his crew to oversee their assembly, but dismantling them was still an operation he hoped to avoid.) To his inexpressible delight, the experiment was a complete success, and his "heart throbbed with gratitude as the huge animals, three to each, marched off with the trucks, the boats upon them, with perfect ease"—a spectacle witnessed by a large and appreciative crowd, for whom the camel had always carried, never pulled, its load.

Also while in Acre, a town which had been bombarded by the English not many years before, Lynch had the unpleasant task of securing adequate guards and guides for his voyage down the Jordan River. He had little taste, again, for what he perceived to be intimidation in the hope of a bribe. The Governor had possession of "the most alarming intelligence" that the tribes of the Jordan Valley, or Ghor, were at war with one another and that Lynch's safety could not be guaranteed for less than about eight hundred dollars, which would secure the services of a hundred of the Governor's soldiers. In support, the Governor had brought a Bedouin sheikh up from the region in question to testify as to the dangers. And testify he did. He warned Lynch that the Bedouin would "eat... [him] up." Undaunted, Lynch responded that "they would find us difficult of digestion." But in truth Lynch was not a provocateur, and he quickly added that though he would travel despite their efforts to dissuade him, he much preferred to go in peace, paying a fair price for services and provisions, but relying on his own arms to protect his party. Finally, the Sheikh, 'Akïl Aga el Hasseé, "a distinguished sheikh of the Bedawin," whom Lynch had described on first meeting as "a magnificent savage, ...the handsomest, and I soon thought also, the most graceful being I had ever seen," joined Lynch's party, having confided that the Governor was a "humbug," as Lynch put it, and had been trying to frighten him away.

The last addition to his party was the Sherîf Hazzâ of Mecca, not governor himself, but from a family who had been governors until deposed, and who claimed lineal descent from the Prophet Mohammad. The Sherîf was persuaded by Lynch to join the expedition of "a far distant but powerful country" to solve a scientific problem and "to convince the incredulous that Moses was a true prophet."

10. William F. Lynch's caravan to the Sea of Galilee. From Lynch's *Narrative of the United States Expedition to the River Jordan and the Dead Sea*, 1849.

At long last, on April 5, 1848, the incongruous band was on the move, setting out inland to Tiberias. "The metal boats, with the flags flying, mounted on carriages drawn by huge camels, ourselves, the mounted sailors in single file, the loaded camels, the sherîf and the sheikh, with their tufted spears and followers, presented a glorious sight. It looked like a triumphal march." The march was rough, but the mule track that joined Acre and Tiberias was a boulevard compared with what they encountered when they reached the high ridge overlooking the Sea of Galilee. "How in the world are the boats ever to be got down this rocky and precipitous path, when we are compelled to alight and lead our horses?... We will... have to brace ourselves to a desperate effort." But they managed, as Molyneux had a year before on the same ridge, and Lynch's two "Fannies" were finally in the water, joined by an old wooden boat, the Uncle Sam, which he added to the flotilla to relieve the burden.

It was an unhappy Tiberias that Lynch found on reaching the lake; the city had been devastated by an earthquake ten years earlier, and Lynch described it as "a walled town of some magnitude, but in ruins." He would have liked to survey the Sea of Galilee, but the season was advancing, so he did little more than take barometrical measurements (arriving at a reading of about minus 653 feet—nearly twice Symonds' figure) before setting his long-conceived plan in motion. His assignments to each crew member were precise: the land party consisted of Dr. Anderson, who would make geological observations; a Mr. Henry Bedlow, who had joined them in Constantinople, would "note the incidents" that occurred; his trusted Lt. John Dale would sketch the countryside; and his own son, Francis Lynch, would manage the herbarium. From the iron boat, Passed-Midshipman R. Aulick would sketch the river and the banks, while Lynch himself would lead in the copper boat and take notes on the course, rapidity, color and depth of the river and its tributaries, the nature of the banks and the countryside, the plants, animals, and birds, and of course keep a journal of events. Finally, four Arabs manned the wooden boat, which carried the party's tents. The greater danger of attack was to the river party, and everyone was armed except the Sherîf, whose priestly lineage proscribed the carrying of weapons. Lynch was boyish in his exuberance; the mood would later fade, but for the first part of the trip he was effervescent. "Bright was the day, gay our spirits, verdant the hills, and unruffled the lake," as they pushed off and headed for the exit of the Jordan.

Lynch's long account of his trip down the Jordan is fastidious, and though he claimed to be "wholly unskilled in author-craft," it makes for compelling reading. The hour and minute of each movement of the party was regularly recorded, as well as estimates of current speed, compass bearings, points of latitude and longitude, and air and water temperatures. The configuration of the countryside was observed in detail, every botanical and ornitholo-

11. The town of Tiberias and the Sea of Galilee, drawn after the earthquake of 1837, by David Roberts. From *The Holy Land*, vol. I, 1842.

gical specimen noted, and each geographical landmark named by the devout Christian who was on intimate terms with the Bible. Lynch's motivation was twofold: his purpose was principally scientific, and he relied on the goodwill of the American public to encourage him: "I felt that a liberal and enlightened community would not long condemn an attempt to explore a distant river, and its wondrous reservoir,—the first, teeming with sacred associations, and the last, enveloped in a mystery, which had defied all previous attempts to penetrate it." But he did not conceal his fervid wish to visit the Holy Land for very different reasons: "The yearnings of twenty years were about to be gratified... My previous desire to visit the land of the Iliad... became merged with an insatiate yearning to look upon the country which was the cradle of the human race, and the theatre of the accomplishment of that race's mysterious destiny; the soil hallowed by the footsteps, fertilized by the blood, and consecrated by the tomb, of the Saviour."

Lynch's trip down the river was trying beyond his expectations. Their hours were spent plunging down one rapid, finding shelter from the torrent in a bay, praying that the other boats would make it, and setting out again for the next plunge. The rapids were so tortuous that at times the men had to swim beside the boats in order to guide them; at other times they had to create artificial channels—at times working hours in waist-deep water—that would permit passage. To give the reader a sense of what the river journey was like from a less precarious standpoint, Lynch included in his account the observations made from the shore as his boats shot down a rapid: "'Soon after we halted [at the ruins of an old bridge], the boats hove in sight around a bend of the river. See! the Fanny Mason attempts to shoot between two old piers! she strikes upon a rock! she broaches to! she is in imminent danger! down comes the Uncle Sam upon her! now they are free! the Fanny Skinner follows safely, and all are moored in the cave below!'" (The Uncle Sam's luck would run out the next day, when it was shattered against the rocks, while the two metal boats showed only dents for the poundings they took. Disappointed to lose the Uncle Sam, Lynch nonetheless found solace in "this conclusive proof of the superior qualities of metallic boats for such service." A decade later, an editor of the *Journal of the Royal Geographic Society* would suggest that explorers enlarge on Lynch's experience and switch to metallic boats for general use.)

Reading Lynch's *Narrative,* one cannot help but feel that he was blessed with a good deal of luck, all his precautions notwithstanding. For one thing, neither the land nor the river party was ever attacked, and that was against the odds. He felt the state of readiness he maintained—the mounted blunderbuss looking formidable,"with its gaping mouth, pointed down stream, and threatening slugs and bullets to all opponents"—was an important deterrent. No doubt he was right, but to what degree is impossible to know; periodic Bedouin raids on Arab farmers indicated at least that potential adversaries were about. Whatever the reason, they were not attacked, and this pleased Lynch greatly, for it was "the dearest wish of my heart to carry through this enterprise without bloodshed, or loss of life."

And, as he himself acknowledged, some luck, too, permitted him to manage the rapids—the fearful and the lesser ones, twenty-seven in all, he would soon report to the Navy from Jericho—with neither injury nor further loss of a vessel. At one point he described a kind of slingshot ordeal by which each boat was held by a rope and eased into place near the head of a 150 yard long rapid, "where she fairly trembled and bent in the fierce strength of the sweeping current. It was a moment of intense anxiety... The Fanny Mason... swayed from side to side of the mad torrent, like a frightened steed, straining the line which held her. Watching the moment when her bows were brought in the right direction, I gave the signal to let go the rope. There was a rush, a plunge, an upward leap, and the rock was cleared, the pool was passed, and, half full of water, with breathless velocity, we were swept safely down the rapid."

In the week that Lynch was on the river, he assembled a large number of details that would give a much fuller picture of the Jordan River and the Ghor than had previously been available. The river was strewn with large rocks, dotted with unnamed islands, and fed by various tributaries, each one named by the Arabs. It sometimes flowed between low banks, and was usually lined by trees. Birds were all about, the tracks of tigers were often to be seen, and the mountains were sometimes visible. The river was falling rapidly, and the elevated terrace could be seen intermittently on either side.

In one of his most important observations, a verification that was awaited by interested parties on more than one continent, Lynch noted that the course of the river "formed a never-ending series of serpentine curves," and that in doing so it lengthened the sixty miles from Tiberias to the Dead Sea to 200. (There is a substantial difference between the length Lynch determined and the one given today, which is about seventy miles less. Former bends in the frequently diverted river's course are deep and numerous, and it is possible that they may account for some of the discrepancy. Lynch himself on one occasion discovered a dry bed spanned by a Roman bridge, and he assumed that in Roman days it was the main channel. Further, one has to assume that his method for measuring was not as accurate as today's.) So serpentine was its course that only after three days out did Lynch note "a long reach in the river; the first straight line we have seen in its entire course, thus far." The river "curved and twisted north, south, east, and west, turning, in the short space of half an hour, to every quarter of the compass." After two days they were but twelve miles on a direct line from Tiberias. That fact, "the tortuous course of the Jordan," held, in Lynch's estimation, "the great secret of the depression between Lake Tiberias and the Dead Sea."

Lynch had a literary sensibility, displaying in his writing a love of poetry equal to his love of science, and an appreciation for literary expression that we today do not associate with career military men: "At intervals I caught a glimpse of the river in its graceful meanderings, sometimes glittering like a spear-head through an opening in the foliage of its banks, and again, clasping some little island with its shining arms." His intimacy with the river was manifested in his personification of it, as for instance when it seemed "desirous to prolong its luxuriant meanderings in the calm and silent valley, and reluctant to pour its sweet and sacred waters into the accursed bosom of the bitter sea."

In his susceptibility to the landscape, Lynch may have written the most impressionistic scientific account of the century: "The scenery became... more wild as we advanced; and as night, like a gloomy Rembrandt, came throwing her dark shadows through the mountain gorges, sobering down the bright tints upon their summits, the whole scene assumed a strange and savage aspect, as if to harmonise with the dreary sea it held within its midst, madly toward which the river now hurried on." Though he may have been given to overexpression, Lynch was also a sharp observer, and his account of a pilgrims' procession to their traditional bathing place on the Jordan River, where the Israelites were said to have crossed and Jesus baptised, is singular in both detail and the effect of a dream-like visitation that it produces. Awakened at three a.m. by a report that "the pilgrims were coming," he hastened to gather up his tents lest they be trampled by the approaching throng, whose torchlights could be seen "moving rapidly over the hills." Those pilgrims he initially spotted, mounted on camels, horses, mules, and donkeys, were but the advance-guard of a much larger assembly that took until dawn to show its entire self on the crest of the ridge: "Copts and Russians, Poles, Armenians, Greeks and Syrians, from all parts of Asia, from Europe, from Africa and from far-distant America, on they came; men, women, and children, of every age and hue, and in every variety of costume; talking, screaming, shouting, in almost every known language under the sun. Mounted as variously as those who had preceded them, many of the women and children were suspended in baskets or confined in cages; and, with their eyes strained towards the river, heedless of all intervening obstacles, they hurried eagerly forward, and dismounting in haste, and disrobing with precipitation, rushed down the bank and threw themselves into the stream... In an hour, they began to disappear;

12. The immersion of the pilgrims, by David Roberts. From *The Holy Land*, vol. II, 1843.

and in less than three hours the trodden surface of the lately crowded bank reflected no human shadow. The pageant disappeared as rapidly as it had approached, and left to us once more the silence and the solitude of the wilderness. It was like a dream. An immense crowd of human beings, said to be 8,000... had passed and repassed before our tents and left not a vestige behind them."

A suitably surreal occurrence, for with it Lynch's trip down the Jordan was virtually concluded and his voyage on the Dead Sea about to begin. Appropriate especially because the next weeks would be characterized by similarly unreal moments—moments that at times contradicted all his experience, and at other times reassured him as to his purpose in life. So, for example, one midnight, when "shadows of the clouds were reflected wild and fantastically upon the surface of the sombre sea; and everything... seemed spectre-like and unnatural, the sound of the convent-bell of Mar Saba struck gratefully upon the ear; for it was the Christian call to prayer." Such reassurance would come later; at this time, his emotions were as stark as the landscape, as they entered the Dead Sea. Later that same day, "awe-struck, but not terrified, fearing the worst, yet hoping for the best," Lynch's party prepared "to spend a dreary night upon the dreariest waste" they had ever seen.

Lynch intended an ambitious program of exploration on and around the Dead Sea, and he would spend the next three weeks at work there. For a few days the party bivouacked at Ein Fashkhah, from where he sent a boat to sound diagonally across the lake, and where he himself was occupied in a shore survey. Nothing lay outside his scope of interest (he observed for example that his boats' draught was one inch less on the Dead Sea than on the Jordan), and if he later felt that certain items were too technical to be included in his *Narrative*, he simply placed them instead in his *Official Report*, published almost simultaneously.

It is useful to remember that Lynch's was not a mission mounted by the U.S. Navy but was one which he personally requested permission to organize and lead. Reading his account, one feels that perfect compatibility encountered in some of the best travel books (Wilfred Thesiger's for example) between an individual's sensibility and the geographical region which he is exploring. In the case of Lynch, that compatibility arose from his intensely religious nature, his devotion to science, his pre-eminent awareness of his obligations to his flag, and—tying those together—his extravagantly romantic inclinations, which found full expression in the Holy Land.

As this might suggest, Lynch is revealed in his book as a man with a two-sided nature. The somber naval officer fulfilled his duty to science and country, reporting changes in scenery sometimes as frequently as every few minutes, and measuring, collecting, assessing along the way, while the poetry-lover reacted on a different level, describing the sea, for instance, as "a huge cauldron, before us—its surface shrouded in a lead-coloured mist." If such a description seems out of place in the account of a naval officer, it may be well to remember that the lake's associations lay heavily on even the most rational minds of that century, and escaping its sway was like breaking loose from a strong magnetic field. Yet what makes Lynch's *Narrative* most memorable is that he made no attempt, not even in the name of science, to free himself from that influence, but provided ample room for the various voices within him. Thus such disparate juxtapositions as the following one, the mind attending to the task at hand, then drifting to less palpable territory, where we see his sensitivity to rhythm and image:

"At 4.15, half a mile from the shore, threw over the drag in ten fathoms water. It brought up nothing but mud.

"4.30, a perfect calm. The clouds hung motionless in the still air, and their shadows chequered the rugged surface of the mountains of Arabia. It was the grandeur of desolation; no being seen—all sound unheard—we were in the midst of a profound and awful solitude."

Arriving at Ein Gedi, halfway down the western coast, Lynch set up his more permanent camp and prepared for his real work—to continue sounding, make topographical sketches of the shore, and take astronomical, barometrical, and temperature readings. From his so-named Camp Washington ("in honour of the greatest man the world has yet produced"), Lynch sent a small party once more across the lake to sound, while he himself advanced to explore the Lisan Peninsula. "The mind cannot conceive a more dreary scene," he wrote, "or an atmosphere more stifling and oppressive. The reverberation of heat and light from the chalk-like hills and the salt beach was almost insupportable." The day's excursion entailed sailing nearly five hours there and five back, with two for exploration, all in ninety degree heat. One can understand, then, what would cause Lynch to exclaim, "The curse of God is surely upon this unhallowed sea!" It was not merely the view of an outsider; one of the Arabs accompanying Lynch commented that "he had often heard of the tyranny of the Franks [i.e. Europeans] towards each other, but never thought they would have sent their countrymen to so desolate a place as this." (This may explain why it was often assumed by the Arabs that travellers from the West were secretly searching for gold and treasure. The constant hammering at the rocks by Lynch's geologist did nothing to persuade them otherwise.)

For the next three days they explored the southern portion of the lake, the first travellers to sail south of the Lisan Peninsula. Camping near Mt. Sedom, Lynch somehow recognized the ruins that Costigan had supposedly identified as Gomorrah. As they later approached the mountain, in barely enough water to keep afloat, they spotted an immense lofty pillar standing detached from the mass of the mountain about fifty feet above the sea and waded ashore to examine it. Contrary to a later report, Lynch did not claim it to be Lot's Wife; in fact he commented in his *Official Report* that it was "with the harmless levity of sailors" that his men called it thus. (His draughtsman certainly embellished the scene, however,

13. William F. Lynch's Camp Washington, at Ein Gedi, named in honor of "the greatest man the world has yet produced." From Lynch's *Narrative of the United States Expedition to the River Jordan and the Dead Sea*, 1849.

for the pillar appears cross-like, set majestically atop a cyclindrical outcrop.)

This tour of the lake's southern basin was probably the most difficult part—physically and psychologically—of the entire journey, and it sometimes seems that Lynch's spirits were flagging beyond the point where he would be able to arouse himself. To him the scene was one of "unmitigated desolation," where "the thought of death harmonized with the atmosphere and the scenery," and where "it was hard to divest ourselves of the idea that there was nothing but death in the world, and we the only living." Indeed, it is this feeling of disbelief that comes across most strongly as he toured the Dead Sea's southern basin—as though he could not quite get used to the idea of where he was. We can see him standing at the prow of his small copper boat, in military dress, staring without comprehension at the water that surrounded him: "The glare of light was blinding to the eye, and the atmosphere difficult of respiration. No bird fanned with its wing the attenuated air through which the sun poured his scorching rays upon the mysterious element on which we floated, and which, alone, of all the works of its Maker, contains no living thing within it." Then, while in full view of the broad, two-caped Lisan Peninsula, he exercised the prerogative of Western explorers, naming the northern extremity Point Costigan and the southern one Point Molyneux, names by which the two points are known to this day. He thus fulfilled the promise he had made to himself while still in Tiberias—to commemorate, if spared himself, "their gallantry and their devotion to the cause of science."

It was during this time that Lynch and his men suffered most, and he wrote in moving detail about what they endured as they attempted to land on the eastern shore: "A hot, blistering hurricane struck us... and for some moments we feared being driven out to sea. The thermometer rose immediately to 102°. The men, closing their eyes to shield them from the fiery blast, were obliged to pull with all their might to stem the rising waves... My own eye-lids were blistered by the hot wind, being unable to protect them, from the necessity of steering the boat." Seeking relief once they gained the shore, some of the men scattered to the shelter of a ravine, others remained crouching in the boats under awnings. One put on glasses to protect his eyes, but had immediately to remove them, for the metal frames burned the skin, as did their coat buttons. The heat increased with nightfall, and they flung themselves on the ground where, even at 104 degrees, it was two degrees cooler. The parched and suffocating crew, encumbered by their weapons and tormented "almost to madness" by the mosquitoes, and fearing an attack in that dangerous territory, slept ferverishly while taunted by dreams of fresh fountains. At daybreak the sirocco broke.

For Lynch the torment was exacerbated by the signs of illness which he read in his men's faces on their return to camp: "The figure of each one had assumed a dropsical appearance. The lean had become stout, and the stout almost corpulent; the pale faces had become florid, and those which were florid, ruddy,... the slightest scratch festered, and the bodies of many of us were covered with small pustules." Though none had yet contracted the fever, the dread of that possibility nearly overwhelmed him, and he considered forgoing an extended excursion across the lake. Like Molyneux before him, he pressed on.

Lynch's mood would revive sufficiently for him to express appreciation for the "wondrous" sea, whose changes are so sudden "as to make it seem as if we were in a world of enchantment." But for most of this part of his journey he was given more to darker feelings, and the *Inferno* became the poetic representation of his travails. A breeze had enabled Lynch to raise sail, and, while not rowing, the men, overcome by lassitude, had dozed. He alone remained awake, and we can picture him studying their faces as the boat made its slow way, his imagination running wild: "The fierce angel of disease seemed hovering over them, and I read the forerunner of his presence in their flushed and feverish sleep." Some of them were bent forward, arms dangling; others were with heads thrown back, cheeks flushed, lips cracked. "The solitude, the scene, my own thoughts, were too much; I felt, as I sat thus, steering the drowsily-moving boat, as if I were a Chăron, ferrying, not the souls, but the bodies, of the departed and the damned, over some infernal lake, and could endure it no longer." On the verge of utter distraction, Lynch shook himself, then woke them all sternly, ordering the sail lowered and rowing resumed. Anything so as not to be left alone to confront their "unnatural stupor."

Ten days still remained of Lynch's sojourn at the Dead Sea, and he would fill his hours on the eastern side continuing their topographical sketch of the shore, verifying positions, and sounding the lake. He visited the site that Irby and Mangles had believed was the remains of Zoar, but was hesitant to confirm their identification. He prepared botanical specimens for preservation and refurbished the much corroded copper boat, to the entertainment of the local Arabs, who had never seen a sailing vessel (according to Lynch, some assumed it had legs). The Arabs believed that "'the sea accursed of God'" was noxious, and on leaving the beach they stuffed their noses with onions to counteract the malaria they may have contracted in their brief visit to the water.

Lynch was dismayed and enraged to hear from the Christians of nearby Kerak, 3,000 feet above the Dead Sea, of the persecution they suffered at the hands of their Moslem neighbors, and he later took a letter from them to present to the American people for aid in building a church. Lynch had few kind words for the Moslems there but found the Christians hospitable and intelligent, an opinion reinforced by obvious bias. He requested that a trip to the southern tip of the lake and the es-Safieh oasis be organized, but his companion 'Akïl warned him of unrest among the tribes, perhaps because the farmers' wheat was soon to be harvested.

Lynch's relationship with 'Akïl merits a comment, for he freely stated that but for him there might have been a "collision" with

14.   William F. Lynch's guide, Sheikh 'Akïl Aga el Hasseé. From Lynch's *Narrative of the United States Expedition to the River Jordan and the Dead Sea*, 1849.

some of the tribes on at least one occasion, yet more particularly because of the high regard Lynch had for him. Earlier he had described 'Akïl as brave and intelligent, "and although a barbarian, he had much of the manners and the feelings of a gentleman." Known for his prowess in battle, he had recently rebelled against the Turks, who had had to settle with him privately to end the uprising. But here, shortly afterwards, 'Akïl was intimating to Lynch that he was prepared to rebel again if the American would support him. Lynch could not even entertain such a notion, and suspected that what 'Akïl really wanted was to rid the tribes entirely of Turkish rule and establish a sovereignty for himself. Lynch not only knew that in his position it would be impossible to aid a rebellion, but believed also that the tribes, accustomed as they were to internecine hostilities, could never be persuaded to fight for a common cause. His comment that "fifty well-armed, resolute Franks, *with a large sum of money*, could revolutionize the whole country" has a prescient ring to it, given the events in Arabia seventy years later. 'Akïl's intent, if Lynch read him accurately, was a few decades too far ahead of its time to be taken seriously.

Lynch was the first undisguised Westerner (except for Irby and Mangles) to visit Kerak since the time of the Crusaders. But he did not stay long, as it seemed trouble was imminent. Descending once more to the Dead Sea, the expedition proceeded north to explore the Wadi Mojib, the Biblical River Arnon, a portion of his journey which will be taken up in a later chapter. On May 10, having arrived back at Ein Gedi the previous night, they broke camp and began the return journey, up the Wadi Kidron to the convent of Mar Saba, whose bell had offered Lynch incongruous solace three weeks before.

He and his men had explored the lake and its environs for twenty-two days and nights, and all but one of them would survive. The young draughtsman Dale contracted "a low, nervous fever, the same which had carried off Costigan and Molyneaux," and he died a month later while they were near Damascus. Sorrowful though he was, Lynch was pleased that they had been able to accomplish so much: details of topography, atmospheric conditions, winds, and currents, as well as extensive soundings of the lake and samplings from its floor. Their journey proved to Lynch, and persuaded the sceptical among them as well as the professed unbeliever, "of the truth of the Scriptural account of the destruction of the cities of the

92

plain." His scientific findings, particularly his work on the lake's depth, were the basis for much research done on the Dead Sea well into this century. His observations have been adjusted and extensively elaborated on, but not in any major respect discredited.

With the Lynch expedition, the first phase of Dead Sea exploration came to an end. The next decade and a half marked a kind of intermediary period, during which the important work of sifting through the information thus far accumulated was continued, thereby preparing the ground for the Palestine Exploration Fund. Its founding in 1865 marked a turning point, as the transition from individual travels to organized expeditions was completed. If the first half of the century was devoted, generally speaking, to pursuing myths and discovering phenomena, the second half concentrated on answering old questions and formulating new ones. It also witnessed an enlargement of interest, so that Dead Sea exploration came more and more to mean exploration of the lake's shores as well, and that in turn meant deeper involvement with the region's natural and human history.

There is no doubt that some of the explorers at the beginning of the century were scientifically sophisticated. Many, though, were eager but untrained, and others were romantic adventurers. The second half of the century belongs to scientists, and a different, widespread sophistication marks these years. While a Seetzen or a Robinson or a Lynch may have appeared in each of the century's early decades, from the 1860s on they would become more the norm. Most of the explorers who came down to the lake were trained in certain disciplines and were prepared to address themselves to specific questions. In general, the travel accounts of the latter part of the century (with certain notable and important exceptions) are less exciting than those of the first part. A certain displacement seems to have occurred—wonder made way for veracity, naiveté for credibility. Not that the narratives reveal less appreciation, just a bit more control and a little less passion, as though their authors were aware that a scientific community was waiting out there, and that professionalism had to be served. This is not to place relative value on the earlier and later literature. The comparison is strictly from a reader's point of view. For the scientist, there is no question that the refinement in the methods of inquiry which the second half of the century saw, and the accompanying categorization of information, mark the real entrance into the modern period.

3

Along the Briny Strand

I N 1800, when exploration of the Dead Sea was in its tentative early stage, there was no central source of information to which a potential traveller could refer in preparing for his trip. Hardly anything had been written about the region, and much of what had been written was so distorted by individual and religious bias that it was of little use to serious explorers. But by the middle of the century, things were considerably different, and by the third quarter, it has been noted, several thousand books and articles had been published about Palestine in general, many of them containing at least some reference to the Dead Sea or its environs.

Explorers of the second half of the nineteenth century inherited from those of the first half a dogged enthusiasm and a wealth of information about this previously little known, much misunderstood, lake, and a good part of their time was devoted to sifting through the material, distilling questions and looking for leads. Given the remoteness of the Dead Sea valley and the diversity of the travellers, the constant exchange of information throughout those decades was remarkable. Some reports were admired, some criticized, some even mocked. But if one thing can be said, it is that there was an eager audience, both lay and professional, for all that was written, and no explorer set out ignorant of the findings and opinions of those who had preceded him.

The second half of the nineteenth century witnessed an enlargement of scope, as interest grew in the cliffs that enclose the Dead Sea. So it should come as no surprise that these explorers concentrated their efforts in the fields of archaeology and human history, zoology and botany, chemistry and geology. And as they

95

immersed themselves in these subjects, they naturally narrowed their focus once again, turning their instruments and eyes to carefully defined questions and honing their skills in service of them. Thus research was broadened in two ways, as expansion of interest and narrowing of observation followed one another in measured breaths.

If one name stands out in the third quarter of the century both for his contributions as an individual and for his role in effecting the transition to organized exploration, it is that of the Englishman Henry Baker Tristram. Surprised at how little had been written about the wildlife of Palestine, Tristram set his sights on doing full-scale zoological research. But he was also convinced that group efforts could accomplish a great deal more than individual exploration. Along with others who were similarly inclined, he took the steps that would result in May of 1865 in the founding of the Palestine Exploration Fund, a society devoted to investigating all the physical aspects of the Holy Land. Backed by Queen Victoria, the Fund immediately received widespread recognition and support from important figures in all the sciences, many of whom were

15. Palestine Exploration Fund logo, as it appeared on the title page of *Tent Work in Palestine*, vol. 1, by Claude Conder, 1878.

already active in the field. The P.E.F. soon became one of the most prestigious scientific organizations of the day. Tristram himself would become known as the father of Palestine zoology, and his efforts nowhere yielded more exciting results than at the Dead Sea. Early on in his field work he identified a black grakle with orange wings that is not found anywhere else in the world. The handsome bird ("the wildest and shyest of the denizens of these desolate gorges") flits in and out of the wadis, whistling a three-note song ("a rich musical roll... of amazing power and sweetness") as his orange wings flash across the cliffs. It soon became known as Tristram's grakle.

Tristram prepared for his major trip of 1863—an undertaking that would result in his landmark work, *The Land of Israel*—by assembling a caravan of thirty-two pack animals and arranging for protection with various sheikhs. He criticized de Saulcy for having paid too much bakshish in 1850, setting a precedent that other Europeans were forced to comply with and rendering it "simply... impossible for ordinary travellers to follow him." The system of bakshish, which allowed for and at times encouraged greed, was foreign to western perceptions; but those explorers who could disengage themselves from occidental attitudes and submit were secure in their travels—and allowing for the luck of the draw, came to respect and even enjoy their escorts. It was a point of honor among the Bedouin that once arrangements were agreed upon, the safety and well-being of the foreigners were of paramount importance.

Those who intended to stay on well-worn tracks had no need of assistance but were forced to comply anyway. Molyneux was impatient with a system he viewed as corrupt, and he suffered for his intolerance. Tristram, on the other hand, was an observer of people as well as of landscape; if he thought the practice venal, he found something to be learned as well, and he cultivated a certain detachment so as not to feel personally victimized: "They were kindly, good-natured, and obliging fellows, those Ghawarineh. £30 seemed a heavy price to pay simply as a fee for not being robbed for a fortnight, and that to the very men who would have robbed us had we not paid it, for no one else could have done so in their territory. Yet the system is recognized and legalised by what pretends to be the government of the country... We became acquainted with their [the Arabs'] habits, we could study their customs, and improved ourselves in their language, while every ruin, cave, and fountain in the district were pointed out to us as they never could have been by any other than the tribe in possession."

Winter found Tristram travelling through the mountains of the Judean Desert en route from Jerusalem to Jericho. The sand-colored mountains are stone-strewn and barren, yet for a brief spell after the winter rains they belie the word desert, as they open into a spread of green thickly speckled with red anemones. The hills, creased and folded into one another, roll toward the valley, while Jericho, below in the distance, is a patch of brightness resting on the plain.

From Jericho Tristram backtracked in order to explore Wadi Kelt, the northernmost wadi on the west side of the Dead Sea. The water of Wadi Kelt slips out of three springs in the hills near Jerusalem and flows through the desert, eventually passing through Jericho and feeding the Jordan River. In the first century B.C.E., Herod had built aqueducts for irrigating his expansive groves and supplying his fortresses and palaces, but by Tristram's day they had long been in disrepair, and the water rushed undiverted through the canyon, nourishing the oasis as it went on to join the Jordan.

Today one can follow the wadi's course on foot for a few miles before it reaches Jericho. From a mountain ridge above the stream, the hiker sees canyon ledges dotted with caves and small hollows. So high is the ridge and so sheer the canyon walls that one looks down to watch birds soaring below, an oddly disorienting posture. The path turns and dips, as if seeking a place to unwind on the unaccommodating cliff. Long, deep curves obstruct the view, so it is suddenly that one comes upon the monastery of St. George, a startling and awesome sight, held as though magnetically to the ledge. The stream of Kelt is a silver ribbon far below.

The remote wadis of the Judean Desert were sought out by monks of the Byzantine period for their tranquility and inaccessibility. Under Justinian, the monastic movement flourished, and by the sixth century C.E. thousands of monks lived in the hundreds of monasteries scattered throughout the desert. At the beginning of the seventh century, Palestine was conquered by the Persians, and the monasteries were decimated. A few years later the Byzantines recouped and expelled the Persians, but the monastic movement never recovered, for in just a few years, the Byzantines were once and for all defeated by the nascent Muslim movement which had swelled out of Arabia. Today, only a few desert monasteries remain, clinging, like St. George, to remote cliffs, their precarious beauty challenging any would-be conqueror to defy God's hand.

Jericho, wrote Tristram, has "a radiancy of atmosphere which converted the eastern mountains of Moab and the Dead Sea into a fairy land of glowing softness." Called a city of date-palms in the Bible, Jericho is the jewel of the Judean Desert, fed not only by Wadi Kelt but also by the more renowned Ein es-Sultan, or Elisha's spring. According to the Book of Kings (II, 2:19–22), the sweet water of the spring was foul "and the land miscarrieth." But Elisha, successor of the prophet Elijah, rewarded the townspeople for their kindness; going to the water's source, he threw in some salt and in

16.   Ein es-Sultan, or Elisha's Spring, at Jericho. From *Landscape Illustrations of the Bible*, by T.H. Horne, 1836.

the name of the Lord he transformed the spring into the freshwater that has since made the oasis famous.

During his strife-filled reign, Herod turned the area into an even more prosperous agricultural center which he could observe from his luxurious winter retreat (ruins of which have been uncovered and recently excavated). So coveted was the town that Antony, to Herod's great dismay, sliced off "the palm-grove... in which the balsam is produced" and gave it as a gift to Cleopatra, who had longed for it. Josephus related the episode in his *Antiquities of the Jews*: "Now at this time the affairs of Syria were in confusion by Cleopatra's constant persuasions to Antony to make an attempt upon every body's dominions;... and she had a mighty influence upon him, by reason of his being enslaved to her by his affections. She was also by nature very covetous, and stuck at no wickedness... She... petitioned Antony to give her Judea and Arabia; and, in order thereto, desired him to take these countries away from their present governors... [Y]et did the grossest parts of her injustice make him so ashamed, that he would not always hearken to her to do those flagrant enormities she would have persuaded him to. That therefore he might not totally deny her, nor by doing everything which she enjoined him, appear openly to be an ill man, he took some parts of each of those countries away from their former governors, and gave them to her." In that way Cleopatra came to be mistress of many of the cities west of the Euphrates, forcing Herod and the Nabatean King Malichus to lease from her their most fertile districts, including Jericho and its environs, where the balsam was grown and "which is the most precious drug that is there, and grown there alone."

This balsam (commiphora gileadensis) was the true prize of Jericho and the other oases on the Dead Sea's western shore. The small, white-flowered desert tree is a native of southwest Arabia and Somaliland, and the origin of its appearance in the Dead Sea region is not precisely known. Some have long thought it was brought from Arabia in seedling form by the Queen of Sheba to King Solomon—a view Thomas Fuller summarily dismissed in 1650, insisting that would have been like carrying water to the fountain. Others agreed that it was in fact indigenous to the Dead Sea region, but only in a wild form from which superior strains were derived. (It is no longer found in any variety in the area, but does still grow in Arabia under similar climatic conditions.)

100

"I have gathered my myrrh with my spice [lit. balsam]," we read in The Song of Songs (5:1), suggesting that its value was long recognized. Balsam was used medicinally and in the preservation of the dead, but it gained its fame as an ingredient in perfume. So treasured were the balsam groves that ownership of them was a national priority. During the war against the Romans, the Jews tried to destroy their groves to prevent them from falling into enemy hands. The balsam survived, however, and also found its way to Egypt. According to legend, Cleopatra had cuttings taken and brought to be planted in the gardens of Heliopolis, where the balsam flourished for a number of centuries before disappearing, as it did from the Dead Sea valley. But before the plant vanished, balsam perfume was a major industry. Not long ago, a perfume factory dating to Herod's time was discovered at Ein Bokek, on the southwest side of the lake, and its several rooms (for crushing and grinding), stove, and plaster-coated pool indicate that the process was a multi-stepped one which ended in the oil being skimmed off the top of the boiled, paste-like resin.

The manufacture of perfume was a state secret for many centuries. In the 1400s the pilgrim Felix Fabri visited Egypt, where the balsam groves were tended as the private property of the Sultan and the resin-extraction process was carefully guarded. Treated to a small demonstration, Felix watched as a cut was made in a branch, whereby thick oil oozed out. Each pilgrim was permitted a dab on the hand, and Felix was delighted that for several days he could smell nothing but the wonderful balm.

This method of extraction had not altered in some fifteen centuries. In describing the Jews for his Roman readers, Tacitus wrote that the Jews' products "are of the same kind as ours, but they possess in addition the balsam and the palm. Their palm-groves are lofty and elegant, the balsam is a tree of moderate height: as each of its branches swells up with the sap, if you cut it with steel, the sap-vessels shrink up, and accordingly they are opened with a broken stone or a potsherd; the extract is used medicinally." Josephus called the balsam "the most valuable local crop" and described the same process whereby their stems were slashed with sharp stones and the resin collected where it was exuded from the cuts.

Josephus described Jericho as "the most fertile spot in Judea," boasting many varieties of palm, differing in taste and name, some

101

of which, when trodden underfoot, even produced a substance like honey. The always curious historian speculated about Jericho's fertility and suggested it was due to the warmth of the air and the power of the water, by means of which plants are able to conserve strength for summer, "when the district is so burnt up that no one goes out if he can help it." He concludes his paean to the ancient town by saying it would be no exaggeration to call the place divine, "a place where the rarest and loveliest things are found in such abundance."

Medieval sources indicate that the palm groves still flourished in the seventh century, but by the nineteenth they were long gone, along with the sugarcane, henna, sycamore, and honey. Still, Tristram found ample reason to be delighted with the oasis: "In zoology, Jericho surpassed our most sanguine expectations. It added twenty-five species to our list of birds collected in the tour, and nearly every one of them rare and valuable kinds."

17. Jericho. From *Liber cronicarum*, by Hartmann Schedel, Nürnberg, 1493 (published by Anton Koberger).

What a stunning array it must have been: the "sociable and noisy" Hopping Thrush, in Palestine found only in the Dead Sea oases; the singular Palestine Sun-Bird, "perhaps the most interesting species of the whole Palestinian Avifauna," belonging to a tropical family and confined to a narrow strip of the Holy Land, where it maintains headquarters at the oases of the Dead Sea's corners; and the Collared Turtle Dove, three species of which meet in Palestine—just to name a few.

Exploring the region, Tristram noted the abundant tracks of wild boar, leopards, wolves, jackals, hyenas, and fox, and he was occupied for the next months identifying and cataloguing everything that crossed his path, while the Arabs in his company carted in a never-ending supply of new specimens—plants, birds, shells— to spread on the table for examination. There sat the bearded English gentleman in his cumbersome tropical dress, spending days on end poring over his notes and planning hikes.

Tristram stands out among the explorers of the day for his uncomplaining good humor and his habit of expressing pleasure rather than chagrin when confronted with the unexpected or the untoward. Most travellers had little favorable to say, for example, of the oasis Ein Fashkhah, today a nature reserve not far down the western side of the lake, other than that the hunting was good. But to Tristram it was much more than a convenient sporting ground: "Our prospects at Ain Feshkhah seemed as bright as at Jericho, and we were already prepared to pronounce the Dead Sea shore to be the shore of charmed life. Water, vegetation, birds and beasts, geology, and hot baths—everything was in abundance. The poor fountain has had, methinks, rather scurvy treatment at the hands of its biographers... Perhaps our tastes were vitiated, or perhaps after the recent rains the mineral element was unusually diluted; but... we found it tolerable. It made good tea and coffee, though with a slight flavor of soda." So content was he that his expedition spent two days at work, someone with a camera, another with watercolors, a third collecting specimens, and Tristram himself exploring the shore.

For many years an interesting debate had centered on Ein Fashkhah. Certain explorers reported seeing small fish swimming in the Dead Sea in the vicinity of the oasis. Others were quick to call those reports wishful thinking, for everyone by then knew that no fish could live in the lake. The respected biologist von Schubert had,

103

it was thought, laid the matter to rest by explaining that the small fish which are brought down by the Jordan "or accompany voluntarily his flood... soon pay for this lovely wandering with their lives." Yet as it turned out, the reports were more than mere fancy. The water of Ein Fashkhah, much lighter than that of the Dead Sea, periodically overflowed its pools and spilled into the lake, sometimes carrying small fish with it. It did not mix immediately with the lake water, but floated on top, conveying its little passengers on a short-lived journey.

Although those fish sighted were actually swimming *on* the lake, not *in* it, it has been known for half a century that the Dead Sea does contain life—microorganic life. The finding in the 1920s that certain microorganisms were not only capable of enduring a saline environment, but actually required salt for their survival prompted microbiologist Benyamin Elazari-Volcani to test Dead Sea water and sediment, and indeed he found an assortment of halophilic algae and bacteria. In what quantities, however, he did not ascertain; that question was first addressed in the 1960s, then more fully so in 1980, when a team of microbiologists from the Hebrew University began an extensive quantitative study. Only in retrospect did these researchers realize how fortunate their timing was. In July they found a very large concentration of *Dunaliella*, an alga which is commonly found in most saline bodies of water. Organic material leaking out of the *Dunaliella* provided fertile feeding grounds for halobacteria, which were found in even greater concentrations, and which, because of their carotenoids, the red pigments which characterize them, gave the Dead Sea a distinctly reddish tint through the fall of that year. Impressive findings; yet even as they watched and measured, both populations began to decrease, and by 1982 had virtually disappeared. The winter of 1979–80 had been an exceptionally rainy one; apparently the floods had been so great as to dilute the Dead Sea's surface water from a life-prohibiting thirty-five per cent to about thirty per cent—optimal conditions, it turned out, for the "blooming" of the Dead Sea. After that, drought year followed drought year, the surface water remained too salty, and the microorganisms, though they undoubtedly still exist in small, latent populations, have yet to reassert themselves.

The story of the Dead Sea's microorganisms extends beyond the confines of the Dead Sea. From the beginning, certain investigators had high hopes for the *Dunaliella*. The alga copes with its saline environment and compensates for the water loss it experiences by accumulating glycerol, an oily substance used, for example, in hand creams. It was thought by some that perhaps the oil could be extracted and converted to a petroleum product. Who knew if one day *Dunaliella* farms, maybe even consisting of the Dead Sea variety, might not dot the Negev Desert, where Israel would finally have "struck oil"? Though experiments were successfully conducted, the project never got off the ground, perhaps because the world drop in oil prices rendered it economically unfeasible.

Other researchers concluded after ten years work that the production of glycerol alone was in any case economically unsound. Yet their interest in *Dunaliella* persisted. They found that the alga also contains Beta-carotene, the reddish pigment that is chemically related to vitamin A. In the green strain that is found in the Dead Sea, this pigment only exists in small quantities and is masked by chlorophyll. Moving to the northern coast of the Sinai, they discovered another strain—a red one where the reverse was true, the green was masked by the red, enabling them to think seriously about extracting both glycerol and the vitamin A-related pigment, a project which continues.

The scientists who began their work at the Dead Sea in 1980 regard their timing as a stroke of serendipity, for had they waited even another year, the knowledge they possess of the lifecycle of microorganisms in the Dead Sea would have been withheld from them for an indeterminable amount of time. It was the good fortune of science that research and nature were synchronized that year.

Lynch had explored the region from Ein Fashkhah to Ein Gedi by boat, and others had made their way along the high ridge. But no one had ever surveyed the shore, for the pathless way was most intimidating. Always game, Tristram had his heart set on exploring the twenty miles that separated the two oases. When told by the sheikh who was accompanying him that it was quite impossible, he replied that the English for "impossible" was "we will try," and with that he was off, the duty-bound sheikh's brother following.

Today the route to Ein Gedi is decidedly different, for a road was built in 1969. Earlier in the century, it would have been impossible for either the Turks or the British to build a road, for until recent decades, when the recession of the lake exposed shore flats, the cliffs plunged almost perpendicularly to the water, leaving no room even for men and horses, let alone vehicles.

Only on his 1863 trip did Tristram venture by the shore route. On his other trips, he, like most others, approached the oasis of Ein Gedi from above, reaching the edge of the cliff after a strenuous two-day trek from Hebron, south of Jerusalem. This way was obviously less convenient than today's—but they were amply rewarded: "The clouds lifted just as we reached the crest," Tristram would write a decade later, "and we looked down on the grand panorama of the sea, and the line of the Moab Mountains beyond... At the risk of being accused of suffering from 'Holy Land on the brain,' by those who can only measure grandeur by bigness, and who can see nothing to enjoy in Hermon or Lebanon because they are only 10,000 feet high and do not reach the Alps or the Himalayas, I must confess that few landscapes have impressed me more than the sudden unfolding of the Dead Sea basin and its eastern wall from the top of this pass." Today, unless one is hearty enough to cross the Judean Desert on foot in order to arrive at the point Tristram described, the only way to recreate this experience is to climb high in the cliffs above the waterfall of Naḥal David, one of the two wadis that form the oasis. From that vantage point, the hiker has the same impressive view of the sea, a blue triangle wedged between the cliffs, with the mountains, obscure but distinctly purplish, beyond.

The largest oasis on the western shore of the Dead Sea and now an extensive nature reserve, Ein Gedi owes its existence to the four prolific freshwater springs which nourish it. The rain which falls high in the Judean Hills collects as ground water and trickles through the rock layers, bursting forth as springs in the cliffs of the oasis. "He who has been to Engedi," wrote George Adam Smith, "will always fear lest he exaggerate its fertility to those who have not." Tristram especially loved the northern of the two wadis, Naḥal David (Wadi Sudeir), and he admired its fine caves "with their stalagmites and luxuriant tresses of maiden-hair fern." The wadi's waterfall, slender but forceful, splashes into a small pool. The wadi is characterized by thick reeds and rushes, and the cliffs take on the faint bluish tint of the eucalyptus-like adiantum which pours out of the crevices. By the pools are huge-leaved elephant's ears, over which hover small sun-birds which beat the air with rapidly fluttering wings as they probe the plants' flowers with their

106

long, curved beaks.

Naḥal Arugot (Wadi Areyeh) is half a mile south and is the southern border of the oasis. It was much less remarked on by travellers of Tristram's day but to this hiker's mind is more special than Naḥal David, more wild and forested. Its waterfall crashes into a deep pool, and below, there are numerous small hollows where the water that has fallen is collected. In places it seems to leak from the solid rock layers of the river bed, where uncounted years of rushing streams have left their mark engraved in swirling patterns. The pools themselves, shallow and clear as light, are pebble-lined and motionless. The water passes through without creating a stir.

The wadi walls rise brown and steep, and watermarks testify to the height of the winter floods. Even in summer one can sense the presence of the awesome torrents which tear down the canyon each year; the wadi course above the waterfall is strewn with immense, sun-bleached boulders which look to have been cast about as stones by a child. Other boulders have been only partly dislodged and are still balanced on the ledges, waiting to be taken down by next season's floods. Some have recently fallen to the bottom of the gorge; still others are rooted in place by trees which sprout from between them. Once they were saplings squirming their way to light; now they are full-grown, and their trunks have conformed to the contours of the boulders which encase them. The stream twists its slow and gentle way, but no one doubts that it is master of the wadi.

In the distant past, radical climatic changes in the world prompted animals to migrate to the Dead Sea region, a location central to three continents, and the area had evolved into a kind of zoological and botanical crossroads, a fact recognized by Tristram over a hundred years ago. "In our first day's expedition," he wrote, "we had abundant illustration of what to the field naturalist is the most marked peculiarity of Palestine, the juxtaposition of northern and southern forms of life, animal and vegetable, within the narrowest limits." Relatively few species adapted to the region, but before wanton hunting depleted the populations, the small valley abounded in all the animals that Tristram catalogued at Jericho.

Animals can only survive in the desert by escaping the heat or adapting to it. Small animals are at a greater disadvantage than large ones, because their relatively large surface-area-to-weight ratio causes them to heat up more quickly and lose water at a faster rate. Rodents, for example, cannot afford to waste water on heat regulation and so do not even have sweat glands. Like reptiles, they come out of their burrows only at night. The rabbit-sized coney, or hyrax (the smallest hoofed animal in the world and an unlikely relative of the elephant), behaves similarly, remaining at home in the cracks of rocks while the sun is high. Large animals, the most popular of which in the Dead Sea region is the Nubian ibex, cool themselves through a process of evaporation and cut down on their water loss by producing only small quantities of concentrated urine while also raising their body temperatures. Unlike most desert mammals, the ibex is active during the day. Known for its nimbleness and surefootedness, it has long fascinated observers with its acrobatics. Tristram was spellbound as he watched a herd through field glasses "as they gamboled, unconscious of our proximity, from point to point... on the heights above us. One fellow I could see, as he leaped from needle to needle, tossing back his enormous curved horns till they seemed to strike behind his tail, and then, in his bound, gathering all his four feet and lighting with them all close together on a little point of rock on the face of what

18.   Ein Gedi. From *Picturesque Palestine*, vol. 2, edited by Charles Wilson, 1881.

seemed a smooth wall of cliff, followed by the rest of the herd in a single file. Once I saw him make a drop, and break the force of the fall by lighting on the front of his horns."

Insects and birds have an easier time than animals in withstanding the extreme heat of the desert. Insects have developed a number of ways of conserving water, one of which is by exuding a wax which coats their bodies and prevents the loss of moisture. Birds, whose normal body temperature is in any case higher than other animals', have the additional advantage of mobility. The larger birds seek higher altitudes, where the temperature is lower; birds that cannot adjust to the summer heat simply migrate. Small birds are often found in the shade of tree branches, mouths open and wings slightly raised—an avian version of panting by which excess heat is released.

Ein Gedi's abundant water and tropical climate are responsible for a particularly wide variety of plant life. Such variety usually occurs only over large areas, but in the concentrated region between the Judean Hills and the Dead Sea there are several distinct regions, each having its own collection of plants. The relative concentrations of salt, moisture, and air in the soil determine which plants will thrive, and the topographical differences in the terrain means that the ratio of those ingredients changes with some frequency. In places where the soil is leached, there is one set of plants; where drainage is poor there is a distinctly different set. Ein Gedi itself is a botanical meetingplace where certain plants reach the northern or southern limit of their distribution.

The problems of survival which face plants in the desert are just as complex as those faced by animals, and their ways of coping with the climate just as varied. They have to adapt to a combination of inhospitable conditions—scarce water, high temperatures, and saline soil. Annuals have a wonderfully simple way of reacting: their seeds remain dormant—for a long period of time if necessary—until a winter produces favorable conditions. Then they germinate quickly, bursting into color and carpeting the desert for a short but intense time. Other plants, having developed means of keeping their water loss to a minimum, have no need to escape the summer. Certain desert plants have fewer leaves than is normal, others have smaller leaves; either means a reduction in the surface area from which water is lost. Some plants have cork around their water-storing parts, others have more roots in relation to shoots and

109

leaves, and still others undergo a subdivision of their main stem into smaller ones, only some of which survive. The salt-secreting system of the tamarisk permits it to thrive in the salt marshes of the southern Dead Sea region where several different species have been identified.

Naturalists have long delighted in the variety of flora found at Ein Gedi. (Tristram was especially appreciative for another, more mundane, reason. The aridity of the region is such, he observed, that plants dried in paper in a single day.) The plant which was of greatest interest to most of those who explored the Dead Sea region was the legendary osher, or Apple of Sodom, a tree bearing large, smooth fruit which when opened are found to be virtually empty.

Probably few plants in the world have been the cause of as much speculation and debate. Recalling the destruction of Sodom and Gomorrah, Josephus reflected that "indeed, there are still marks of the fire from heaven and the outlines of five cities to be seen, and ashes still form part of the growing fruits, which have all the appearance of eatable fruit, but when plucked with the hand dissolve into smoke and ashes." Tacitus took the catastrophe to have been more far-reaching in its effects, saying that "all natural growths, as well as what is sown by hand... become black and hollow and moulder as it were into ashes." The medieval belief was similarly Scripture-related. Maundeville described trees "that bear apples very fair in colour to behold; but when we break or cut them in two we find within ashes and cinders, which is a token that by the wrath of God the cities and the land were sunk into hell."

With time came scepticism, and Maundrell explained the phenomenon differently: "As for the apples of Sodom, so much talk'd of, I neither saw, nor heard of any hereabouts: nor was there any tree to be seen near the lake, from which one might expect such a kind of fruit; which induces me to believe that there may be a greater deceit in this fruit, than that which is usually reported of it; and that its very being, as well as its beauty is a fiction, only kept up, as my Lord Bacon observes many other false notions are, because it serves for a good illusion, and helps the poets to a similitude." One poet so helped was John Milton, who in *Paradise Lost* wrote of a fruit "...like that which grew/Near that bituminous lake where Sodom flamed."

Others agreed that the fruit was an invention, and some considered it an allegorical representation of the illusory pleasures

110

of the world. Most, however, at least by the nineteenth century, were certain of its reality and were eager to identify the elusive tree and explain the oddity of its hollowness. Maybe it was actually a dried-up pomegranate, said one. Most probably a large apple whose interior had been attacked by worms and turned to dust, asserted another. "Who would not imagine," wondered Chateaubriand, "that the question had been set completely at rest, by the authority of Hasselquist, and the still greater authority of Linnæus, in his *Flora Palæstina*? No such thing. M. Seetzen, also a man of science and the most modern of travellers... does not agree." Seetzen had been shown a silk-like material used by the Arabs in matchlocks for their guns and told it came from a fig-like tree called the aoeschaer which grew in the Dead Sea valley. The cotton-like interior, which was not suitable for weaving, was contained in its pomegranate-like fruit, and Seetzen went on to say that "by making incisions at the root of the tree, a sort of milk is procured, which is recommended to barren women." In short, Seetzen's report confused matters, and Josiah Conder exhorted travellers in the 1830s that it would be "inexcusable if they leave this question undecided."

Edward Robinson soon after untangled the knot by observing that actually the odd fruit, though filled mostly with air, also contains a slender pod in which may be found the silky material used for tinder by the Arabs, who preferred it to regular matches because it required no sulphur "to render it combustible." So it is likely, after all, that all the references were in fact to the same plant, the Apple of Sodom (calotropis procera). The small tree, found in the Dead Sea, Jordan, and Aravah valleys, is a tropical shrub that grows to not more than fifteen or eighteen feet. Its leaf is thick and ovular, its star-like flower white and purple, and its grapefruit-size fruit smooth and green. When opened, the fruit is often found to contain a cotton-like substance; at other times, depending on its maturity, its interior is more accurately described as dust-like or powdery.

Such conditions as are found at Ein Gedi were bound to attract settlers from earliest times. The remains of a temple which served a community around 3000 B.C.E. are still standing, and cult objects fashioned from copper and found in a nearby cave are thought to have belonged to the Bronze Age community. Ein Gedi figured in

111

the Biblical story of David's flight from Saul, when he hid in the wilderness there. A camp at the top of the cliffs was called in the Book of Samuel the stronghold of Ein Gedi, and the town was mentioned in the Book of Joshua as one of the wilderness cities given by him to the tribe of Judah. In the Song of Songs it was praised for its vineyards, the source of the town's fame in ancient days: "My beloved is unto me as a cluster of henna/In the vineyards of En-gedi." (1:14)

Several factors insured that Ein Gedi would be an agricultural center. Climatic conditions were ideal, and there was no shortage of space for groves and vineyards, since the population was fairly small. It was secure, being protected by mountains on the west and the Dead Sea on the east. And it came to be on an important trade route. When King Solomon fortified the Red Sea port of Eilat many years before, during his reign in the tenth century B.C.E., he had also established posts in the Negev Desert, in the southern half of Israel, to protect the caravans which crossed the Negev on their way from Arabia to the Mediterranean ports with their valuable cargoes of incense, perfume, and spices. But Solomon's control could not be maintained by his successors after the kingdom divided; by the seventh century B.C.E., the central government of Judea had become too weak to protect its desert outposts, and the Negev trade route was gradually abandoned. It was then that Ein Gedi assumed importance; its first agricultural settlement dates to this time, when all the oases from Jericho to the southern end of the Dead Sea were used for the cultivation of rare Arabian plants, eliminating the need for a long, trans-desert route. Date palms were grown for fruit and their leaves woven into baskets; grapes for wine, henna for cosmetics, and the secret balsam—all made the town famous. It was part of the royal estate, and its famed industries were run in the service of the king.

Ein Gedi as a Jewish town flourished from the seventh century until 582 B.C.E., when Nebuchadnezzar, having sacked Jerusalem and sent the Jews to their Babylonian exile, destroyed it. It was then rebuilt as a Persian town which lasted about a century. During those years the settled area was expanded and the buildings themselves enlarged. After a lull, the Hellenistic period saw a revitalization of the settlement under the Hasmonean kings, until the line was expelled from the throne by Herod, who seized power with the help of his Roman patrons in 40 B.C.E. The town's history

112

continues through Herod's rule, as well as through his sons', until the country was overrun by the Romans. In 68 C.E., the town was burned, only to be rebuilt by the Romans themselves, and it flourished again. By the time another half century had passed, it was once more inhabited by Jews, though it was assigned as the personal property of the emperor to serve as a base for a Roman garrison.

The area deteriorated after the Romans put down the Jewish revolt of 135, but from the third to the sixth centuries Ein Gedi was revived. The Writings of the Church Fathers attest to the fact that in those days it was home to a sizeable Jewish community, and Eusebius described it as being well-known, once again, for its dates and balsam. One of the most important and beautiful finds in the excavations at Ein Gedi was a mosaic floor from a Byzantine synagogue. Part of it is an inscription that has puzzled scholars; it calls down a curse on "anyone causing a controversy between a man and his fellows or who slanders his friends before the gentiles or steals the property of his friends, or anyone revealing the secret of the town to the gentiles..."—the last curious phrase aimed, it is thought, at those who would divulge the secret of the balsam industry.

Even in Tristram's day, before anyone thought to undertake excavations, it was obvious to the discerning observer that Ein Gedi had once been the site of a complex agricultural center. That the hills had once been extensively terraced was clear to anyone whose eye scanned the rocky slopes. "Everywhere through this barren wilderness," Tristram noted, "were the traces of the old terraces where once grew the vines of Engedi." According to pilgrims, the groves were neglected but nonetheless still impressive well into the fourteenth century. Burchard claimed that even in his day there were "some exceeding noble vine-stocks on Engaddi; but Saracens do not tend them, and no Christian, who would tend them, live there." Von Suchem declared that comparable vineyards are not found elsewhere in the world, and he wrote that in his time, 1350, they belonged to the brethren of the Hospital of St. John at Rhodes. Once before they had been the property of the Templars and had been tended by Saracen prisoners, an interesting detail that can be assigned to Crusader times.

The vineyards' reputation evidently lasted into the nineteenth century, for one of Lynch's stated goals in exploring the region of the Dead Sea was to examine the "soil in which grapes of such extraordinary size are said to grow... to ascertain if the chemical composition has any influence on the size of the fruit." It was hard not to be impressed by the terraces' crumbling, vestigial beauty, and one explorer would even suggest repairing them and resuming cultivation, though the land had not been farmed in some twelve centuries.

Although the signs of extensive agriculture were apparent to Tristram and to others, they had no idea of the extent to which the reluctant earth had been coaxed to produce. The entire eastern slope below the springs was at one time cultivated, and plaster-coated irrigation pools are evidence of the sophisticated techniques employed. Farmers were not the only ones whose skills were essential; engineers were brought in to work out methods for harnessing the spring water and guiding it down to the terraces in open channels. As long as there were no obstructions, the channels were dug; if a cross-stream interrupted the flow, a bridge was built; if bedrock impeded the way, the channel was quarried. The channels flowed into pools which were strategically located where they could provide water for large areas. Their walls were of double thickness, plastered to prevent leakage, and supplied with stoppers. With the water carefully parcelled out to selected terraces, about five hundred acres were cultivated.

Ein Gedi was and would remain one of the major attractions at the Dead Sea and maybe the major one of the western shore. Not long after Tristram was there, one of the leading figures in the Palestine Exploration Fund's survey of western Palestine explored Ein Gedi with a peculiar purpose—to identify the cave in which David hid from Saul nearly 3,000 years before. It was an unlikely mission (though half a century earlier John Stephens had described what he took to be the famous hideout) for two reasons. There were no artifacts by which to identify the cave, and one of the distinguishing features of the wadis on the lake's western shore is the numerous caves which were created by the same forces of erosion that produced the canyons themselves. William Allen described "the precipitous cliffs [which were] hollowed into numberless caves, [and] were formerly inhabited by men, whose hearts and minds, scathed by wild passions, found congenial responses in the horrors of the glen."

Allen may have gotten a little carried away, but he was not

wrong. For many centuries people had either made the caves of the Dead Sea valley their homes, or had sought sanctuary in them. Most famous were the Essenes, a communal Jewish sect of the second century B.C.E. to the end of the first century C.E. who fled the corruption of Jerusalem. It is presumed that they lived in the caves of various wadis, but they were concentrated at Qumran, twenty miles north of Ein Gedi, where flour mills, storage bins, a pottery factory, a manuscript room, ritual baths, and cisterns have all been uncovered. Like the farmers at Ein Gedi, the settlers at Qumran were plagued by one practical worry which overshadowed all others—the acquisition and storage of water. Wadi Qumran has no springs, which made the problem even more acute. They had no choice but to rely on the winter floods; patience, persistence, and no small amount of engineering brilliance enabled them, by means of a channel, part of which had to be chiselled through a hundred feet of solid rock high in the cliff, to trap and guide the precious seasonal water to the cisterns.

The Essenes were an apocalyptic sect believing in the struggle between the sons of light and the sons of darkness at the end of days. Viewed from Rome, they were described by Pliny with a mixture of fact and exaggeration as "a people that live apart from the world, and marvellous beyond all others throughout the whole earth, for they have no women among them; to sexual desire they are strangers; money they have none; the palm-trees are their only companions. Day after day, however, their numbers are fully recruited by multitudes of strangers that resort to them, driven thither to adopt their usages by the tempests of fortune, and wearied with the miseries of life. Thus it is, that through thousands of ages, incredible to relate, this people eternally prolongs its existence, without a single birth taking place there; so fruitful a source of population to it is that weariness of life which is felt by others."

Josephus was more knowledgeable than Pliny, and his description of the Essenes goes on for several pages. (There has also been speculation that he lived among them for a time.) "They eschew pleasure-seeking as a vice and regard temperance and mastery of the passions as a virtue. Scorning wedlock, they select other men's children while still pliable and teachable, and fashion them after their own pattern—not that they wish to do away with marriage as a means of continuing the race, but they are afraid of the promiscuity of women and convinced that none of the sex remains

115

faithful to one man." Today the Essenes are best known for their library. The so-called Dead Sea Scrolls, found mostly in caves near Qumran, are considered one of the most important archaeological finds of this century. Fragments of all but one of the books of the Old Testament have been identified, and most of the manuscripts were written in Hebrew, pre-dating by a thousand years the oldest previously known Hebrew text of the Bible.

While the caves may have been home to some, they served as sanctuary for others, most notably the followers of Bar Kokhba during the second, ill-fated revolt against the Romans in 132 C.E. The war became localized in the Judean Desert two years after it broke out. There the rebels banded together, striking at Hadrian's army, then retreating to the caves of Nahal Hever and Wadi Muraba'at, on either side of Ein Gedi. The incensed Romans laid siege to the caves, as the remains of their military camps high in the wadi attest, cutting off food until the rebels and their families died of starvation. Letters and documents found in the caves (along with cloth, vessels, date pits, and the remains of human plaits) illuminate the life the Jews led during the three years of the tragic revolt.

In the early Christian centuries, the caves were inhabited by the most devout and reclusive solitaries. The nineteenth-century editor of one of the collective biographies of the fathers of the desert pointed out that certain regions of the Holy Land were composed of limestone from which the elements had carved out caves, which had then been enlarged by human hands and occupied. Because in the pre-Christian era they were used as graves, it was sometimes related in the lives of the anchorites that the desert fathers lived in tombs.

From Ein Gedi, Tristram travelled south fifteen miles to Masada, the 1,500 feet high rock set in stark desert relief by deeply incised canyons. The way there is bland; the shores spread out and the white hills left from the prehistoric lake which occupied the Dead Sea valley become the landscape's dominant feature. Carved by thousands of years of rains into a maze of badlands, the hills reflect the sharp sun in a piercing glare. Even the easy-going Tristram felt a want of life: "It was a dreary, desolate, hungry ride, more truly reaching the popular notions of the Dead Sea than anything we had yet met with. All around us was utterly lifeless and brown, with the cliffs and mountains glaring red in the sunshine, and the soft alluvium below dazzling our eyes by its whiteness."

Edward Robinson, "the prince of Palestine geographers," was given credit for identifying Masada thirty years before Tristram's time, but Robinson acknowledged that it was his companion, Eli Smith, who first suggested that the rock the Arabs called Sebbeh might actually be the famous site. Another century would pass before it was excavated, but though the crumbling walls told hardly a thing about what had gone on there eighteen hundred years before, nearly every explorer was familiar with Josephus' graphic account.

Situated just inland from the Dead Sea, Masada was long recognized as a natural fortress. It is an isolated plateau whose eastern side, facing the Dead Sea, plunges almost vertically to the shore, and whose three other sides are all protected by canyons. Josephus pointed out that the cliffs were so sheer that no animal could get a footing except in two places where with great difficulty the rock could be climbed. De Saulcy described his ordeal attempting the ascent: "After some minutes' progress, the path becomes more difficult, and goats alone might be content with it, supposing they were not over-difficult to please." Van de Velde,

19. View of Masada. From *Narrative of the United States Expedition to the River Jordan and the Dead Sea*, by William F. Lynch, 1849.

who characterized de Saulcy's account as so filled with contradictions, erroneous quotations, and false hypotheses "that to refute them all would require a book as large as that of M. de Saulcy himself," had a moment of rare agreement as he struggled up the rock: "Previous experience had led me to put a little bottle of eau-de-cologne [smelling salts] in my pocket, and I was thereby preserved from a fall that would infallibly have killed me." Tristram, on the other hand, claimed that the difficulty had been exaggerated, asserting that "an English lady could accomplish it easily." But what he neglected to say, and probably didn't realize, was that he climbed the ancient Roman ramp behind the rock, while all the others seem to have made the ascent by the tortuous so-called snake path which was described by Josephus, and which was not outfitted with the stairs that aid the modern hiker.

The Hasmonean ruler Alexander Jannaeus, descendant of the Maccabees, probably fortified Masada in the first century B.C.E. But it was Herod who made it famous, and the Jewish zealots who insured that its name would never be forgotten. After Herod was placed on the throne of Judea by the Romans, he refortified Masada, storing enough weapons there to stave off an army, cultivating the flat top in case he should ever be cut off from a food line, and constructing cisterns that a single hard rain could fill with a year's supply of water. His ambitious precautions were not the result of idle paranoia. "It is believed," wrote Josephus, "that Herod equipped this fortress as a refuge for himself, suspecting a double danger—the danger from the Jewish masses, who might push him off his throne and restore to power the royal house that preceded him, and the greater and more terrible danger from the Egyptian queen, Cleopatra. For she did not conceal her intentions but constantly appealed to Antony, begging him to destroy Herod and requesting the transfer to herself of the kingdom of Judea... Such were the fears that made Herod fortify Masada, little dreaming that he was to leave it to the Romans as the very last task in the war against the Jews."

Soon after Herod's death in 4 B.C.E., a Roman garrison took up position at Masada and remained there until 66 C.E. when, with the outbreak of the Jewish war, the fortress was captured in a daring surprise attack by a band of Jewish zealots who held it for the next seven years. When Jerusalem fell in 70, the Roman commander Titus, convinced that it would be dangerously imprudent to allow

118

any Jews to remain unsubdued, even in isolated desert pockets, ordered the elimination of all resistance. Conquered first was Machaerus, the Herodian mountain-top fortress on the northeast side of the lake where John the Baptist had been beheaded. Then the Romans moved on to Masada, which was not to fall so readily. It took Flavius Silva nearly a year to overpower this final stronghold. The siege ended with the mass suicide of 960 men, women, and children who preferred death at their own hands to capture and enslavement by the Romans.

Tristram's observations give a sense of what it must have been like to endure the Roman siege: "As I sat astride a projecting rock on the north peak, I could look down from my giddy height, 1,500 feet, on both sides and in front; and yet so clear was the atmosphere, and so extraordinary its power of conveying sound, that I could carry on conversation with my friends in the camp below, and compare barometers and observations." It is one thing to be surrounded by eight enemy camps, and for months to contemplate defeat and enslavement, all the while watching the Romans at work on their battering rams and assault ramp. But it is quite another to hear them as well; how much closer the Roman legion must have seemed, how much more imminent vanquishment. "Looking down from the top," Tristram wrote, "the whole of the Dead Sea was spread out as in a map... It was a picture of stern grandeur and desolate magnificence, perhaps unequalled in the world. All round at our feet we could trace the wall of circumvallation by which the Romans hopelessly enclosed the devoted garrison. In the plain to the east beneath us, and on the opposite slopes to the west were the Roman camps, with their outlines and walls as distinct as on the day when they were left."

Tristram travelled on down the coast to Mt. Sedom, the six-mile long jagged mound of salt which is the only topographical feature on the lake's southern shore. Because the salt is highly erodable, the mountain is punctured with caves which at places permit entry deep inside. The air is still, the way dark, but then a sharp breeze signals an opening. Soon light from the sky pours through, and one finds oneself in a cathedral-like chamber. Stepping into this so-called chimney is like being inside a finely fluted column of salt and viewing it from the inside. It was formed as millennia of annual rains splattered down on the mountain, wearing it away until a hollow was reached and the chimney opened up.

The erosion has also created pinnacles on the mountain's flank, and they stand out as pillars until eventually washed away and replaced by others. Tradition has it that the most prominent pillar is the petrified remains of Lot's wife. As it is related: "And it came to pass, when they had brought them forth abroad, that he said: 'Escape for thy life; look not behind thee, neither stay thou in all the Plain' ...But... [Lot's] wife looked back from behind him, and she became a pillar of salt." (Gen. 19:17, 26) Josephus retold the event in the *Antiquities*, adding about the pillar, "I have seen it, and it remains at this day." Unsettled by the claim, which was confirmed by travellers much later, Josephus' eighteenth-century translator William Whiston admonished sternly in his 1737 edition: "Whether the account that some modern travellers give be true, that it is still standing, I do not know. Its remote situation, at the utmost southern point of the Sea of Sodom, in the wild and dangerous deserts of Arabia, makes it exceedingly difficult for inquisitive

20. Lot's Wife, with view towards the Dead Sea. From the colored frontispiece to *Desert of the Exodus*, part 1, by E.H. Palmer, 1871.

21. Lot's Wife, with view from the Dead Sea. From *Narrative of the United States Expedition to the River Jordan and the Dead Sea*, by William F. Lynch, 1849.

travellers to examine the place; ...When Christian princes, so called, lay aside their foolish and unchristian wars and quarrels, and send a body of fit persons to travel over the East...we may hope for full satisfaction in such inquiries, but hardly before."

At the beginning of the nineteenth century, travellers didn't doubt that the pillar existed, and they occupied themselves trying to explain it. "There is surely nothing irrational in the idea," wrote Jolliffe in the 1820s, "that a human creature, when struck by lightning and reduced to a state of torpor, might be so completely encrusted and wrapped around with the sulphureous matter, as to be indurated into a substance as hard as stone, and assume the appearance of a pillar or statue." A few decades later, de Saulcy offered a completely different explanation, a strikingly modest one considering it was he who had claimed to identify Sodom and Gomorrah: "At the moment when the huge mountain was heaved up volcanically, there must have been throughout its whole extent tremendous falls of detached masses... Lot's wife having loitered behind, either through fright or curiosity, was most likely crushed by one of these descending fragments, and when Lot and his children turned around to look towards the place where she had stopped, they saw nothing but the salt rock which covered her body."

Researchers even well into this century were interested in the larger question suggested by this particular phenomenon—namely, the origins of the story that made its way into Genesis. It is generally believed that some kind of cataclysm may actually have taken place nearly 4,000 years ago, well before the Bible was written, but that so awful was the destruction of the Cities of the Plain that memory of it was retained as part of oral tradition until it was recorded. Most investigators finally ruled out the possibility of volcanic destruction (William Albright called that theory "thoroughly obsolete" in 1924), and the theory developed that the real agent of devastation was earthquake-provoked explosions of natural gases that had been seeping out of the earth under the plain that would become the Dead Sea's shallow southern basin.

Sporadically, over the last half century or so, a kind of debate has taken shape concerning the exact location of the Cities of the Plain. For a number of years some investigators had favored the north end of the Dead Sea as the place they likely occupied, but by the first third of this century, opinion was more or less unanimous that the

122

towns probably sat at the southern end. Exactly where, though, was the question; and would remains ever be found?

Albright is credited with the 1924 discovery of Bab edh-Dhra (though he himself credited Père Mallon), an Early Bronze Age site situated about five hundred feet above the southeast shore of the lake. To him it was clear, in the absence of appropriate debris, that Bab edh-Dhra was not a town but had been a place of summer pilgrimage for the town dwellers. Thus he took the site to be confirmation that the cities themselves had been located on the plain below. As for remains, he felt they would never be found, since the shallowness of the southern basin meant that they would have been levelled by storms and currents. He believed that approximate locations (which he went on to suggest) were the most that could be hoped for.

About a decade later, Nelson Glueck expressed his agreement with Albright, that the cities themselves were located below, and that Bab edh-Dhra was abandoned after the cataclysm that wiped them out early in the second millennium B.C.E. Glueck went on to surmise, after an aerial survey of the region in the mid 1930s revealed no traces of ruins in the shallow southern end of the Dead Sea, that millennia of saline deposits probably covered what remains there might be.

Nothing is quite neat in the field of archaeology, so it hardly came as a surprise to find Albright and Glueck challenged, at least indirectly, in recent years. Archaeologists Walter Rast and Thomas Schaub had an opportunity to examine the then nearly empty southern basin in the mid 1970s and concluded that there were no remains of any towns to be found. Further, Rast and Schaub's experience had taught them that in any case Early Bronze Age towns were located higher up, as Bab edh-Dhra was. Continuing their work, they located four additional towns, and discovered some evidence of fire destruction. One can guess already what the tempting conclusion is—and so may be surprised to note the near complete absence of references to the Biblical story in Rast and Schaub's detailed reports. Indeed the authors' studious avoidance of such reference is most striking to one who has read accounts of their work in the more popular Biblical archaeology journals, where more eager parties drew the conclusion for them that the Cities of the Plain had been found. In describing his own work, Professor Rast felt he could not conclude that Bab edh-Dhra and the other sites must be the cities, for to him it was important not to confuse archaeological concerns with questions that are essentially extraneous to his work in the field. He does expect to publish his own interpretation in the future, but feels that those who, on the basis of his work, have drawn the conclusion that he has located Sodom and Gomorrah, Admah and Zeboi'im, have done so over-hastily.

In his journey of 1863, Tristram was prevented by the complications of tribal territorial control from going around the Dead Sea as he wished. It would be another decade before his dream of exploring the eastern side, the Biblical land of Moab, would be realized. Tristram was the last major explorer to work alone at the Dead Sea, and his later work, the *Fauna and Flora of Palestine,* was done in conjunction with the Palestine Exploration Fund's survey of Palestine. The P.E.F. came into the fore by the late 1860s, and from then on, most of the names associated with Dead Sea research were connected to it. Tristram's travels marked the end of the transition period and inaugurated the very sophisticated era of the Fund, whose story continues, for our purposes, through 1913, a year which

22.   The Destruction of Sodom. From *Liber cronicarum,* by Hartmann Schedel, Nürnberg, 1493 (published by Anton Koberger).

can be said to mark the close of the nineteenth century. The outbreak of the First World War resulted in a suspension of scientific activity in the Holy Land, and the war, bringing the dissolution of the Ottoman empire, marked the beginning of a new, different era under the British.

There are reasons why the second half of the nineteenth century saw a shift from the Dead Sea itself to its surroundings. Just so much could be accomplished with the tools available in those days; after Lynch did his thorough soundings, there was not much to add until new equipment was developed. Further, the curiosity of explorers was insatiable; once access to the region was offered, travellers ardently pursued routes into every hidden corner, detective-like seeking their past. Yet the lake was a powerful magnet, and gradually attention was once again turned to it, as a new project which promised to yield further clues to the mysterious life of the sea caught the imagination of explorers.

It was no secret that the Dead Sea did not maintain a constant level but rose and fell, sometimes sharply, from season to season as well as from year to year. In 1855, William Allen proposed a systematic study of the lake's level in connection with his idea of a Mediterranean–Jordan River–Dead Sea–Red Sea canal. Evidence suggested that the lake was in a state of equilibrium, but Allen was worried it might be slowly falling. As we will see, in his day and for the next half century, the opposite was the case. A year after Allen's proposal, a member of Britain's Royal Geographic Society recommended that the Society undertake to determine the relation of inflow to evaporation, but again, no project was initiated.

For years, travellers had traded stories about certain landmarks being submerged or reemerging, and in an effort to prevent the exchange from being wasted, a member of the Palestine Exploration Fund went down to the Dead Sea in 1874, fixed piles for measuring, and in the next issue of the Fund's *Quarterly Statement* requested that travellers report any observations made with regard to them. Though not very reliable an approach, it did mark the first attempt to devise a system for measurement. At the same time, another member of the P.E.F. set graduated poles by the lake's edge, but they were stolen before anyone could report on the extent of their submersion.

Such was the state of affairs at the turn of the century, when

125

someone suggested that a rock in the vicinity of Ein Fashkhah be designated for long-term observation. Taking up the idea, a P.E.F. scientist went down in 1900 in search of something suitable. At the only break in the thick reeds between Ein Fashkhah and Ras Fashkhah, a promontory two miles south of the oasis, he chose what is still known as the P.E.F. rock, a huge boulder at that time protruding twenty feet out of the water, next to which was a smaller rock convenient for standing on. The rock, rediscovered by Ze'ev Vilnay shortly after the 1967 Arab–Israeli war, was slightly sloped, which meant that the tape could not be dropped exactly perpendicularly, but it was as good and near a one as they could find, and they turned back to Jericho to find a stone mason. The nine-inch line which he cut was fourteen feet above the lake's surface, and under it the letters PEF were carved, the mason having been successful on his second attempt, as one can still see.

From that point, Edward Masterman—he who told parts of Costigan's and Molyneux's stories—took over, and his name became synonymous with observation of the lake's level. For the next thirteen years he came down twice annually to read and report on the sea's seasonal and annual variations. Masterman turned the sea-gazing which had been practiced in an interested but haphazard way for decades into a matter of serious scientific inquiry which has been carried out intermittently to this day.

There were three points of reference by which European travellers, with the help of their Arab guides—who had lived all their lives in the region and knew the Dead Sea most intimately—could gauge its fluctuations, and it was to these that most of them referred in their accounts. The first, at the northern end of the sea, is today a barely recognizable heap of stones lying at least a quarter of a mile from the water's edge. Called by the Arabs Rujm el-Baḥr—castings of the sea (Maganit Ha-Melaḥ in Hebrew)—the mound of rocks, originally assembled as a port probably in the eighth or seventh century B.C.E., was either a peninsula or an island throughout the nineteenth century and well into the twentieth, though at times it was completely submerged and at other times sat on the beach.

The incidental notes kept by travellers become of great use in tracing the vicissitudes of Rujm el-Baḥr. In 1807, Seetzen noted that it was a peninsula connected to the shore by a narrow strip of land, but his Bedouin guides told him that just ten years earlier it had been an island, the neck of land submerged. If his guides were correct, and they generally were, then it would seem that the level of the lake was falling in the early part of the nineteenth century. Other travellers confirmed that the point remained a peninsula for a few decades; Lynch saw it as such in 1848, as did de Saulcy two years later. But de Saulcy also noted that the isthmus which connected it to the mainland was covered with shallow water. Apparently he was the last European to see Rujm el-Baḥr as a peninsula; by the mid-1850s the connecting strip was no longer visible, though the water could still be forded. For the next several years the isthmus was alternately visible and not, until the slow rise gained force. Tristram had easily forded the water in 1858, but in 1864 he was not able to. Arabs guiding a P.E.F. party assured them that the isthmus had been submerged for twelve to fifteen years. Into the 1880s a hearty few swam out to the island, but in 1892, after several successive years of heavy rains, it disappeared altogether. Just after the turn of the century, the island was apparently so far underwater that Masterman could find no evidence of it whatsoever.

It could not be denied that the level seemed to have risen considerably, at least at the northern end of the lake. But there were always the sceptical few who clung to the possibility that the lake's bottom had risen or that the island had sunk, giving the appearance of a rise. Unlikely as it may seem, the notion could not be automatically ruled out, for there was enough seismic activity in the valley to lend some credence to their hypothesis. It happens not to have been the case, as most were convinced early on, but the suggestion made for a stimulating exchange in the pages of the P.E.F. journal.

The second landmark by which the rise or fall of the sea could be watched was the causeway that had existed at certain times throughout history between the Lisan Peninsula and the western shore of the Dead Sea. The lake consists of two basins which were almost completely separated by the broad peninsula, the straits separating it from the western shore named after Lynch by a nineteenth-century German geographer. The straits were at times shallow enough to be forded, and there were also times when the very shallow southern basin probably did not exist; indeed, as scholars have pointed out, there is a good deal of historical evidence to suggest that well beyond Biblical times the Dead Sea was limited to its northern basin. In the Book of Joshua, the territory of Judah is said to extend from the "tongue" (i.e., peninsula) southwards; the valley of salt referred to in both Samuel and Kings is probably the empty southern basin; and the sixth-century Madaba map shows only one basin.

Seetzen was prevented by high water from crossing the straits in 1807, but five years later, Burckhardt learned that a drop in the level made it possible—a sequence which is in accordance with what had been reported about the northern end of the lake. Irby and Mangles' famous reference to a caravan crossing means that it was still possible to ford in 1818, but since then no one seems to have been able to. Tristram's guide on his trip in the mid-1870s pointed out the place where he used to ford as a youth, sixty years before. And though by 1910 there was no trace at all of any way across, a Bedouin guiding one explorer assured him of the same thing, "that when the hair first appeared on his face, it was so narrow that the people of his tribe used to sit on the edge of the Lisan and parley with Arabs from the west as to the return of cattle that had been stolen by one or other of the parties," and that in his youth, large caravans of camels and mules used to be driven across.

The third geographical touchstone was a path that ran in front of Mt. Sedom and which was used by all those who wished to avoid climbing or circling the mountain. Between 1838 and 1855, all the maps drawn by various explorers showed a wide beach running between the mountain and the sea. It now seems inconceivable that there were also times when no path existed, for today a paved road runs the same route, with plenty of room to spare on either side. In 1890, it was still possible to squeeze in front of the mountain, but in the next decade the water crept up so close that passage was cut off. If we recall that 1892 is given as the year of Rujm el-Baḥr's disappearance, then it is hard to avoid the conclusion that the lake experienced a considerable rise in the last two thirds of the nineteenth century. Those who had entertained the notion that the lake's bottom might have been thrust upwards were slowly silenced, their views gradually fading from the pages of the Fund's journal.

The discussion of the lake's level, carried on each quarter in the P.E.F.'s journal, lasted many years and drew numerous speculators and scientists. But no participant had as much authority as Masterman, who filed his first lengthy report a year and a half after the rock was chosen and engraved. In light of where it now

128

Comparative photographs, taken from the same place (P.E.F. Rock)
in the 1930s and again in the 1970s. The first shows the Dead Sea
and its shore before the recession, with water reaching the reeds
and cliff. The next decades witnessed a dramatic lowering of the
lake's level, and the second photograph shows the water so receded
from the cliff as to leave room for a two-lane paved road. Courtesy
of the Kibbutz Ein Gedi photo archive.

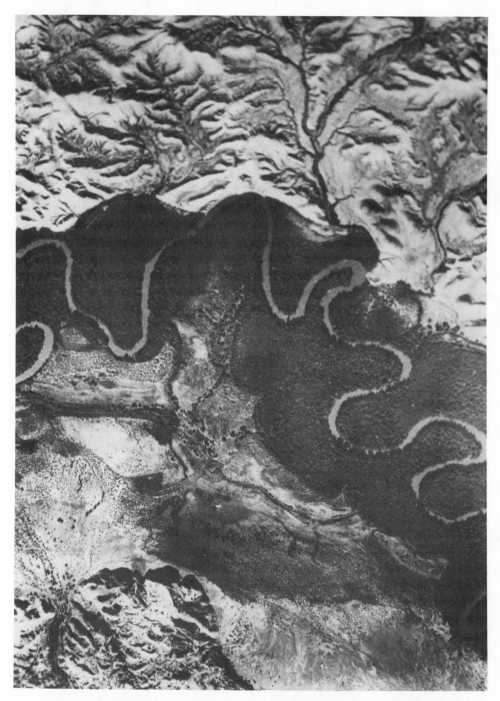

Aerial view of the Jordan River twisting its way through lush banks
to the Dead Sea, 1929. Courtesy of Keren Kayemet.

View of the Jordan River. Courtesy of Keren Kayemet.

The boat used by the explorer Thomas Molyneux in his 1847 voyage on the Dead Sea. Courtesy of Keren Kayemet.

Aerial view of Masada, the Herodian Mountain fortress on the western side of the Dead Sea. Courtesy of the Israel Government Press Office.

Ein Fashkhah, an oasis on the western shore of the Dead Sea.
Courtesy of the Israel Government Press Office.

Salt-encrusted trees reemerging from under the Dead Sea with the
recession of the lake. Courtesy of the Kibbutz Ein Gedi photo archive.

The American explorer William Francis Lynch, who journeyed to the Dead Sea in 1847–1848. Courtesy of the Museum of the Confederacy.

ים המלח

View of the Dead Sea, with Turkish sailing vessel, and caravan passing along the shore, circa 1915. Courtesy of the Central Zionist Archive.

Scene on the Dead Sea: Arabs harvesting salt, circa 1918. Courtesy of the Australian War Memorial, negative no. B3132.

The fish ponds at Kibbutz Beit Ha'Aravah, May 1944. Courtesy of the Israel Government Press Office.

A member of Kibbutz Beit Ha'Aravah channelling water from the Jordan River into the fields near the Dead Sea to wash the salt from the soil in preparation for cultivation, May 1944. Courtesy of the Israel Government Press Office.

Moshe Novomeysky (center), founder of the Palestine Potash Company, his partner Thomas Tulloch (left), and an unidentified worker, Sedom, 1930s. Courtesy of the Dead Sea Works.

Harvesting minerals, then: hand-harvesting of carnallite at the Palestine Potash Works, 1930s. Jewish Agency photograph; courtesy of the Central Zionist Archive.

Harvesting minerals now: a modern floating harvester, run by two workers, producing what it would take 10,000 workers to produce in a comparable amount of time. Photograph by Shimon Fuchs; courtesy of the Dead Sea Works.

Ibex, denizen of the canyons on either side of the Dead Sea. From *The Flora and Fauna of Palestine*, by Henry Baker Tristram. Reproduction prepared by the Kibbutz Ein Gedi photo laboratory.

Salt formations in the Dead Sea, formed as the water evaporates in shallow areas. Courtesy of Keren Kayemet.

View of the northwestern shore and the Dead Sea. Photograph by
Shai Ginott.

sits—about twenty feet above the far side of the road which runs parallel to the Dead Sea—it is odd to read his description of the difficulties his party had merely in reaching the site. Forced to leave their horses at Ein Fashkhah, they proceeded part of the way along a trail, skipping the rest of the way rock-to-rock. All westerly breezes were shut off by the mountains, he wrote, making that part of the trip, in the sweltering heat, extremely taxing. A truly perpendicular rock might have been found a little further south, but he confessed it would not be worth it, for any longer a hike would have been unendurable. To compensate for the imperfection, he vowed to take extra care with his measurements and to drop the weighted tape several times to be sure of his readings. Though the rise in his first year of observation was smaller than many had supposed it would be, it was indisputable that there had been a general rise of about twenty feet in the last decades. Further, the rise toward the end of that period must have been sudden as well as substantial; on the southeast shore, trees, hunting grounds, and farmland had all been inundated, suggesting that the lake rose to a height not achieved in many decades.

In 1913, having completed more than a decade of observation, Masterman drew his project to a close and filed a final report with the P.E.F. Correlating his readings with a record of rainfall that had been kept in Jerusalem since 1861, he concluded that the overall rise of the last decades did have to do with increased rainfall. But he quickly added that even all of his findings together could not relate the whole story. He assumed that the influence of snow on Mt. Hermon, at whose base the Jordan River originates, must also be great. (One cannot help but recall Burchard, who in the year 1280 or so had written, "At times this sea overflows, owing to the melting of the snow on Lebanon and the other mountains," as well as the flooding of tributary rivers and rain.) Not only was volume an important factor, Masterman suggested, but so was melting time. That is, a cold spring would delay the melting of the snow, so that the amount of water pouring into the Jordan and finally into the Dead Sea late in the season would be much greater than when the snow melted early. Obviously a late flooding of the Jordan would also delay the onset of the lake's annual shrinkage by some weeks. These circumstances (or their reverse) would of course have affected Masterman's readings, but his measurements were taken at the same time every year regardless of climatic conditions in the

129

north. Masterman's speculation was well-founded, and the variables he named, as well as temperature and winds, are important to anyone drawing conclusions about the lake's fluctuations. But nuances aside, the foremost fact is that the lake experienced a very considerable rise in the last part of the nineteenth century, a rise that held until the 1930s, when the lake's fortunes were reversed and the recession which continues to this day began. Trees which were lost under the encroaching water finally reappeared in the 1960s, and their salt-encased trunks and branches told the graphic story of where they had been.

After 1913, no regular measurements were taken until 1927. In the early 1960s, the level was estimated, based on new readings, to be more than seventeen feet lower than when Masterman began his observations, which meant a drop of about thirty-seven feet from its high point near the turn of the century. The P.E.F. rock had been unusable—stranded too far from the water's edge—since 1935. A relic of the lake's recent history, it is also a kind of modest monument to those whose energies were spent writing that history.

The second half century of exploration ended quietly, not with the immediate resonance of the first half, but with a subtle, prolonged echo of its own. It was a less spectacular half than the first, but not less fruitful; and tedious though some of the work might have been, the results were every bit as exciting as the century's early years had forecast. The time had been devoted to exploring the ancient sites around the Dead Sea and studying the flora and fauna of the valley; then attention shifted back to the lake itself, as Masterman, and others less remembered but not less dedicated, strove to understand the life of this slowly revealed body of water. Some of the P.E.F. explorers, those connected to research at the Dead Sea and those who pursued their work elsewhere in Palestine, went on to greater dramas. Kitchener appeared in Khartoum; Lawrence went on to Arabia. Many others would never be known beyond the pages of the geographic journals to which they contributed. But together, over the course of the century, the adventurers and eccentrics, explorers and scientists, illuminated one of the world's darkest bodies of water, lifting from it the shroud of superstition which had consigned it to a place in pilgrims' texts and exposing its beauty and wonder.

PART III

Origins and Evolution

In all my wanderings I have never seen anything so likely, on a cursory view, to create belief in preternatural agency. Yet by degrees, and most involuntarily... impressions and features seemed forced upon me, as bearing the indubitable stamp of natural and progressive action.

William Allen
The Dead Sea: A New Route to India, 1855

4

The Life of a Lake

O NLY WITH a great effort can we project ourselves far enough
back in time to reconstruct the early years of our planet. Few
are supplied with such natural elasticity of imagination, and the
mind resists the elaborate stretching exercises it is called on to
undertake. Yet geological history requires this extension, for only
when we are thinking comfortably in terms of millions of years can
we begin to visualize how the configurations of the earth came to be.
What we may customarily refer to as sudden and dramatic
upheavals which altered the earth's surface forever were indeed
dramatic, but sudden only in the way that a few hundred thousand
years in the course of four billion may be considered so.

Our sense of time is gradually altered as we stand by the shore of
the Dead Sea and consider the creation and evolution of this
comparatively young lake, one of the youngest important bodies of
water on earth. Eons of geological history are exposed in the sharp
cliffs that tower over it, and we are asked to imagine figures such as
a hundred million years as we extend back to its ancestry. We work
our way slowly from there into the more manageable five million
year range. Before we know it we have arrived at the era of its
immediate predecessor, a mere 60,000 years ago, a figure with
which we can feel quite at home. The Dead Sea itself is probably
only about 12,000 years old, and so expanded has our sense of time
become that its birth seems now to crowd the history of human
civilization, which began roughly around the same time at, from all
indications, nearby Jericho. Abraham's migration somewhere in the
second millennium B.C.E., marking the advent of western religions,
seems within this context as accessible as our own childhoods, and

133

the Byzantine period, which saw the last extensive settlement at the Dead Sea until this century, strikes us as not just recent, but virtually contemporary. The alteration in our perception of time is startling. As the antique becomes familiar and ancient civilizations merge with our own, the brevity of human history is emphasized and the unity of our species seems attainable.

Pinpointing the origins of the present day Dead Sea is to some extent arbitrary. Every process that might be identified as the beginning was caused by something else, and at some point we have to cast aside the past and define a place as broadly acceptable as possible. The time most often chosen as having seen the beginnings of the processes that would prepare the way for the Dead Sea millions of years later is in the Cretaceous period, which ended 65 million years ago, following the extinction of the dinosaur and the division of the earth's land mass into continents.

Over the course of many millions of years, the single mass that made up the earth's land surface was redistributed, as the plates which modern geology has learned make up the earth's crust began moving. The earth experienced severe seismic disturbances, and the period was characterized by the levelling of old mountains and the raising of new ones, as well as by the inundation of vast tracts of land by the sea. It is the events that make up this scenario that ultimately led to the birth of the Dead Sea. The movement of land masses and their flooding by the ocean, processes that would determine both the configuration and composition of the region for eons to come, were not isolated phenomena but were in keeping with world-wide geological events of the age.

It was probably then, in the late Cretaceous, that the Arabian land mass began to move northward away from Africa, splitting the earth in a hairline fracture that ran from Africa to Turkey, eventually opening up the Red Sea, and passing between today's Israel and Jordan from the Gulf of Eilat north through the Aravah Valley and the Dead Sea, continuing up the Jordan Valley, through the Sea of Galilee and the Ḥuleh Valley. In its early stages, this part of the tear in the earth's surface was a shallow depression that was periodically filled in. But gradually, with the continued slow movement north of the Arabian block—about sixty miles in all by our day—a modest trench became outlined. That trench became substantial enough to hold a lake only around three million years

134

ago, when the northward movement of the Arabian peninsula shifted to the east, pulling open the valley. By that time, the earth had matured through eons of adolescence and had experienced many of the serious traumas that would make of it the planet we know today. The valley, though not as deep as it would become, had pretty much acquired its present shape.

Slow then was the creation of the Great Rift Valley, or Syrian–African Rift, a valley stretching 3,700 miles from eastern Africa's Zambezi Valley to the Taurus Mountains of Turkey. The Great Rift, which looks in satellite photographs like nothing more than a slight scar, is not one continuous valley but rather a chain of basins loosely strung together and of varying depths and ages. When it initially opened, it was as though a wedge were being driven slowly up the plain, the force of it opening one gap after another, some of the earlier ones being filled in as new ones came into being. The long narrow fissure which cuts through what are now mountains, crosses stretches of land that have become deserts, and passes through the open sea, and whose deepest inland section contains the Dead Sea, reveals the stele-like engraved evidence of the processes that have marked the maturation of our planet in the last few million years.

To the observant non-scientist, the lines of the tablet are as distinguishable as to the scientist, though the language is beyond his grasp. "To one traveling along that dreary road [south of the Dead Sea]," wrote John Stephens, "every step opens a new page in the great book of Nature." A decade later, Lynch would scan the same pages and write: "All our observations have impressed me forcibly with the conviction that the mountains are older than the sea." All the major expeditions included a geologist, but it was not until late in the nineteenth century that a specifically geological mission was undertaken. The foremost geologist of the time was the P.E.F.'s Edward Hull, whose 1883 journey resulted in two major works, one of which concentrated on the geology of Palestine. Though much of his reasoning was later proven faulty, Hull's work is important to anyone wishing to trace the evolution of geological theory concerning the Dead Sea valley and the Aravah.

The east and west sides of the Dead Sea valley differ surprisingly given the fact that they are only six to twelve miles apart. The exposures—that is the visible rock formations—are much older on the east. The igneous rocks, one of the main components of the earth's surface, are covered with the 400 million year old red Nubian sandstone that has made the mountains of Moab famous for their beauty. The western cliffs are not as high as the eastern ones, and their brown exposures of chalk, limestone, and dolomite date back only to the initial opening of the Rift. The visual discrepancy is unavoidable, and so impressive that one of the first questions a traveller is likely to ask is how it came to be. The answer lies in the very forces that created the Rift Valley; if we look on the west side for a match of the reddish sandstone mountains of the east, we do find it—but not directly across the lake. Rather, the mate is to be found sixty miles south, the distance being evidence of the movement of the Arabian peninsula, movement that continues at its slow but inexorable pace.

The last important movement in the Rift Valley took place in the geological period immediately preceding ours, during which time the valley continued to sink. Familiarly called the Great Ice Age, the Pleistocene was an epoch of glacial periods and interglacial thaws alternating over a large part of the earth. Every time the ice melted, perhaps four times in all, soil would reappear on the cold planet, bringing with it vegetation in these interim periods, each of which lasted around 200,000 years. Areas south of where the ice sheets spread reveal traces of lakes where today there are none, as well as evidence that certain extant lakes were once much larger. All of this suggests that those regions experienced periods of intense precipitation and a low rate of evaporation; it is believed that these pluvials coincided with the ice ages of colder regions, and that the lakes shrank during the interglacials, when the climate turned dry. This cycle of the expansion and contraction of lakes characterized the Pleistocene in warm regions and is important in the evolution of the lakes in the valley.

Before any lake existed there, another process was taking place that would have the most pronounced effect on the composition of the Dead Sea valley. As the rift opened around three million years ago, the Mediterranean washed inland down to the Jordan Valley in a bay-like extension. The bay's story is one of alternating penetration and recession that lasted hundreds of thousands of years. The climate was dry and the rate of evaporation high, ideal conditions for the precipitation of salt, which sank to the lowest point in the basin, the part that would one day be occupied by the Dead Sea. Eventually, probably around two million years ago, the connection with the sea came to an end, perhaps because the valley's further subsidence left high land as interference. From then on, both the level and salinity of whatever lake occupied the closed depression would be determined by the relationship between inflow and evaporation. But though the link to the ocean was a thing of the past, a permanent mark on the Dead Sea valley remained—a bed of salt that drilling has established to be almost two miles thick, and which could be twice that.

The story of this salt deposit continued as the dry period during which it was accumulated turned humid. When flooding began, enormous quantities of rock and sand were washed down into the basin, where they settled on the salt bed. As the floods continued, the new layer—at least a mile deep—grew thicker and heavier, until the rock salt was softened by the great pressure. Squeezed against the sides of the basin, it sought an escape through faults and began to seep upwards, eventually floating all the way to the surface of the lake under which it had lain. Geologists explain the effect in terms of a bucket of mud into which a large flat stone is placed, forcing the mud to creep up the sides of the pail. In this case, the "mud" became on one side the Lisan Peninsula, whose cliffs may rise as much as 150 feet, and on the other side Mt. Sedom, later thrust up to 600 feet high. The mountain is composed of a core of solid rock salt, and its nearly vertical stratifications—very different from the horizontal ones found in most mountains—attest to this origin of intense pressure. But we are now somewhat ahead of the story of the Dead Sea itself, as the raising of Mt. Sedom came late, coinciding with the last important movement in the depression.

There have been a number of lakes to occupy the deepest section of the Great Rift, but little is known of the very early ones. Investigators believe that they ran the whole spectrum from fresh to hyper-saline, and they think that in the not too distant past, around 100,000 years ago, the lake which was formed by a return to a humid period was a freshwater one. Whether it was a single lake or a system of smaller ones is not clear, but this so-called Samra extended the length of the Jordan Valley. When the rains which created it stopped, it became increasingly saline and was converted, by virtue of this change in composition, into the important Lisan Lake, the immediate precursor of the Dead Sea. The rains returned, and the young Lisan grew enormously, stretching far beyond the territory that would be covered by its successor. Extending at its maximum from beyond Tiberias in the north to Hatseva in the south (further than the southern limit of the Dead Sea), the Lisan was six times as long as the Dead Sea and, though it was probably not as deep, had a volume of water four to five times as great.

During the first part of the lake's existence, torrents of water raged down the mountains, joining the rains which poured into it. The low rate of evaporation was nowhere equal to the task of countering the inflow, and the lake rose to a height of 660 feet higher than the Dead Sea is today. The evidence of this may be found in the cliffs. In the long ago post-pluvial summers, when evaporation was very high, aragonite, a white mineral, precipitated to the lake's bottom in a thin layer. In the winters, floods washed down clay and small fragments of stones which also settled to the bottom, in a thin brownish layer. After thousands of years of a seasonal cycle that must have been much more extreme than today's, the bottom of the lake had come to consist of a thick bed of this thinly laminated marl, its white layers clearly distinguishable from the brown. As the lake shrank, its floor was exposed, and the laminated deposits left by its recession have been found in the cliffs as high up as 660 feet. Spread from the Sea of Galilee in the north to Hatseva in the south in the shape of flat-topped hills as much as 100 feet high or more, this so-called Lisan Formation may be the single most distinguishing feature of the Jordan Valley. It is proof of the great length of the Lisan Lake and is accepted as irrefutable evidence that it once swept the shores at extraordinary heights.

The Lisan Lake reached this high level about 23,000 years ago, after which an arid period caused it to plunge to a level well beneath the current level of the Dead Sea. Although some of the lowering was caused by subsidence rather than actual shrinkage, dramatic changes in the climate had unmistakably taken place. The reduction in inflow and escalation of the evaporation rate were such that the mammoth prehistoric phenomenon came close to disappearing about 18,000 years ago. Evidence suggests that at one time it was as low as 2,100 feet below sea level, more than one and a half times lower than the Dead Sea. Exploration of the Dead Sea floor has revealed valleys cut into the sediment. These valleys were once the wadis that carried whatever flood water there was down the slopes and into the sea. The only way they could have been cut was if the lake were for a period of time as low as the now submerged river beds.

During this severe recession of the Lisan, its two major basins were exposed. The northern Beit Shean basin today contains the Sea of Galilee, and from the end of the Lisan period ceased to be connected with the evolution of the Dead Sea. The other basin would come to hold the Dead Sea, a lake differing greatly both in size and composition from its predecessor. As the composition of the Lisan distinguished it from its freshwater parent, so the slow development of the Dead Sea's singular composition would mark another turning of the generations. The approximate age of 12,000 years which has been assigned to the Dead Sea roughly coincides with these two foremost factors—the confinement of the post-Lisan Lake to a vastly smaller area, and the markedly different composition once that basin refilled. In addition, its great depth (some 1,000 feet) may be attributed to further tearing of the valley's floor, a process which filled those interim millennia.

Like the Lisan Lake, the Dead Sea has been prone to quick and severe level changes. (On both the east and west sides of the lake, one can see the horizontal lines that mark prehistoric shorelines.) But although its level has varied considerably over the years, the lake has been in a relative state of equilibrium, for the huge water loss which it experiences through evaporation has been compensated for by inflow from various sources. The primary source, contributing sixty per cent of all the replacement water, was until the 1960s the Jordan River. But the largest contributor now (taking into account annual variations) is the winter floods, and we should perhaps look at the Dead Sea environment in order to understand its phenomenal influence.

The lake lies in a desert that occupies the eastern flank of the Judean Mountains, which run north and south through the central portion of Israel. The Judean Desert is not part of the belt that includes the Sahara, Sinai, Negev, and Arabian deserts. Rather, it is a rainshadow desert; its situation on the lee side of the mountains, where it is shielded from most of the moisture-bearing winds that come off the Mediterranean, is responsible for its aridity. Jerusalem, some 3,000 feet above sea level, receives an average of twenty-five inches of precipitation annually, but when the rain clouds descend into the valley, they are warmed and in effect dehydrated; thus the northern end of the Dead Sea receives only four inches. Once the clouds reform and scale the Moab Mountains, they are cooled, showering the eastern range as they had showered the west. Only the Dead Sea basin itself remains dry.

The rain that falls on Jerusalem and the surrounding hills runs a slippery course down to the valley. The Judean Mountains, composed of limestone, are fairly impervious to water. Most of the rain is not absorbed but slides down the slopes and pours into the lake in a quantity that now accounts for more than half its replacement water. Jerusalem may be only nineteen miles away from the Dead Sea, but its 3,000 foot elevation, coupled with the 1,300 foot depth of the Dead Sea depression, means that the winter floods are plunging well over 4,000 feet in the space of those nineteen miles. It is not hard to imagine what has been happening in the region for thousands of years. The erosion of the eastern slopes of the Judean Hills has produced a network of canyons that laces the mountains' flank. If the Judean Desert is characterized by anything, it is by these deeply incised canyons that have been carved as the seasonal floods pound their way down to the lake. "The mind is lost in the bewildering extent of past geological æras," wrote Tristram as he studied one gorge, "when we try to conceive the length of time that must have elapsed since the furious torrents of the once watered hills tore down that ravine, and ploughed through the flinty rocks."

The dry river beds *(wadi* in Arabic, *naḥal* in Hebrew) provide the most striking contrasts with the desert. The same floods that have engraved them into the hills support a vast array of plant and animal life, and the rainy season brings on a short-lived but brilliant burst of color that extends, scrappy but distinct, well into the long dry summer. Only those wadis which are spring-fed retain their streams throughout the year. The rest run dry by early summer, but lone bushes scattered in uneven rows across the desert persist to mark their courses, stubborn evidence of the will to exist.

Winter is another matter. It is too easy to be deceived by the gentle brooks. The weather is perfect for hiking, and nothing could be more pleasant than wading in the streams rather than walking the tentative route along the cliffs. Yet it is a temptation that should be resisted, for the desert is prone to flash floods of stunning and sudden power. If it rains in the Judean Mountains, a flood can materialize with no advance warning, crashing through the wadis with a force that rips boulders from the hillsides and slices chunks from the asphalt road below. The tell-tale rumble often comes too

140

late for any possible escape, and nearly every year a hiker is carried away by the unpredictable and unforgiving torrent.

The force of the torrent is greatest toward the mouth of the wadi, not only because of the obvious accumulation in volume and increase in speed, but also because of a particular feature that characterizes all the ten to fifteen wadis on the Dead Sea's western shore. Each wadi typically has what is called a dry waterfall, a formation that looks exactly as its name suggests. About a mile in from its mouth the river course is interrupted by a severe break. (The few wadis on the west side that have springs have actual waterfalls, but most of them are only seasonal and are thus called dry.) The dry waterfalls were all created by erosion, and although they vary in age, they have a common origin; their creation was made possible by the subsidence of the basin when the valley snapped off at a point of weakness and sank further down. Most of the wadis have one or two sheer breaks of this sort. It is not known why, but the dry waterfall of Wadi Daraja, north of Ein Gedi, is broken into fifteen or twenty smaller but formidable steps which make for an exciting—but difficult and dangerous—hiker's descent.

Although the wadis have been created by water flowing down the channels for thousands of years, their mouths have changed since the Dead Sea basin began to subside. They were initially sketched in pre-Lisan days, so that when the Lisan came into being and rose nearly 700 feet higher than the present-day Dead Sea, the channels were already actual river beds. A constant flow of water passed through them, carrying large amounts of sediment which accumulated on the lake floor. As the Lisan shrank, the deltas which had been underwater were exposed, and the broad mounds of sediment obstructed the courses, forcing the streams to find new routes to the lake. As the dessication continued, the ancient deltas were left stranded; they can still be discerned as high as 600 feet above the Dead Sea (Kibbutz Ein Gedi, situated part way up the cliff, may actually be sitting on one of them).

Deltas can be found at the mouth of every wadi, where the stone-laden floods fanned out just as they reached the sea and deposited the broad mounds of sediment. To be exact, those mounds are usually not deltas, but alluvial fans, a close relative. Both are formed when a wadi course levels off and the energy of the water flow is diffused, causing the stream and its sediment to spread

141

out. They differ from one another not in appearance but in origin; a delta is built up gradually by a perennial flow of water, while a fan accumulates only seasonally. Strictly speaking, there is no such thing as a modern delta on the west side of the Dead Sea, for none of the major streams is perennial. On the eastern side there are actual deltas, but they are less pronounced because of the much greater water depth there (a consequence of the rift's main fault line being off center).

The relationship of the wadis to the cliffs is most apparent from a boat. One can see the fans extending into the lake, each raised, green-flecked promontory resembling a spread freckled hand. The wadis themselves look like notches that have been chiselled into stone, and they are generally distinct enough to be easily counted; if a break in the cliff is not apparent, a sprinkling of green is unmistakable. One's sense of proportion is altered by this vantage point. Despite the marked recession of the sea in recent decades, the cliffs seem to meet the water in a perpendicular line. One has no impression at all of shore flats, though they are ample; the primary impression is that of being at the bottom of a deep, steep-sided basin, and the feeling of its immutability is powerful.

Although the wadis of the western side of the Dead Sea were much frequented and fully appreciated by travellers of the last century, long-standing, if tacit, consensus had it that the two most magnificent gorges were to be found on the east. Few explorers actually entered the Wadi Mojib, directly across from Ein Gedi, but several described it from a distance. Those who went close were awed by its perpendicular walls of red sandstone, a mere hundred feet apart at 1,600 feet up, with palm trees growing from cracks overhead.

Lynch was one of the first to sail between the towering cliffs, noting that the chasm ran in a straight line for 150 yards, then bent gracefully to the southeast. The water was not very deep—between four and ten feet—and they remarked, from having seen traces of an Arab camp, that there must be some way down to the ravine. He spent only one evening examining the canyon, perhaps because one crew member's health signalled a possible outbreak of the fever which had "heretofore attacked all who had ventured upon this sea." Still, when his troubled eye scanned the Mojib, it was arrested in spite of itself. In the single page he devoted to the canyon he managed at least to hint at its splendor, observing that the cliffs

WADY MOJEB.

23.　Wadi Mojib. From *Narrative of the United States Expedition to the River Jordan and the Dead Sea*, by William F. Lynch, 1849.

were "all worn by the winter rains into the most fantastic forms, not unlike Egyptian architecture. It was difficult to realize that some were not the work of art."

Twenty-five years later, in his careful exploration of the eastern side of the Dead Sea, Tristram described his approach from the plain above: "The rolling slopes come close to the precipitous descent, the plain being perfectly level on either side, breaking away abruptly in limestone precipices to a great depth. No idea of the rift can be formed till the very edge is reached... The boulders have rolled down the slopes in wild, fantastic confusion, and add much to the effect and grandeur... An almond-tree was in full blossom near the top; tufts of asphodel and gorgeous scarlet anemones [pushed] out among the stones." Tristram made the difficult descent to the mouth of the river, probably the first European to do so, and he planned to return to follow its course back between the narrow canyon walls. To his regret he was never able to.

North of the Mojib is the Wadi Zerka Ma'in, the outlet of the famed hot springs of Callirhoe. At the beginning of the nineteenth century, a travelling companion of Irby and Mangles watched in amazement as their Arab guide took "a vapour-bath" above the water, which itself was too hot to touch: "Over a crevice, whence issued one of the springs, a bed of twigs and broom was laid, at a distance of about a foot from the water, upon which he placed himself... and remained... for several minutes." Pliny described the Greek-named spring as "remarkable for its medicinal qualities, and which, by its name (i.e., fine stream or fair-flowing), indicates the celebrity its waters have gained." Indeed, the hot baths had been attracting a hopeful clientele for centuries, none more famous than King Herod, who made the pilgrimage just before his death in 4 B.C.E., counting on the therapeutic waters to cure him of his agony. The irrepressibly moralistic Thomas Fuller would recall Herod's futile effort when he described "two springs of contrary natures. One hot and sweet, the other cold and bitter. Both which meeting together make a most excellent Bath, cordiall [sic] for several diseases. As if nature would thereby lesson us, that moderation, wherein extremities agree, is the best cure for all distempers. These waters are approved excellent for the contraction of the nerves, either inwardly taken, or outwardly applied. *Herod* the king being sick... was hither directed in vain by his physitians [sic], the water refusing to be guilty of such a Tyrants recovery... And now what pity is it that such precious water should presently be spilt into the *Dead Sea*! But what remedy? Fair and foul faces must meet together in the grave."

For Tristram, the Zerka Ma'in rivalled the Mojib in grandeur. As he descended near the famous baths, he was enchanted by the gnarled and contorted iron-red rock, the tall palms and dense undergrowth, the hidden stream given away only by "the bright cascades leaping down the rocks." In the three-mile wide plain, Tristram counted ten springs ranging in temperature from ambient to 140 degrees Fahrenheit, and from mildly to hyper-sulphurous. Once he reached the bottom, Tristram stood at the mouth of the gorge and looked back: "Picture a wild ravine," he recommended, and went on to describe the six hundred foot high rugged red cliffs, the water rushing to the sea, its course fringed by emerald maiden-hair fern all the way.

The consummate scientist, Tristram was by his own admission susceptible to seduction by "less scientific propensities." What a scene he paints as he and his companions try to make their way back up the gorge: "Now leaping, with guns slung on our shoulders, from rock to rock; now stumbling among boulders, up to the hips in the warm water of the dashing stream; now struggling through tangled jungle; now climbing slopes of rotten debris that looked impassable a few minutes before; now crawling up a jagged rock on hands and feet; at length we reached a point, on a shelf at a dizzy height above the stream, where we had just room to stand... A short rest, and another tremendous climb was before us. Alas! the folly of attempting such a feat as heavily weighted as an unfortunate British soldier on a march, with gun, pistol-belt, compass-case, field-glass, powder, two shot-belts, bowie knife and cartridge case, flask, and other *impedimenta* on one's person." His hiking was apparently not nearly as nimble as his prose, as he recounts his travails negotiating the terrain: "Now, to have one's head-gear repeatedly abstracted by some thorny creeper, and to be in danger of plunging headlong into a lake the temperature of 120° Fahr., as you clutch convulsively at the excrescences of an overhanging rock, which are provokingly rounded and smooth, is somewhat trying at the end of a day of eleven hours under an eastern sun."

The wadis of the eastern side of the Dead Sea are not only less accessible than those of the west, since the broad headlands with coves and beaches soon give way to the sheer cliffs, they are also more fertile than those across the lake, and Tristram was perpetually thrilled with what he found. "We pass the crest," he wrote from his vantage point high in the cliff, "and are treated with another series of landscapes of bewildering grandeur; while at our feet every black [i.e., basalt] boulder is framed in the loveliest flowers—a setting, springing one can hardly see whence, and living one can hardly think how. Geraniums, iris, ranunculus, red poppy, and composite plants of endless variety... delight us all, and glut Haynes' collecting cases."

As we saw, the lives of Costigan and Molyneux might have been saved by the drinkable, if not tasty, water they could have found at any of the springs along the lakeshore. Perhaps they underestimated the danger of going without water. We know that Molyneux was reluctant to land on hostile shores, but Costigan, according to his servant, slept on the beach nearly every night and could not have

24. The eastern shore of the Dead Sea. From *The Land of Moab*, by Henry Baker Tristram, 1874.

146

avoided spotting some tell-tale verdure. For the springs are not hidden, and it is their very accessibility which provokes puzzlement over what seems to have been the explorers' unnecessary misery.

Most of the numerous springs of the Dead Sea valley are located at low points, at the bottom of wadis or along the shore, and all of them are connected to the fault line of the Rift. The springs on the western shore range in temperature from cool to very warm; those on the east, being much closer to the main fault line, are generally a good deal hotter. There is also considerable variation in the nature of the spring water. The chemical composition of each is determined by several factors: how long the water has been trapped underground; how deep its point of issue; the type of rock over which the water passes as it rises; and whether or not it is diluted by freshwater on its way up. For these reasons, springs that are close in proximity may be different in make-up.

Those springs that are hottest and highest in mineral content and radioactivity are the ones that have been most prized since antiquity for their therapeutic qualities. The Callirhoe probably ranked first, but others, on both sides of the lake, were also highly valued. There is, for example, archaeological evidence of a kind of health resort on the southwest side near Ein Bokek, which is thought to have been popular in the Herodian period. Together, the springs contribute about ten per cent of the Dead Sea's replacement water, their contribution being greater when the lake is low because then the water table is higher in relation to it.

Tristram's desire to follow the Mojib upstream was fulfilled instead by the little known Rev. Putnam Cady in the winter of 1898. Responding to a P.E.F. call for new photographs of the east coast, Cady took a twelve-foot flat-bottomed boat large enough for three and set out from the mouth of the Jordan in order to survey the northern third of the east coast. At first he found the shore to be marked by broad beaches that made landing easy, and the many large trees standing in the water sixty feet from shore indicated that the lake had risen in recent decades. The trees were encrusted with salt, Cady noted, "and looked ghastly in the early light." To Irby and Mangles eighty years before, they had seemed like "fine white coral"—yet another instance of simple descriptions revealing the mood of an expedition. Indeed, alluding to illness and fear, Cady called the lake a sea of death and expressed the hope that it would be kinder to future travellers than it was to him. So was the entire coast of the Dead Sea surveyed by the turn of the century. Yet while one acknowledges Cady's service to the P.E.F., it is a small detail of his experience that stays in the mind—his collecting lumps of asphalt along the shore.

The Greeks called it Lake Asphaltites, after the asphalt that periodically came to its surface. The substance was prized for its water-proofing and medicinal applications and was bought by the ancient Egyptians for use in embalming. The Dead Sea was the region's primary source of the substance, and whoever controlled the lake became wealthy from the lucrative trade with Egypt. None were more successful in mining and marketing the asphalt than the Nabateans, who possessed most of the lake's east side by the second century B.C.E. According to Diodorus, the barbarians, as he called the sophisticated Nabateans, "take the asphalt to Egypt and sell it for the embalming of the dead; for unless this is mixed with the other aromatic ingredients, the preservation of the bodies cannot be permanent." (During his trip through Egypt in 1836, John Stephens inadvertently corroborated the ancient use when he commented on the fact that many of the tombs had been robbed of their mummies, which had been sold to travellers. Momentarily irreverent, he went on, "The Arabs use the mummy-cases for firewood, the bituminous matters [i.e., asphalt] used in the embalment being well adapted to ignition: and the epicurean traveller may cook his breakfast with the coffin of a king.")

It is not completely clear how the asphalt is formed, but it is probably related to the remains of oil deposits which have shifted elsewhere. Lumps of the substance, some weighing as much as several tons, still rise very occasionally to the surface of the lake, generally at the same places close to the Rift's main fault. Its release is thought to be connected to movement in the earth's crust; Arabs guiding Europeans in the last century assured them that chunks of the substance are only found in the lake following earthquakes, as in 1834 and again after the severe quake of January 1837, when a house-size mass was supposed to have been discovered on the sea. (According to the report available a few years later, the Arabs swam out to it, cut it up with axes, and brought it to shore, from where they conveyed it up the pass at Ein Gedi on camels. In all, that one harvest brought them several thousand dollars in sales.)

So unusual a phenomenon was the asphalt, and so important a commercial product, that it was widely discussed by the Greeks and

Romans. The Dead Sea, explained Strabo, "abounds with asphaltus, which rises, not however at any regular season, in bubbles, like boiling water, from the middle of the deepest part. The surface is convex, and presents the appearance of a hillock. Together with the asphaltus, there ascends a great quantity of sooty vapour, not perceptible to the eye, which tarnishes copper, silver, and everything bright—even gold. The neighboring people know by the tarnishing of their vessels that the asphaltus is beginning to rise, and they prepare to collect it by means of rafts composed of reeds. The asphaltus is a clod of earth, liquefied by heat; the air forces it to the surface, where it spreads itself. It is again changed into so firm and solid a mass by cold water, such as water of the lake, that it requires cutting or chopping (for use). It floats upon the water, which, as I have described, does not admit of diving or immersion, but lifts the person who goes into it. Those who go on rafts for the asphaltus cut it in pieces, and take away as much as they are able to carry.

"Such are the phenomena. Posidonius says, that the people being addicted to magic, and practising incantations, (by these means) consolidate the asphaltus, pouring upon it urine and other fetid fluids, and then cut it into pieces. (Incantations cannot be the cause), but perhaps urine may have some peculiar power (in effecting the consolidation)...

"It is natural for these phenomena to take place in the middle of the lake, because the source of the fire is in the center, and the greater part of the asphaltus comes from thence. The bubbling up, however, of the asphaltus is irregular, because the motion of fire, like that of many other vapours, has no order perceptible to observers."

Modern geology's explanation, though more sophisticated than Strabo's, is not radically different. Geologists believe that the substance, partly liquified by the heat of the inner earth, seeps up to the bottom of the lake and, being lighter than the dense water, rises to the surface, cooled and solidified.

Strabo's description of the gathering of the asphalt found support in Josephus: The lumps of asphalt "are in shape and size like headless bulls. The lakeside workers row to the spot, seize the lumps one by one and haul them into their boats. When these are full, it is not easy to get the asphalt away, as the boats stick to the glutinous mass until they loose it with a woman's menstruous blood and

149

urine, to which alone it yields." Tacitus called the purported use of menstrual blood the story of ancient writers, and it is odd that he would know more about it than Josephus. Myth or not, the belief survived into the medieval period, Burchard explaining that bitumen, also called Jews' pitch, is brought up from the bottom of the lake "when wind stirs the sea." Then the asphalt "clings together and is cast up on shore in great quantities. It is strong and medicinal, [and] cannot be melted save with menstruous blood." From these various descriptions, one can easily understand the popular medieval view that the Dead Sea "casteth up clots of glue."

Today there are enough sources of asphalt so that the Dead Sea is of virtually no importance, and far too little rises to make an industry feasible anyway. That which does surface is hauled to shore as a curiosity. Though the substance may be rendered soft by the desert sun—as an asphalt road in summer—it is not nearly as sticky as the ancient writers had it to be, nor does it require any unusual means of detaching.

Given the uniqueness of the Dead Sea's more than thirty per cent salt content, one can imagine that the question of the salts' origin must have provoked the interest of many investigators. Indeed, though the question would remain unanswered well into this century, theories had been put forth since early in the 1800s. It was known that all lakes receive a certain amount of minerals from incoming rivers and that they are carried out again by exiting streams, of which the Dead Sea has none. It was also known that the rate of evaporation is a factor in the concentration of salts in any body of water, and that the rate in the Dead Sea valley was obviously very high. But while such knowledge helped explain why the accumulation increased, it did not explain how the large quantity of minerals came to be there in the first place.

Seetzen surmised in 1810 that the Dead Sea owed its saltiness to the salt mountain by its shore, which presumably was being slowly dissolved, but hardly anyone else took up that erroneous line of thought. As time went by, different theories were put forward. At the beginning of the twentieth century it was suggested that the salts came via the atmosphere from the Mediterranean. (Farfetched as it sounds, some salts are in fact transported by wind and rain from the sea, though that study greatly overestimated their impact on the total accumulation in the Dead Sea.) Some researchers

150

suggested that the salts were brought down by the Jordan River, and others regarded them as having flowed in from the hypersaline springs (which, because they are often saltier than the lake, contribute an amount disproportionate to their water contribution). In the late 1920s, a marine origin for the salts was suggested, a hypothesis that would find support in the work of later researchers.

The 1950s and '60s were decades of revelation. Not only did the sophistication of the tools catch up with that of the investigators, but the simple development of the Dead Sea valley—construction of roads, for example—made the lake more accessible. In 1959, the American/Israeli team of K.O. Emery and David Neev began a systematic study of the physical, chemical, and geological aspects of the Dead Sea. The study which they published in 1967 was the most comprehensive since Lynch's 120 years earlier, and it quickly became a cornerstone of modern Dead Sea scientific exploration.

One of the difficulties in establishing the source of the Dead Sea's salts was determining their age. At around the time that Neev and Emery were working, test borings at Mt. Sedom were made in connection with oil exploration. The deep salt which the drills penetrated was analyzed and found to contain ordinary pollen which had been carried by some prehistoric wind and had settled on and been preserved in the salt mound. Coincidentally, a method for dating pollen had recently been developed, and when the Mt. Sedom pollen was dated at three million years old, Neev and Emery could conclude that the salts of the Dead Sea were also that old—a far cry from the age of as much as 500 million years that scientists early in the century had estimated. Dating the salts was the single most important event in verifying their source. Not everyone agreed, but it is widely accepted today that the Dead Sea derives its salinity from the same source as the Lisan Lake.

This answer calls upon us to return to the valley's early history, and recall that the Mediterranean had at one time washed into the rift, depositing, after hundreds of thousands of years, a salt bed more than two miles thick. Though the bulk of the salt had collected at the basin's lowest point, large quantities were also stranded throughout the valley. The Lisan Lake, as we saw, dates to the time when it came to encompass enough of those salts to turn its freshwater forerunner saline. By virtue of its size alone, it dissolved a vast quantity, and as it dried up, it left them behind, the bulk gathering once again in the depression's deepest section. When the

151

basin began to refill—this long geological moment that saw the birth of the Dead Sea—the water mixed with the residual brine of the Lisan Lake, but in a much smaller area than that which the Lisan had covered, making the mineral concentration much higher.

If the source of the Dead Sea's salts is the ocean, one would expect the lake's mineral content to correspond with that of the ocean; yet it doesn't. The ocean contains primarily sodium chloride, the Dead Sea a very large quantity of magnesium and calcium chloride. The discrepancy is based partly on the different precipitation tendencies of minerals. As water becomes saturated, sodium chloride falls out of solution much before magnesium chloride, which is among the last compounds to crystallize. So though the Dead Sea itself is high in magnesium, examination of its sediment reveals, as expected, a very high sodium content.

As the Jordan River flowed to the Dead Sea, it washed over the Lisan marl which coated most of its course and brought down additional salts. The early scientists who suggested that the lake's salts must have originated in the Jordan were at least partially right in a sense. The Jordan did bring down minerals, though not a major portion by any means. What they of course did not know was that those salts were not the Jordan's own, but those of an earlier era reactivated by the washing action of the river. Recycled, as it is, the salt of the Dead Sea is much older than the lake itself, dating back to the penetration of the valley by the open sea three million years ago.

Early studies of the Dead Sea took in every phenomenon that could in any way be seen, felt, or measured. Once an explorer made an observation, the next decades might be filled with conjectures about it, or denials of it. The question of currents, one of the most complex of Dead Sea phenomena, was no exception. When Lynch experienced currents in 1848, he conjectured that the tons of water flowing from the Jordan River every day were pumped with such force that a strong southward current was created down the center of the lake. The jet of water struck the Lisan Peninsula and bounced off northward, generating currents along the east and west coasts. Lynch, it seems, was wrong, but then it would have been most remarkable had he been right. There are many factors involved in creating currents, some only dimly understood to this day. Because currents may be detected on windless as well as on windy days, there must be invisible forces at work which greatly complicate matters. Nonetheless, two major ones were identified by Neev and

Emery as a result of modern analytical methods. Their role in the Dead Sea drama goes back to the lake's early years.

When the long flat-bottomed dish that is the Dead Sea depression cracked several million years ago, its two basins were created, evolving from that point on as independent units. Any subsequent movement in the valley did not affect them equally, and the difference in their respective depths became more and more pronounced. The last major movement left between them a raised rim (which eventually cracked) that separated the two basins so effectively that the lake was probably confined, as we have seen, to its northern basin until well into historical times.

So great is the difference in the depths of the two basins that it seems at first improbable: the northern basin is as much as a thousand feet deep, the southern averaged around fifteen. Because of its shallowness, the southern basin more immediately responded to atmospheric conditions than did the northern one. It was more prone to temperature changes and experienced an even greater rate of evaporation, meaning that the salt concentration increased more rapidly than in the north. (De Saulcy, for one, had first-hand knowledge of that peculiarity: "The water of the Dead Sea, at the northern point, is atrociously bitter and salt," he complained, "but it is lemonade in comparison with what we so rashly tasted [in the south]." The southern basin is about five percent saltier than the northern, a variation far greater than that found within other bodies of water.)

The discovery of this difference by Neev and Emery turned out to be a key to understanding the currents. The southern basin's greater density had created, in effect, a slope; magnet-like, it pulled the water from the north, producing the southerly current that had been observed by early explorers, and sending back a northerly stream in return. Through isotopic analysis, modern investigators were able to "see" the different composition of the currents much as early observers could see the muddy Jordan flow into the lake. The Coriolis effect produced by the rotation of the earth determined that the southward flow would shift to the west coast and the northward one to the east.

As the shallowness of the southern basin yielded some explanation of the currents, so the currents partially explained yet another tendency. Many travellers to the Dead Sea described strange lines of foam that ran across the lake, sometimes in apparent patterns

153

and at other times randomly. Having seen them near the shore, one explorer wondered if they were not caused by the lapping of waves, but that did not explain their occurrence in the middle of the lake. In mid-century, an American visitor noticed that the sea was bordered "by a line of white, thick, creamy foam, though there was scarce a ripple on the lake, and several streaks of a similar appearance lay upon the green and purple waters far away." More than half a century later, Masterman suggested a correlation between their direction and changes in wind direction, an observation that would prove to be important. For similar foam lines, or slicks, are found in the ocean, and like those, the ones in the Dead Sea are caused by friction, whether within one current divided by the wind, or by the rubbing of a current against a shallow bottom. They can also be seen where springs, floods, or streams enter the lake.

From early in the century, individuals with practical interest in the nature of the Dead Sea had noticed that the lake's salinity was not constant at various depths and that in fact the sea appeared to be quite sharply stratified. Neev and Emery noted that the northern basin of the Dead Sea consisted of distinct layers of water which differed sharply in temperature, density, and salinity. There were two major layers, sandwiching a middle one. The so-called upper water mass extended from the surface down 120 feet, and the lower mass down to the bottom. So extreme was their difference that simultaneous evolution was thought to be out of the question. The lower layer might be characterized as a fossil water body—one that has been completely sealed off for so long that it has ceased to interact in any way with the atmosphere. The upper layer must have accumulated relatively quickly for this to have happened. The question was what sequence of events brought it about.

This question brings us into thorny territory, for in order to identify such events, the upper water mass had first to be dated, and that was a most complicated and uncertain task. Neev and Emery determined an approximate age of 1,500 years, and looked to the end of the Byzantine period for an explanation. For many centuries the region had been intensively farmed, and water conservation had been a major enterprise; the torrents which today rush unchecked down the wadis were once corralled instead into reservoirs. The Arab conquest of the 630s C.E. brought a rapid disintegration of agriculture, for the Moslem conquerors were not farmers. The

154

25.   View of the Dead Sea. From *Picturesque Palestine*, vol. 3, edited by Charles Wilson, 1881.

aqueducts fell into disrepair, and all the water that had been trapped annually by a thousand years of Jewish, Roman, and Byzantine efforts flowed undisciplined into the Dead Sea, raising it, Neev and Emery believed, by 120 feet, the volume of the upper water mass. To say that there is no unanimity of opinion on this question is an understatement. Other researchers did a calculation based on the age of radioactive isotopes and arrived at an age of only about three hundred years—a discrepancy so great as to remind one of the discussion of the depth of the Dead Sea depression nearly a century and a half earlier. Still others looked for a climatic context. The seventeenth century was fairly wet in this region, and the eighteenth dry. Beginning around 1820, another wet period, as we saw, began raising the level of the lake for the next century. Some researchers, their argument bolstered by specific gravity measurements, believe that the upper water mass could only have been as old as that recent accumulation, namely, 150 years.

The Dead Sea itself can no longer divulge the answer to this question. Since 1975, it had been clear that the surface layer of the lake was becoming increasingly saline, probably because of the tapping of the Jordan River system. By 1976, the difference between the layers was negligible, and by mid-1978, the upper layer was actually saltier than the lower. Stratification, however, was maintained because of the temperature difference between them. That winter, with the cooling of the upper water mass, a dramatic event took place: the lake "overturned," its water becoming more or less homogenized for the first time in at least 150 years.

The question of the age of the fossil water body and the origin of the upper water mass may never be answered because of the "overturning." Yet it seems that if human intervention may be recognized even as a possible element, then it is useful to consider the implications of human activity in general. Factors have been introduced in the last decades that have already had a pronounced impact on the lake, and it is almost certain that before this century is out, human beings will once again exert a major influence on it; for better or worse has yet to be seen.

PART IV

Further Exploration

...I never felt so unwilling to leave any place. I was unsatisfied. I had a longing desire to explore every part of that unknown water ; to spend days upon its surface ; to coast along its shores ; to sound its mysterious depths...

John Lloyd Stephens
Incidents of Travel in Egypt, Arabia Petræa, and the Holy Land, 1837

5

A Gentleman from Siberia

L ONG BEFORE scientists and engineers turned their thoughts to the
multiple potential of the Dead Sea, those who lived by its shores
were finding a livelihood in its unusual treasures. Asphalt, though
the most prized, was also the least predictable. A much more
mundane substance was harvested with absolute reliability. After
visiting the Dead Sea in the early 1740s, Pococke described the
Arab practice of digging small pits on the beach. With the melting
of the snow in the north, he explained, the Jordan River would
swell, causing the lake to rise and overflow into the pits. When the
water evaporated, the hollows would be left filled with inch-thick
cakes of salt which were then collected. In this way, the tables of the
surrounding countryside were supplied. In subsequent years, a
number of travellers mentioned meeting salt-laden caravans en
route to Gaza, Jerusalem, and Bethlehem. At mid-century, an
Englishman spoke of camels being brought to Mt. Sedom, rather
than the Dead Sea, to be loaded with salt. The Arabs received ten
shillings per load of five hundred pounds on their arrival in
Jerusalem, he noted, in addition to which the purchaser was
required to pay a duty to the Turkish Government. Evidently this
commerce was eventually made illegal, and much of the contraband
was transported during the night. One unhappy explorer, camping
at Ein Gedi in the 1870s, complained about being kept awake all
night by the running conversation his sentries carried on with the
Arabs of a caravan as they led their camels up the narrow pass.

Less than half a century later, the extraction of minerals from the
Dead Sea would far surpass this long-practiced salt-farming, and
the combined efforts of idealists and pragmatists would result in

achievements that probably few had ever dreamed of. The development of the Dead Sea valley in the last decades has been extensive—so much so that there are those who are fearful lest radical and irrevocable changes, whose consequences cannot be forseen, be wrought on the landscape, and permanent harm done to the lake and its fragile environment. It is difficult not to admire the imagination and energy of those who took on the desert and conceived of ways to make it not only accommodate, but also yield, life. Yet the fear that the Dead Sea will be overwhelmed in a flood of technology and the increasing needs of the two countries that share it is a well-founded one, and in these years of extraordinary inventiveness and ambition, excitement over man-made marvels need be tempered by anxiety for the natural one.

In 1831, a Jew named Novomeysky from the Russian town of Novo Miasto near what was then the Prussian border was arrested on the charge of having aided rebels of the Polish uprising the previous year. Sentenced to exile, he and his fellow prisoners set out for Siberia on foot, the 4,000 mile forced march almost to the Chinese border taking them four years. Novomeysky's wife had been allowed to accompany him, and once there, they settled in and raised a family. By the time their grandson Mikhail, later to be called Moshe, was born in 1873, the village of Barzugin, on the shores of Lake Baikal, had become the family's home.

Like his father, Mikhail had an inclination for mining, and after studying mining engineering in Germany, he returned to Siberia and threw himself into his work. His fellow scientists were occupied for the most part in mining copper and gold, but Mikhail's active imagination was already focusing on something quite different. Even at that young age he had large projects in mind, projects that would revolutionize the mining industry in Siberia and energize the economic life of the region. One such idea was to develop a method for extracting minerals from the nearby lakes, and by 1900, when he was just twenty-seven, he had built the necessary chemical factory and was supplying the local glass-works with the refined salts, a great improvement on what had been available to them. Novomeysky had the rare gift for turning imagination into realities, and by the time he emigrated, after more than twenty years of work in Siberia, he had become a pioneer in Russia's exploitation of natural resources.

160

Novomeysky was the third generation of a family with distinct radical propensities, and his activism was as evident as his grandfather's had been. For a time he was an adherent of the Social Revolutionary Party, and when he became disillusioned with it, he began to lean towards the Social Democrats. But he could never align himself with them unequivocally, mainly because of their stand on the question of nationalities. Although he had not been especially moved by the First Zionist Congress in 1897, he did have a definite feeling for Jewish nationalism. In 1903, when the Social Democrats split, he was put off by the debates on the Jewish question. That same year he attended the Zionist Congress in Basel, where the contact he had with young Russian Zionists spurred him in their direction. In 1905, when he was imprisoned for revolutionary activity, he spent seven months reading Zionist literature. Novomeysky's early commitments were strong, and he was still far from emigration, but the year's two conferences seem to have been responsible for the change in direction his life would later take.

One of Novomeysky's jobs in his radical circle had been to forge identity papers and passports, and he eventually found himself doing that very thing for himself in 1906. Released from prison, he had no assurance that he would not be arrested again, and he thought it wise to leave the country for the time being. His trip to Germany, where he had been a student, was the final element in his conversion to Zionism—though he confessed that his involvement with the Zionist circles in Germany was more or less compensatory: "Divorced suddenly from active engineering and social work," he wrote, "I was momentarily without anything to do." He made the acquaintance of the botanist Otto Warburg, whom Herzl had recruited to the Zionist cause, and their association, which was both scientific and political, served as a stimulus for Novomeysky. When he expressed his long-standing interest in studying the natural wealth of undeveloped nations, Warburg allowed him to read an unpublished report on Palestine's natural resources, prepared by the geologist Max Blanckenhorn at Herzl's request. The paper included a detailed description of the Dead Sea, and Novomeysky was excited by the similarity between its chemical composition and that of his Siberian lakes. By 1907, he had already inquired about the possibility of obtaining permission from the Turks to extract salts.

Yet he was very much a political man, and despite his enthusiasm and desire to conduct experiments, he remained committed to affairs in Russia. Returning that summer, he once again became involved in the struggle. "During the punitive expeditions' work," he would write of events that took place during his absence, "the gallows and firing squads had been constantly busy without waiting for any trial, and the bloodthirstiness of the happenings, of which I only learned when I returned, so affected me that all I had learned in the Warburg Institute about Palestine and about the Dead Sea and its waters ceased to have any real interest for me. For months I was restless and simply could not work. My only feeling, and one which never left me, was that those crimes of the Cossack general could not be forgotten, and should not remain unpunished." He became involved in an assassination plot, and it was only the sudden reassignment of the general responsible for the atrocities that prevented its being attempted.

Five years later, in 1911, Novomeysky finally arranged the trip that had been conceived of in Germany. "My eye was certainly inured to deserted, uninhabited places," he would write of his first view of the Dead Sea valley, "but this was something of quite a different order from anything I had known." No two climates could be more dissimilar than those of the Siberian *taiga*, the dense forest where the very subsoil is permanently frozen, and the barren, hot Dead Sea basin. Obviously his process of extracting minerals from Siberian lakes, which entailed freezing them out of solution, was impossible at the Dead Sea. But Novomeysky had a suspicion from the start that his already proven technique would provide him with the key to devising a method adapted to extreme heat. He measured the water's specific gravity, took numerous readings of air and water temperatures, and investigated the practicality of constructing the evaporation pans he envisioned. Taking ample specimens with him, he returned to Siberia and began his experiments.

It would be a number of years before he returned to Palestine. The First World War, the Russian Revolution, his mining projects, and, not least, his deep attachment to Siberia all prevented him from going back. But his thoughts turned increasingly towards Palestine. A country with only 700,000 inhabitants ("a population much less," according to a report in 1921 of the British High Commissioner, "than that of the province of Galilee alone in the time of Christ"), it was as devoid of industry as Siberia had been when he began mining there twenty-three years before, and he

162

longed to play a part in the country's economic development. His love for his native country was great, but not great enough to keep him there after the Revolution. "After a period of great perturbation in Russia, living through revolution and civil war and the loss of all our property, I had made up my mind that there was no other course for my family... but to begin a new life, and that this should be on new soil."

Making his way back to Siberia to say a temporary goodbye to his family, he left by the eastern route, legally but none too soon, as he was soon after denounced by an acquaintance who turned against him. The following year he sent for his family and settled them in the small village of Gedera, near Tel Aviv. "My whole training and philosophy of life had taught me and experience had shown me that there was no more satisfactory way to [secure the family against misfortune] than the fundamental way of establishing them as tillers of the soil. Industries and towns may rise and fall, but basic agriculture must always remain."

Nine years earlier, when he had conducted his first tests on the Dead Sea water, he had been encouraged by the results. "At last my early hunch about the feasibility of exploiting the salts of the Dead Sea had taken new shape. The idea now seemed much nearer to realisation." But as he had had no way of knowing that nearly a decade would pass before he would resume his work in Palestine, so he had no way of knowing that yet another would be spent obtaining permission to undertake his project. On his return in 1920, he immediately began what would be a long, frustrating procedure of negotiating with the British for the rights to construct a potash plant on the northern shore of the Dead Sea.

Why potash? In 1840, a German scientist had made the connection between potash (potassium chloride) and plant growth, and for twenty years before Novomeysky's time it had been considered essential to healthy crops. Plants draw potash out of the soil for various uses: it prevents stems from breaking, regulates the flow of water, protects the plant against cold, and increases the starch in grain and the protein in other plants. By 1900, scientists recognized that overworked soil needed its supply of potash replenished. A mine containing a large quantity was found in Germany, which became the world's sole producer. With World War I, the price per ton increased almost tenfold, and England began searching for another source. Their need was all the more

163

acute because of a much less benign application of the substance: it happened to be an ingredient in explosives. England's desire to break the German monopoly would figure in the Dead Sea concession battle.

The story of how this slender, rather formal, gentleman from Siberia, his straight nose and firm lips set under a resolute, even stern, gaze, was able to obtain the coveted concession is one of extraordinary determination, impressive ingenuity, and no small degree of diplomatic skill. The odds were against him, and his perseverance and resilience make for an exciting chapter in Dead Sea history—one that could serve as a useful prototype.

Novomeysky was not alone in recognizing the Dead Sea's potential, and the struggle for the concession was an arduous, sometimes unpleasant, one. At first his rivals were individuals like himself (his primary competitor, the Scotsman Major Thomas Tulloch, soon became his partner), and it looked as though he would achieve an early victory, after just four years' labor. But the inquiry which he thought was the last step in the negotiations (an inquiry in which his British examiner expressed doubts that any white man could live at the Dead Sea) proved far from that, though not because he failed to answer any question to the committee's satisfaction. Sir Herbert Samuel was just ending his term as High Commissioner in 1924, and, suddenly fearful of a Novomeysky monopoly, he made the abrupt decision to throw the whole matter of the concession open to public bidding.

Novomeysky was perturbed, but sympathetic. Samuel, a Jew, had not long before been the target of criticism from Parliament for granting a concession to another Russian Jew—"a very dangerous kind of animal!" quipped Novomeysky. "Thus I had no more grudges against Samuel, and my reason approved of action which was causing me great hardship and strain. It remained for me to be patient. I had now no other course than to write off the first chapter in my battle for the concession, a four-year chapter, and wait for the Press advertisements which would throw everything open to tender." In Mandate Palestine, one had to cultivate patience or accept defeat; the previous year, when Novomeysky had thought he should not be able to bear any more postponements, he had discovered that he was "getting a little inured to unexpected delays, and to the leisurely beat of the pulse of the official world."

The irony, however, in Novomeysky's being treated as if he were a powerful corporation intent on gaining a monopoly of the Dead Sea's resources was that when the advertisement was read in America, applications for the concession were submitted by none other than General Motors, Du Pont, and Standard Oil. The lake contains a billion tons of bromine, which had recently been discovered to be an octane booster and anti-knock agent in gasoline, and with the automobile industry burgeoning in America, they all had their eye on the lake's store. "I was now very alarmed indeed," wrote the troubled Novomeysky. "Idle to say that this Goliath of a combined competitor did not want potash as well... If, dazzled by their greatness, the British authorities conceded the Americans what they wanted, would they bother very much about me and my proposals?"

A period of either confusion or double-dealing—probably fair measures of both—ensued. The spokesman for the corporations insisted to Novomeysky that because they were not interested in the potash they might consider a joint venture, since the two chemicals were related in the extraction process. But their British attorney made it clear to him that sharing was out of the question. He did not know whom to believe, and the whole affair was very disconcerting to a man well-accustomed to adversity, even pettiness, but unfamiliar with prevarication. "In the limited Dead Sea area," he paraphrased a friend's explanation, "a concession to the Americans would amount to a monopoly, and although there had been talks about joining forces with my group, the impression was that these talks were not serious, merely intended to keep me quiet while the Americans walked away with the concession." Informed that the British had decided to award the Americans the bromine concession, Novomeysky contemplated defeat: "It would be of poor advantage to the Palestine in which I believed, and of which I was now a citizen, to allow foreign capitalists to have a controlling interest and to exploit the Dead Sea, having only commercial profits in mind."

But he had not spent all those years struggling for nothing, and Novomeysky would not be intimidated. Instructing his attorneys to write a strong letter of protest to the British Colonial Office, he assured them that he was able to produce evidence of financial resources great enough to put him on an equal footing with the Americans. The letter had a persuasive effect, the Office replying noncommittally but positively enough for Novomeysky to feel that

165

"the American danger had been baulked." From there, maybe it was a matter of his passion simply being greater than theirs, or his will more resolute. His application was finally accepted, in principle, in 1927—seven years after he first submitted it.

Novomeysky was not the only party who felt abused by the unpredictable decision-making machinery of the British Government. As early as 1918, and unknown for some time to Novomeysky, a chemist named Dr. Annie Homer had submitted an application for a Dead Sea concession, also for potash. Since a source had been sought by Great Britain for two years, it is difficult to understand the Government's long delay in coming to a decision. In any case, when the matter was opened to public bidding several years after Dr. Homer first inquired, her group, referred to as the British Group, was not a little surprised and distressed; obviously she had expected to win the concession, and to discover some seven years later that the Government was advertising for additional applications was a major blow. A year later, in 1926, there was a possibility of a merger between the British Group and Novomeysky and his partner, but it didn't materialize, apparently because Novomeysky wanted control.

Soon after, the Government determined that the British Group had the best proposal after all, yet as a result of "certain financial intrigues," as one finds it called in a memorandum, they lost their backing. In the meantime, the Colonial Office offered the concession "in principle" to Novomeysky, requiring from him that he produce in the whole seventy-five years of the concession an amount of potash less than the amount produced world-wide that year. The British Group was understandably angry, charging that Novomeysky was given "undue preference" in the form of almost unlimited time to provide financial guarantees (it took him sixteen months), while their 1925–26 application was turned down because financial support was for the moment withdrawn.

At the end of 1929, the British Group submitted yet a fifth formal application, claiming there was no binding agreement with Novomeysky, and charging that the Novomeysky scheme involved "a negligible output" in comparison with theirs. But they were informed that a preliminary agreement had been signed, and that negotiations with other parties was ruled out.

Two and a half more years of strife were still before Novomeysky. For one thing, the arrangement was contingent on his raising a

166

large sum of money. That meant persuading backers that the project was not a pipe dream, but grounded, as his own faith was, in years of technical experience in a part of the world no more congenial to human occupation than this. Wrote the forty-seven year-old engineer, "I was not a youngster, stirred by momentary enthusiasm, and my determination was based on much practical work in Siberia in hard and trying circumstances."

But by far the most unsettling part of his battle to gain the concession ("the worst obstacle I had so far known") was against those parties who were "bitterly opposed to the Jewish national idea in Palestine." His vanquished rivals from various countries (there were French and Australian claims as well) sang a litany of criticism, but the objections that were hardest to bear came from both Houses of the British Parliament. The protests at first concerned technicalities such as ultimate ownership of the plant when the concession ran out, and what to do in the eventuality that Novomeysky devised a way to extract the small amount of gold contained in the lake. But the decision to award Novomeysky the concession led to a concerted effort to dissuade the Government. In the two major debates that took place in the House of Lords, in May 1928 and March 1929, discussion at times degenerated, revealing not only anti-Zionism, as might be expected, but not so skillfully disguised anti-Semitism. ("I do not know whether he is a Russian Jew or what he is," said one. "I have noticed that a certain number of people seem to think that Jews have a historical right to Palestine.")

The inquisition into Novomeysky's suitability was at times crass, but it is difficult to untangle the unremitting anti-Zionism of some of the Parliamentarians—even their anti-Semitism and their innuendoes that he was a German agent of some sort—from their real fear of the German monopoly, as well as their concern about serving the majority, i.e., Arab, population of Palestine and Transjordan. It was urgent that the monopoly be broken, and here was an opportunity for Britain to do it. If a concession were to be awarded, argued one, surely it must be to a group that was known to be entirely free of the existing monopoly and that had no inclination to work even indirectly with it. It seems that the names of Novomeysky's backers had been withheld, and his antagonists in the House of Lords demanded to know why the Government was concealing their identity, since this group would be operating an undertaking of "first-class national and Imperial importance." The speaker, Lord Islington, had opposed "the unfortunate experiment which is known as the Zionist Home in Palestine," and he worried that the future company would "be tied up in the meshes of the Zionist organisation," or that it would be so international in its make-up as to conform with the existing monopoly. He recommended that the Government look favorably instead upon the application of the other group, the British Group.

With the realization that the British Parliament attached such value to the concession, and worried, for reasons that were tantamount to national security, that the concession may not serve British interests, one is increasingly astonished that Novomeysky did prevail, even if not so easily. By early 1929, opposition to him was so strong that he had lost almost all hope, once again, of attaining his goal. Moving quickly, he managed to satisfy the Government that he had £100,000 beyond the figure he had submitted. More important, he was able to assemble a Board of well-known Londoners and a British chairman; he firmly believed that had it not been for that, he would not have been granted the concession. At last, in August 1929, a seventy-five year concession was awarded to him and his British partner. On the first of January, 1930, it was transferred to Palestine Potash, Ltd., a further victory for which Novomeysky credited a New York Jew named Israel Brodie.

Novomeysky had been sufficiently optimistic for a long enough time to turn his attention to the project itself. He had actually begun the practical work several years earlier, before the League of Nations Mandate was even conferred on Great Britain. At that time, the British, though they were administering Palestine, had no authority, not even to grant Novomeysky a lease of a few acres of land by the Dead Sea where he could set up an experimental station. Novomeysky did a little investigating and discovered that there was a small port on the lake already, equipped even with a motor boat, and a few huts nearby. It all belonged to an Arab who during the war had supplied the Turks with wheat from Transjordan, and Novomeysky arranged to buy the equipment and take over the lease to the land. He planned to set up a modest import–export business, bringing wool and wheat from across the lake in exchange for consumer goods from Palestine. That project never got off the ground, but at least he managed to establish himself on the lake and secure a place to construct experimental evaporation pans.

It was in 1925 that Novomeysky set into motion the project's next phase, a phase which owed its success to his young assistant, Moshe Langotzki. A fellow Siberian, also a scion of Jews exiled early in the nineteenth century, Langotzki was born around 1900. He got caught up in the civil war, and in 1918 escaped the fighting by fleeing east. After two years wandering in Mongolia, China, and Manchuria, he encountered a Zionist youth organization and made his way to Palestine, where he obtained work at Novomeysky's family's agricultural community. A few years later, he became a victim of a Novomeysky ruse—one for which he would be grateful all his life. In April of 1923 there was to be a ceremony to open the Hebrew University, and Novomeysky pretended it was very important that Langotzki travel with him to Jerusalem. Afterwards, Langotzki prepared to return to Gedera, at which point Novomeysky stopped him and asked where he was going. Back to the farm, the puzzled man replied. No you're not, Novomeysky informed him; you're coming with me. Where to? To the Dead Sea.

One can imagine the slight, balding boss, perhaps dressed in the khaki shorts and safari hat of later photographs, accompanied by his tall, strong, curly-haired charge who was wondering where they were headed and for what. They rented a car and started down.

Now of course Novomeysky had been to the Dead Sea before, but never unguided. The Siberians drove, and searched, and wandered, and searched some more, and couldn't find the lake. Ending up in Jericho, they went to the police station to ask directions. They would not find it alone, they were advised; they could spend the night there and a guide would be provided the next day. An inauspicious beginning, one might say, but the pair seem to have been undaunted. They arrived the next day at the two-room earthen-floored hut which would serve as both living quarters and laboratory and settled down to work, subsisting on canned food and water carted several miles from Jericho.

They took water samples from various locations and learned that the concentration of salt increased enormously with depth: precipitation required twenty-six days in the surface samples but just two days in those taken from further down. Because of these experiments, they decided early on that should they win the concession, they would use water pumped from the lower stratum for the production of potash. Seven years later, they would lay the pipe—thirty inches in diameter and half a mile long—at a depth of 175 feet.

When Novomeysky brought Langotzki down to the Dead Sea, it was not his intention to remain with the young man, though Langotzki hardly had a notion of what the place was. Friends advised them that Langotzki would not be safe there alone, that he would surely be killed. So they concocted a plan, and when Novomeysky left shortly after their arrival, it was not a farmer or even a chemist he was leaving behind, but a doctor. Langotzki had donned a white coat, wore a stethoscope, and, armed only with medical booklets of the most elementary kind, he set up in his hut a little "pharmacy"—a row of bottles filled with water of different colors.

Before long, as he told it, word spread on the other side of the Jordan that a new doctor had arrived, and patients began coming to him. Considerably chagrined—he had expected the disguise to remove anxiety, not provide it—he had no choice but to "treat" the Arabs crossing the river to obtain medical aid. He would ask each patient to choose from among the colored-water bottles, and he would prepare an injection accordingly. He had no intention of risking injury to anyone by injecting him with water, so he would tell each to lie on his stomach, warning him not to turn over lest he die, on which he gave him a poke with the needle and squirted the water onto the floor. Somehow, to his dismay perhaps, his rate of cure was very high, and he earned a reputation as the best doctor at the Dead Sea, his patients bringing him many gifts, and of course more patients. Meanwhile, Novomeysky was in England fighting for the concession, and he wired his assistant to ask how things were going with the experimental evaporation pan, and did he perhaps need the help of a chemist? No, Langotzki hastily replied, but please, send another doctor.

Langotzki originally thought he would spend two weeks at the Dead Sea. He spent over forty years. In those decades he never had anything but good relations with the Arabs; to them later on he was Abu Yusef (father of Yosef), and Novomeysky would single him out as being "the principal protector and patron of the Arabs." Writing much later, Novomeysky declared that in all his years watching Langotzki deal with the plant's mixed staff (mixed in accordance with the terms of the concession as well as with Novomeysky's ideals), he never saw him make a distinction between Jew and

170

Arab, and his fluent Arabic, which had seen him through his early career as regional "doctor," always served him well. One might ask what motivated Langotzki to stay; after all, the heat, the isolation, the danger, the uncertainty would have been enough to conquer even a brave heart. A close friend of his tried to explain: for one thing he was instructed to stay, and he revered Novomeysky. For another, he was not a man to desert a cause, and he possessed great physical courage in addition. Finally, he loved his new country and was perhaps looking for a task to which he could devote his life. Whatever the reason, Novomeysky knew that in the project's early days especially, it was Langotzki who was responsible for the realization of his dream.

Novomeysky was in the meantime travelling to various places, honing his skills in preparation for the challenge of actual production. He went to Egypt to watch production of table salt at Port Said, to America to see the salt works in Los Angeles and San Francisco and to visit the salt-extracting operation at the Great Salt Lake. Most of his education, however, came from Germany. Novomeysky was instructed by some of that country's most prominent mining engineers, and though the Germans mined potash from the ground, he was helped considerably by studying their methods. He returned to Palestine secure in what he was planning and more confident than ever that his enterprise was technically feasible.

But Novomeysky prepared for the years ahead in other ways as well. He considered it his responsibility to have good relations with the Arab population in general and with the administration of Transjordan in particular. In the spring of 1921, Mandate Palestine had been partitioned into Palestine and Transjordan, and soon after, Novomeysky met with Abdullah, then emir of Transjordan. Abdullah had been born in Mecca into the Hashemites, a prominent family claiming descent from Mohammad. He joined the British to defeat the Turks in 1917 and was rewarded, after England received the League of Nations Mandate, with the territory east of the Jordan River.

Novomeysky's concession included the entire lake, but because half of it lay in Transjordan, the profits would be shared. According to Novomeysky, Abdullah was convinced that Transjordan could become a state and develop only by means of a joint effort with the other mandate territory, and he was just as interested in cooperat-

171

ing as Novomeysky was, for they both saw the Dead Sea as being central to the economic growth of their shared region. Their political roles in their respective countries were vastly dissimilar, for Novomeysky wielded no power at all. But in Novomeysky's view they were of the same mind on more than one issue, perceiving the conflict between their two peoples as based on a misunderstanding rather than on anything truly substantial. Although Abdullah would invade the new Jewish state along with the other Arab armies in 1948, Novomeysky did not believe that he was a hater of Jews nor even fearful of Zionism. He and Novomeysky became friends, and to the extent that was possible, given the pressures exerted on the one and the constraints imposed on the other, they labored for the mutual benefit of both territories until Abdullah's death in 1951.

Work on the potash plant at Qalya—from the word *kalium*, meaning potash in German, but also a Hebrew acronym for *Qum l'ha'im, yam ha-mavet* (Rise Up to Life, Sea of Death)—began when the concession was awarded. As soon as the malarial swamps were drained and turned into a system of evaporation pans, the construction crew set to work. Trucks streamed in from Jerusalem loaded with lumber, cement, iron piping, and assorted other equipment and provisions. Before long workers' huts had been raised and the first pipes were laid—some to convey Dead Sea water to the evaporation pans, others to bring water from the Jordan River. A small harbor was built, with a fleet of barges, one specially equipped to transport drinking water from the Wadi Zerka Ma'in. "And the finest feature of all in this work," Novomeysky beamed, "was the unhindered enthusiasm of all the men engaged there, as they saw industrial life developing in this waste corner of the desert of Judaea." Just one year later, the first fruits of their labor, a quantity of bromine, was on the market in England, and the following year they began production of potash, the first shipment arriving soon after in Baltimore.

The terrain at the northern end of the lake did not permit unlimited expansion for evaporation pans, so in 1934 Novomeysky opened a second plant, at the southern end of the lake by the foot of Mt. Sedom. The climate there was even more forbidding than in the north; it received half the rainfall (two inches annually) and was a good deal hotter as well as far more isolated. There was, however, topographical compensation; the shore was broad, flat, and less subject to seepage than the north, and the es-Safieh oasis, the same as had revived and delighted so many travellers of the previous century with the sweetest water in the region, was just across the way. Before long, Novomeysky had arranged to buy water from Abdullah, and it was piped into the southern camp.

The attraction of the Dead Sea valley went beyond its industrial potential. In 1938, the confluence of three factors was responsible for the founding of Kibbutz Beit Ha-Aravah, the first agricultural settlement at the Dead Sea. First, one of the best-known pioneers of Dead Sea development, Yehuda Almog, persuaded the members of a youth group to come down to the Dead Sea. Around the same time, a certain Moshe Isakevitch, from a kibbutz near Jerusalem, concluded successful experiments raising crops in hypersaline soil. And finally, in 1938 the British issued the White Paper that restricted Jewish settlement in Palestine and forced Almog to find a way of circumventing the law in order to establish a kibbutz.

Almog recognized that any kibbutz at the Dead Sea would have to be legally tied to the potash works because Novomeysky had an unretractable lease to the land surrounding the lake. Almog persuaded Novomeysky (who did not need much persuading) to turn over part of his land to the still unborn kibbutz. And so in September of 1939, a group of some forty boys and girls, all of them eighteen or nineteen years old, arrived at the Dead Sea. They worked in potash production to support themselves, but their sights were set on the ambitious goal of turning an area whose soil contained a prohibitive seventeen per cent salt into a full-scale farm. (Nearby, the salt content was only five per cent, which is what today's kibbutzim have to contend with, but they had no choice about their location and had to accept the much higher concentration.)

The process of washing the soil of salt was long and painstaking. First the designated plots of land had to be levelled so that when they were covered with water, the pressure down on the soil would be constant. The kibbutzniks worked with plots roughly 150 feet square which they kept submerged by means of a pipe about a mile and a half long which flowed from the Jordan River. The continual water pressure caused the salt to sink to lower levels, and when tests showed that the salt had been carried down the required twenty or so inches (a process that took up to six months), they then fertilized the soil and prepared to plant.

They were successful beyond their most sanguine expectations. In two years they were producing tomatoes, a winter crop unheard of in the region, and one that made them famous in tomato-loving Jerusalem. By 1943, they were known throughout the country, and their 100-family kibbutz was the most successful of its age group—so much so that the anxious English authorities tried to persuade them to leave, offering to pay off all their debts and compensate them as well. The kibbutzniks declined, and since the farm was legally tied to the potash company, the British were powerless.

By 1944 or '45, the scene must have been striking; the kibbutz's eight acres of living area, surrounded by lawns, palm trees, tamarisk, cypress, pine, and eucalyptus, not to mention flowers, which they raised for sale in Jerusalem, were encircled by 250 acres either under cultivation or serving as fishponds, which were made from land that could not be levelled for agriculture. By the time the Israeli War of Independence broke out, most of the members of the kibbutz had left the mining industry and were being supported by agriculture. About their relationship with the Arabs, suffice it to say that in the days when no Jew was allowed to cross the Jordan, those from Beit Ha-Aravah were permitted to; and in all the years of animosity between Arabs and Jews, no violence was ever done to the kibbutz until the actual outbreak of the war. The farm was destroyed after the Jews evacuated, but the name has not been forgotten; it remains associated with physical and social challenge and with achievement amidst natural conditions as unwelcoming as any on earth.

It is hard to overemphasize the importance of the Palestine Potash Company to the Dead Sea region and beyond. From the late 1930s until the war broke out, the potash works employed an Arab and Jewish staff of 2,000 workers. The southern plant was by far the largest industry in the region stretching across the desert to Saudi Arabia, and it attracted laborers not only from nearby villages but from as far away as Yemen, from where Arabs would come to work a three-year stint and go back with enough money to support a family. About 100 Jewish families lived at Qalya, which also employed Arabs from Jericho, but most of the Jews commuted weekly from Jerusalem and the nearby kibbutz, Ramat Raḥel.

The two plants, separated by forty-eight miles of water, were linked by telegraph. In addition to the potash plants and living quarters, there were recreational and cultural facilities at both ends of the lake, and a kindergarten and grade school for the Jewish families of Qalya. The northern plant had the advantage of proximity to Jerusalem, and occasional lecturers would come down from the university. Movies were shown, concerts offered, and athletic events arranged. Qalya became a tourist center as well, and by the mid-1930s, a privately owned hotel (with its invitingly named Sodom and Gomorrah golf club—a British contribution) attracted foreigners and natives alike. By 1947, the two plants were producing 100,000 tons of potash a year, worth seven million dollars and second only to citrus, and Novomeysky claimed that the industry was responsible for the livelihoods of ten to 15,000 people. Novomeysky's fleet numbered thirty vessels, including the passenger boat M.S. Lieutenant Lynch, which ran the route from north to south—the first trading vessels on the lake since the time of the Crusaders. Novomeysky looked back on those years with pride and pleasure in both the industrial and social achievements, and he stated that his most cherished memory was that of Arab and Jew working together. "There were incidents of friction among the Jewish workers, and also among the Arabs, but I cannot recall a single case of Jewish–Arab hostility."

Novomeysky has been described as an Anglophile, perhaps even a colonialist, who sat in the director's chair and oversaw operations below. According to a long-time associate, he had an old-fashioned notion of the division between management and labor, but he believed in the education of the workers and was responsible for turning the Dead Sea industry into an important place of learning. His early belief in a binational solution for Palestine may have colored to some extent his depiction of the relations between Jews and Arabs. But from all accounts, he was accurate in his basic declaration that there was harmony. To say, as those from Beit Ha-Aravah were able, that no shot was fired between them in all those angry years is to indicate something of the mutual need and respect that existed. The Arab employees of the Palestine Potash Company took no part in the anti-Jewish riots of 1936–39, nor was there any fighting between them until the war began. Novomeysky claimed that even on the eve of the Arab invasion in May of 1948, the Arabs of the potash works asked protection from militant Arabs trying to instigate them to violence.

When the British Mandate was about to end, there was still hope among the Jews that Abdullah could be persuaded to stay out of the war. In his famous secret meeting with Golda Meir, who crossed the Jordan in disguise to implore the king not to attack, he had given his word that he would not, but it was a word he would have to retract under pressure from the other Arab armies. Novomeysky approached him in those tense days, too, trying to strike a deal that would at least spare the potash works that were so valuable to both sides. Abdullah was receptive, and in the first week of May, just ten days or so before Israel would proclaim its independence, a delegation of two Arabs and an Englishman from the Arab Legion came down to the Dead Sea to discuss with Novomeysky the possibility of neutralizing the Qalya plant. They proposed an agreement according to which the plant would be signed over to Jordan, in whose territory the United Nations partition plan placed it, while maintaining relations with Israel.

Novomeysky had also been interested in arranging a way by which the potash of the southern plant, which would remain Jewish, could be transported through Arab territory—north on the sea and then up to Jerusalem—as it had been for fourteen years. It seems he would have liked Jews to remain in the north, helping the Arabs in production, in return for transportation rights. But John Glubb, commander of the Arab Legion, made the deal contingent on the Arab Legion's presence at both plants. Novomeysky does not say whether or not he was willing to accept this extraordinary condition; there are those who remember him as being ready to pay just about any price to save the major work of his life, and perhaps he would have agreed even to this. In any case, a second meeting was arranged with the Arab/British delegation for the following week. But before the meeting took place, Novomeysky had to be in Tel Aviv, and while he was there, there was a blackout during which he was struck by a car or a motorcycle. His leg broken (no slight injury for a man nearly seventy-five years old), he was placed in a hospital and effectively removed from the negotiations that were fast reaching a climax. To replace him at the second meeting, he sent someone who represented the American interest in the potash company, and on May 17, two days after fighting broke out in the rest of the country, the American, accompanied by an officer from the Haganah, the Israeli defence force, met again with the Jordanians.

Meanwhile, that morning an Arab informer had come to the Jews

176

at Qalya and told them that contrary to what the Arab Legion wanted them to believe, they had no military presence in Jericho, as they were engaged in fighting in the rest of the West Bank, and that the Jews should not give in so quickly to a deal that would neutralize them. On the basis of this information, and with seven or eight hundred men and women ready to defend Qalya, the leaders of the kibbutz came out against the proposed deal. But the American, acting on his own initiative, signed the agreement anyway.

Agreements are not abided by so easily in times of war, and at least three factors worked against the implementation of this one. First, the Jewish settlement at Kfar Etzion, south of Jerusalem, had been wiped out just a few days before, and mistrust was in the air at Qalya. Even more important, a similar agreement had been signed the previous week at the Rutenberg electric plant at Naharai'im, up the Jordan River, but the agreement had been violated by the Arabs, who took the Jews as prisoners of war for exhibition in Amman. In light of that violation, it became difficult to argue in favor of neutrality. Yet the decisive factor was the Jewish leader, David Ben Gurion, and his aversion to the pact. Those were precarious days for the Jews of Palestine, and they had no way of knowing what the outcome of the war would be. Ben Gurion reasoned that the northern end of the lake was going to Jordan in any case, but how could he be sure that the southern end could be held? Fearing that they might lose everything, he was unwilling to agree to the neutralization of eight hundred potential soldiers then sitting and waiting at Qalya and Beit Ha-Aravah (which had also been a clandestine Haganah training center), and he decided to make a concerted stand at the southern end of the lake with the combined forces. Against the wishes of the men and women (mothers and children had already been evacuated) who wanted to defend the settlement, he ordered evacuation.

It was planned for May 20, when boats and launches would take them and whatever they could load on the seven-hour trip south, scheduled for midnight to minimize the risk of being detected and bombed. Working as quietly as possible that evening, they either destroyed or incapacitated whatever machinery they could not take. They drove tractors into the sea, removed pistons from the giant diesels (a few months later, they were supplying power in Amman), and in various ways made certain the plant could not be re-opened.

177

The site was nevertheless filled with millions of dollars of valuable machinery and piping, and the next day the plant was totally dismantled and destroyed by looters.

Novomeysky maintained secret contact with Abdullah even after the war, when he still had hopes that production at the southern end of the lake could be resumed. The pipeline from the es-Safieh oasis had been sabotaged, and he met with Abdullah, by then king of what had become the independent Hashemite Kingdom of Jordan, to see about repairing it. According to Novomeysky, Abdullah had other things on his mind as well—he was interested in talking about real peace. What happened subsequently Novomeysky does not say, but all hope for a future of coexistence came to an end with Abdullah's assassination two years later, at the hands of Arab extremists, some believe, because of his desire to make peace with the Jews.

Novomeysky was not a utopian but a practical visionary who had an abundant faith in his ability to turn ideas into fact. A chemist who worked beside him for many years made a telling comparison between him and Pinḥas Rutenberg, the recipient of the other major concession under the British. Rutenberg received the concession for the electric works by persuading people that using the Jordan River in this way was a great pioneering effort, though he later produced electricity conventionally. Novomeysky, on the other hand, won the backing he needed by understating from the start the project's complexities and convincing people that what was actually a preposterous scheme was not in the least out of the ordinary, though it had never been done anywhere else in the world; and that his experience in Siberia, of all places, gave him the necessary credentials. Modest to such an extent that one has often to fill in between the lines of his memoirs in order to get an idea of his achievements, he reserved his energies for the important work in which he believed. Ironically, that very lack of flamboyance may be the reason that he is hardly known in Israel today. Very few people have heard the name or can place it, let alone know anything substantial about the man or his accomplishments.

Novomeysky's rivals for the Dead Sea concession were numerous and at times formidable. But in the final analysis, it does not seem that any of them had a fraction of his drive. He wanted the concession, he knew he was the one who should be granted it, and he proceeded as if shielded by blinders from the obstacles on all sides. A man with better peripheral vision might have been utterly discouraged long before Novomeysky evinced even the slightest disappointment; but he drove on, shuttling for nine years between Palestine and Paris, London and New York, raising money, garnering support, facing criticism. And what did he achieve by all this? Practically speaking, he laid the foundation for one of Israel's major industries. And his moral achievement, if one may speak of that, was at least as impressive. During years of bitter hostility between Jews and Arabs, he created a little island of cooperation in the Dead Sea valley, turning that part of the desert into an outpost of mutual regard that one only hopes could be emulated.

6

A Lake Divided

AFTER THEIR evacuation from Qalya, the potash workers and kibbutzniks remained for months under siege at Sedom. On their release from the army a year later, the kibbutzniks split for ideological reasons into two groups and went north to found two new kibbutzim in the Galilee. Left at the plant was a group of six men: an Egyptian, a Turk, a Druse, and three Jews, one of whom was Langotzki. And there they stayed, isolated and idle, for four years, until the road from Beersheba was completed and contact with the rest of the country restored. Then they hauled in supplies, drilled for water, and prepared to resume production. The scientists at the potash works also contrived to make use of the surface water of the Dead Sea. At that time the influx from the Jordan River was still so great that it could be skimmed off the top of the lake and used for washing the evaporation pans of their salt residue.

Novomeysky suffered bitterly in those days. It was not only war, partition, destruction, the ruin of everything he had spent a quarter of a century building that he had to bear, but, he felt, the betrayal of his own people, as well. No help, no sympathy was offered from official quarters for his loss. Not one expression of understanding did he hear for the fact that his company was struck down in its prime through no fault of his own; instead, he claims, only slanderous words came his way. The situation was complicated and unpleasant. The Government had no interest in the business; after all, the plant was entirely cut off from the rest of the country, besides which the machinery had rusted. But there were those who were convinced anyway of the importance of a Government takeover, and they persuaded Ben Gurion to form a Dead Sea committee to investigate. Such a committee was appointed in November 1949, purportedly to examine the problems connected with exploitation of the Dead Sea. Yet its real purpose, Novomeysky accused in an angry pamphlet published in 1950, was to fabricate an excuse for nationalizing his industry by discrediting management so thoroughly as to sway the public and leave the Government no alternative but to take over.

Novomeysky quoted from two newspapers, one left-wing, the other centrist, and summarized the charges against him: negligence, incompetence, a willingness to surrender the country's resources to "imperialist monopolist capital." (Insinuations about the surrender of the northern plant, its "destruction in mysterious circumstances," and payment to Transjordan, "are so beneath contempt that they can be ignored as a whole.") Further, he was accused of not having recognized national authority in matters of security (perhaps this had to do with his continuing relationship with Abdullah, which alienated him from the Zionist establishment and may have earned for him the ill-will of Ben Gurion). Finally, he was criticized for not having paid adequate workers' compensation. About the latter charge, he repeated that it was the war, not his own caprice, that resulted in the workers' dismissal; that in fact he had spent £70,000 on assistance; and that no agreement on compensation could be reached until he was able to raise new funds. Twenty years earlier, he recalled, such calumny came from "some British Antisemites"; now it came from his fellow Jews. He concluded by noting scathingly that surely a case could be made for nationalizing his industry without "slavishly copying the cheap methods used by the gutter press in countries which have brought civilisation into disrepute."

After the war, Ben Gurion had given Novomeysky six months to raise enough money to reopen. Not surprisingly, given the plant's singularly unpropitious location, Novomeysky had failed to find investors. Ben Gurion gave him another six months. When he failed a second time to come up with sufficient funds, they spent a year discussing the company's future, and in the end the dispirited Novomeysky gave up and the government assumed control in 1952. One long-time associate of the Dead Sea Works, as the company was called after the war, carries in his mind a sad picture of the once dynamic man—small, fragile, quiet, unsmiling, sitting down for a big midday meal at Sedom and eating only mashed potatoes and yogurt. But for Mordechai Makleff, the new managing director, Novomeysky was no outcast but a hero, and he kept him on as advisor, not merely out of kindness, but common sense as well. Nonetheless, Novomeysky eventually moved to Paris, where it could perhaps be easier to bear age, defeat, and bitterness. He died in 1961 and was brought back to Jerusalem to be buried. Until his own death, Novomeysky's faithful ally Moshe Langotzki made a lone pilgrimage to the grave every year on the anniversary of Novomeysky's death.

Times would remain hard, even under the leadership of the much admired Makleff. Between 1952 and '56, the Dead Sea Works suffered severe setbacks and nearly folded. The name itself was synonymous with failure, and it was said that nothing could sink in the Dead Sea except money. Only utter idealists or those enticed by the relatively high wages would come to work in the desert; one of the former, who went down in the '50s and would devote his entire adult life to the region, claims that his family hid the news of his whereabouts from relatives, so great was the shame. Sedom, ironically, would be plagued by social problems, including drugs and, according to some, prostitution. In 1957, Makleff took the drastic step of closing down the workers' camp there and insisted that from then on no transient labor would be hired. He encouraged and persuaded families to move to Beersheba and the new development town of Dimona, from which they could commute.

Seeking to reverse the fortunes of the company, the management initiated a new program in the early 1960s. A Dutch company designed a system of dikes, construction of which was begun by an American firm. But that company took huge losses and backed out. Following a complicated legal battle, Israel finished the project—without any prior experience—and the entire western side of the southern basin was turned into an evaporation pan. Another American company built a new refinery, and once it was adapted to the special conditions of the Dead Sea Works, the experience of the company has been more in keeping with the promise it showed in its early years under Novomeysky. The Dead Sea Works projected a figure of two million tons of potash for 1985, a goal which was met. (To put this figure into perspective, it might be noted that Canada, the Soviet Union, East Germany, and the United States produced eighty percent of the 45 million tons mined worldwide in 1980.) Production will eventually level off, because the amount of potash that can be extracted depends on the size of the evaporation area, which can be enlarged no further.

For many years, the Dead Sea Works was the only company in the world (except for a small American firm working at Utah's Great Salt Lake, whose process is very different) that mined potash from a body of water, a distinction it now shares with its Jordanian counterpart, the Arab Potash Company. The advantage in mining from a lake, rather than from an exhaustible vein, is that a large part of the initial phase is done passively, by the sun and the force of gravity alone. The principle involved is easy enough: at various degrees of saturation, certain salts fall out of solution in crystalline form. But the process itself is far more difficult, mainly because the concentration of potassium chloride in the lake is comparatively small. Of the 44 billion tons of salts in the sea, only two billion are potash. There is no way that the mineral can be extracted unless its concentration can be greatly increased, to twenty-five per cent.

The key to the process which Novomeysky invented (which remains essentially unchanged today) is twofold: the ability to bring the water to the saturation point, and the more critical ability to control precipitation. The process begins in an enormous evaporation pan in which the water is reduced in volume by one half. The first mineral to precipitate is sodium chloride, and while that is happening, the potash is doubling in concentration. When most of the common salt has precipitated, and the water has turned into a heavy brine, it is channelled elsewhere, where continued evaporation turns it into a thick white foam. By this time a new compound has begun to precipitate, and it is this carnallite that contains the potash. But it also contains magnesium chloride as well as the rest of the sodium chloride, and the remainder of the process is devoted to separating the potash. The frothy mixture is scooped up from the bottom of the pans by large tractor-like dredgers and is sent for washing, passed through vibrating screens—like panning for gold—spin-dried, refined, and sorted. The rate of attrition for the machinery is high because of the salts' corrosiveness, and an on-site repair plant, operating night and day, turns out 30,000 different replacement parts.

The magnitude of the industrial achievement becomes clearer when one realizes that an enormous amount of freshwater is needed to produce the potash. Not for washing the salts—that water comes from the brackish wells—but for energy. The plant runs on electricity produced from steam generators which require huge quantities of freshwater every day. If the well water were used, the generators would be ruined in a matter of weeks. There is no alternative but desalination, by far the most expensive part of the process.

The story of Jordan's potash plant is decidedly different. There is no single, driving figure at the center, no Siberian-like connection, no intrigue or struggle with a foreign power. But it is exciting in its own way, and many feel its success is as important to the region as the Israeli enterprise. The Arab Potash Company was founded in 1956 as the first-ever pan-Arab project. The objective was to construct a mineral-extracting operation like that of the Israelis; but various difficulties, political and technical, delayed it for nearly twenty years. In 1975 the Company was resurrected and a feasibility study was carried out by an American firm. The study concluded that the 420 million dollar plan was sound, and efforts were directed at preparing the way for large-scale production of potash. Over two hundred million dollars was borrowed from an array of government and international agencies, and planners set to work awarding contracts. It has been an international venture. The American firm was overall supervisor; a British company constructed the dikes and evaporation pans; an Austrian firm built the processing plant, and Germans the power station. The construction workers, 2,000 mostly British and Arab, were accommodated in a township assembled near the Lisan Peninsula by a South Korean firm and slated to be home to the Jordanians who will eventually run the plant.

The project was placed high on Jordan's list of national priorities, as spelled out in its five-year plan for 1976–80. With the most modern technology, the most efficient equipment, great financial resources, and the vital es-Safieh oasis nearby, the Jordanians opened on schedule in September of 1982. The Arab Potash Company planned to produce its full capacity of around 1.2 million tons in 1985, but as of 1984, the Company had taken a loss. International competition, lower prices, and the difficulty of perfecting the extraction process meant that production had to be drastically curtailed. Obviously management expected to see better times, and indeed by 1986, production was up to some eighty per cent of full capacity. Jordan is one of the few countries in the world that possesses huge quantities of both phosphate and potassium,

184

which along with nitrogen are the essential ingredients in fertilizers. The Arab Potash Company could soon become the largest producer of fertilizers in the Arab world, and Crown Prince Hassan noted not long ago that the Dead Sea industries could develop into the backbone of Jordan's economy. Jordan and Israel are currently competing on the world market, though they serve different clients. Jordan's main customer is Japan, and Israel, though it now ships most of its potash to the West, is currently cultivating a major Far Eastern market.

Although it seemed in the last several years that the Israeli Dead Sea Works had taken a permanent turn for the better, and that the Arab Potash Company could look forward to a secure future, something else was happening that produced still another challenge. Until the mid-1960s, the seasonal rises and falls of the Dead Sea had been largely dependent on natural factors. The Jordan River was responsible for about two thirds of the annual replacement water, and as long as the snow on the Hermon melted and rain fell each year—a kind of Birnam Wood prophecy—the annual cycle of the lake would be roughly the one it had obeyed for millennia. But both Israel and Jordan are water-poor countries and have had to turn to the Jordan River system. Since the Jordan is part of their common border, one can imagine that the issue of water-sharing has for decades been endlessly complicated and has thus far eluded solution on a unified regional level.

In 1944, the American land conservationist and hydrologist Walter C. Lowdermilk advised in *Palestine, Land of Promise* that so far as the utilization of water resources was concerned, there was no doubt that a regional approach based on the agreement of all parties would greatly benefit all concerned. In 1953 the United States sought to initiate a program by which Israel and the Arab nations would share their combined water resources. This so-called Johnston Plan (named after President Eisenhower's envoy and worked out by the Tennessee Valley Authority) allocated certain amounts of water to Syria, Jordan, and Israel. But the Arab states objected that Israel's share was too large, and they spent a year negotiating with Johnston over proposed allotments. Israel, on the other hand, had hoped for a greater share and also submitted counter-proposals. Johnston tried to put it all together, and in 1955 presented his Unified Plan. But though it had at first been endorsed by both sides, it was rejected that year by the Arab League, perhaps because acceptance meant tacit recognition of Israel. Israel never ratified it either, and from that point on both sides proceeded unilaterally.

Israel was ahead of Jordan in implementing a comprehensive water-diversion program. Development of the Negev Desert had already begun, and Israel had started work on its National Water Carrier, which would use the Sea of Galilee as a reservoir and convey water (about the amount stipulated in the Johnston Plan) southward. The Arabs were furious, and in 1960, four years before Israel's National Water Carrier would even open, they proposed to divert the Jordan before it reached the Sea of Galilee, thus derailing the Israeli irrigation project. The proposal was approved, but never implemented, perhaps because of inter-Arab disagreement about water-allocation. But the issue remained a provocative one, and in 1964 they met again. Rejecting the idea of immediate war, they proposed a second time to divert the Jordan's sources. That alone, had the plan ever been put into motion, might have been enough to provoke a confrontation; but the summit conference also took the step of recognizing the newly formed Palestine Liberation Organization, which in the next few years initiated terrorist raids in Israel and prompted reprisals. Hostilities increased in all directions, not just between Israel and Jordan and Syria, but among the Arabs as well. Within a few years the 1967 Arab–Israeli war broke out, and with the capture by Israel of the Golan Heights, the question of Arab diversion of the Jordan's sources was resolved, for they lay in the conquered territory.

Jordan has not lagged far behind in irrigation projects. The East Ghor Canal, for irrigating the Jordan Valley, was conceived in the late 1950s. Extending from the Yarmukh River (the Jordan's main tributary and once accounting for half its volume), its first section was opened as early as 1961. The Yarmukh is Jordan's most important source of water, and its conservation has long been considered vital. In recent years the United States has been aiding Jordan in the construction of a dam initially considered in the '50s and postponed for various political reasons. That dam will increase the capacity of the East Ghor Canal, which is now being lengthened. Both sides have been industriously pursuing water projects on their own, but in such a way, it has been noted, that should peace between them ever come about, they could be integrated into a central system. To some observers, early participation in the Johnston discussions suggests a mutual recognition that a single unified plan is ultimately the best solution for the region.

As one can see, great demands have been placed on the Jordan River in the last decades, and so severely reduced had its flow become by the mid-1970s that its contribution to the Dead Sea had been cut in half. By around 1980 it was contributing less than the winter flooding and less too than the Wadi Mojib, and now, in mid-decade, the Jordan has to a large extent ceased its year-round flow. (Winter produces a river, but in the summer the flow is reduced to a trickle.) It is an ironic—and pyrrhic—victory for those nineteenth-century travellers who complained, in the words of one, that "the abounding waters of the Jordan are at present wasted on the thankless corpse of the Dead Sea." Ironic because the Dead Sea never was a corpse except in their projections, and its lifecycle was always intertwined with the Jordan's.

There are various opinions about what the essential loss of the Jordan ultimately means to the Dead Sea. Climatic changes have been inducing a recession of the lake since around 1930, and it was shrinking perceptibly year by year. The northern basin has shown the effects, as the water backed away from the cliffs. But the shrinkage was experienced much more critically by the southern basin, whose shallowness meant that it would absorb the brunt of the recession. As Irby and Mangles noted more than a century and a half ago, a reduction in inflow means not merely a lowering of the level, but a shortening of the lake; sure enough, year by year the Dead Sea's southernmost point was creeping further and further north—around eighteen miles in half a century.

It did not take unusual imagination to see that the Dead Sea was disappearing, and not so slowly, from its southern basin, and that by the end of the 1970s it would be gone. The loss would be bad enough from a conservationist point of view, but the practical consequences would also be serious. The recession of the lake was leaving the Dead Sea Works stranded at the far end of a muddy, salt-encrusted plain. Half a century of painstaking labor was at stake, as well as an expensive system of dikes. To counter the recession, Israeli engineers built a channel leading to the southern basin from the northern one, and a pumping station to supply it as needed with water. Today the southern basin no longer exists as a natural phenomenon; though it is not generally recognized, what is there is a large artificial pool. The Lisan Peninsula is no longer a peninsula but a land bridge, a broad salt plain extending the full width of the lake; for the first time since the Byzantine era, the Dead Sea once again occupies, strictly speaking, only its northern basin. The Jordanian side of the southern basin was dry in 1981, but a year later, construction on their dikes was completed, and their pumping station was ready to fill the pool. As long as the northern basin exists, both countries can channel water south and maintain a level compatible with that of their dikes.

Although the amount of potash that can be mined from the Dead Sea is ultimately limited by the area of the evaporation pans, the Dead Sea Works and the Arab Potash Company will continue to expand, extracting other minerals as well. Magnesium chloride accounts for roughly half the minerals in the Dead Sea, making the lake one of the largest magnesium mines in the world. But a prohibitive amount of energy is needed in its production, and so for the time being the Israeli company is producing only a small quantity, for use in bricks that line the kilns of steel mills.

Meanwhile, Israel is expanding its bromine production facility, as Jordan will also. Since Novomeysky's days, a subsidiary of the Dead Sea Works has been extracting magnesium bromide, which was used to raise the octane level in gasoline. By the mid 1970s, the company was mining 12,000 tons, by 1985 80,000, and by 1986 100,000. In five years it should be twice that, accounting for half of world consumption. The reason for these high expectations is that of the many new compounds recently developed, two appear to have great potential. One is used in pesticides, where the toxicity to humans and animals is evidently lower than that of conventional pesticides; the other is as a fire retardant which may one day be used in building materials. The store of bromine in the Dead Sea makes Israel and Jordan the world's largest possessors of it; there is enough in the lake's billion tons to satisfy world demand for centuries.

The key to industrial expansion is inexpensive energy, which Israel has no means of producing; and Jordan, though it receives money from OPEC, is itself oil-poor. As long as seventy years ago, Novomeysky recognized that the long-range success of his project would depend on an energy source. The geological report he read before coming to Palestine indicated that there were oil shale deposits not far from the Dead Sea, and he thought the shale might solve what he termed his "power difficulties." He journeyed to Nebi Musa to gather samples and sent them to Berlin for tests by a leading authority on mineral fuels. Yet although Israel possesses enough of the chalk-like rock to meet its energy needs for several decades, a method for turning oil shale into efficient energy has eluded researchers for years. Only in the mid-1980s has the first oil been produced at an experimental plant, and research will continue also to determine if shale might not be burned directly, as coal is.

And the search for oil has gone on for most of this century. We read in the P.E.F.'s *Quarterly Statement* of 1914 that two companies were engaged in oil prospecting at the Dead Sea. The American Standard Oil Company was in the midst of constructing a road fifty miles long from Hebron to the lake, at great expense and with 2,000 men at work. "They are evidently quite satisfied that oil will be found," wrote the correspondent, "and are bringing out by special steamer a great quantity of machinery and eight motor trucks and automobiles." An English company was similarly employed on the east side and appeared "equally hopeful of success." For many years, Leo Picard, who conducted a geological survey of the entire country, worked both in association with Novomeysky and alone, searching for oil, as well as doing mineral research. In 1967, Israel's oil needs were partially satisfied when after the Arab–Israeli war it found itself in possession of the oil-rich Sinai. But the peace agreement with Egypt and the return of the Sinai stipulated the relinquishment of all the oil wells, pre- and post-'67, and since then Israel has been drilling in its own desert. In 1980, an American geologist announced the location of an oil deposit just south of the Dead Sea, where drilling continues; drilling has also been done (so far unsuccessfully) near Masada and was recently begun at Mt. Sedom as well. That there were at one time oil deposits beneath the Dead Sea is almost beyond a doubt, the evidence being the asphalt that periodically rises and the petroleum that leaks out of certain rocks on both sides of the lake. Several explorers referred to the latter phenomenon in the region of Wadi Mojib; and a wadi on the southwest side of the lake—where an important Neolithic discovery was recently made—is called Nahal Hemar, or asphalt, in recognition of the phenomenon. But so extensive is the seismic activity in the Rift, and so fluid the oil, that it is assumed those deposits have long shifted elsewhere.

In the 1950s, David Ben Gurion expressed faith in the future of solar energy, and he pressed for research and whatever application was possible. Indeed for years now Israeli homes have been characterized by water drums sitting on their roofs with adjacent solar collectors. But the emphasis Ben Gurion placed on the development of solar energy was not extended by his successors, and as long as oil was inexpensive and plentiful, the call for alternatives had no ring of urgency. Still there were always those few whose foresight or plain curiosity prodded them on, and in the last years additional scientists have once more been looking to the sun for a solution to Israel's needs. The sun shines on the Dead Sea all but a handful of days every year. If those rays could be collected and stored, then why not converted to electricity? The story behind this question goes back several decades.

In 1935, Novomeysky, dissatisfied with the rate of evaporation in the pans of his potash works, sought the advice of a physical chemist named Rudolph Bloch, a Czech Jew then living in Paris. Novomeysky invited Bloch to come to London, where the Palestine Potash Company had its offices (impressive ones near the royal palace), and showed him aerial photographs of the evaporation pans on the northern shore of the Dead Sea.

Now Bloch was one of those responsible for discovering the cause of an ailment, the so-called glassblower's cataract that was commonly found among glassblowers because of their long hours in front of the intense light of open furnaces. It had been thought that their cataracts were caused by infrared light, but Bloch had learned this was not so, that it was the visible light which was at fault. His studies had made him aware of the different properties of light, and as he looked at Novomeysky's photographs, he was struck by what now seems an obvious detail. The evaporation pans, he saw, were white, which meant that while the infrared rays were being absorbed by the water, the visible light was being reflected back off the pans. In short, Novomeysky was losing much of the light that could have been absorbed. At that time, the engineers of the potash works thought that wind, not light, was the cause of evaporation, and Novomeysky himself, as outstanding a chemical engineer as he was, was not familiar with the subject of light absorption.

This was the late 1930s, and Bloch, not allowed to take his money out of Czechoslovakia, invested it instead in experiments; in his words, if he was not permitted to take money out of Europe, he would take out knowledge in its place. The point of the experiments he requisitioned was to determine what dyestuff would be suited to the evaporation pans—which, in other words, would be both resistant to sunlight and soluble in a concentrated salt solution, not common characteristics of dyestuffs. After having two hundred substances tested, he discovered an appropriate one (it happened to be green), filed for a patent, and notified Novomeysky. Strangely enough, Novomeysky took Bloch's discovery rather casually and resisted paying him for the patent, and the two men, who would ultimately become friends and work together in the potash industry, ended up in litigation. All the more strange because the litigation was being played out even as Bloch's experiments over the next two years were increasing the rate of evaporation by twenty-five per cent, and by 1939 had increased potash production by forty per cent.

Resented by some of the company's engineers as an outsider, Bloch gained credibility by teaming up with a Hebrew University scientist, Laszlo Farkas (who was killed in a plane crash in 1948) and Farkas's student, Zvi Littman. The main problem with which they had to contend was that of washing the evaporation pans. In producing one ton of potash, eight tons of salt were produced and remained in the pans, which every winter had to be washed out with water from the Jordan. The engineers of the potash works had resisted Bloch's idea of dyeing the water only partly out of resentment at being taught their trade by a stranger. Their practical reason was that the dye would increase the amount of residual salt in the pans. But Bloch felt that in any case there must be a more efficient way of going about the washing. In the course of their investigation, Bloch, Farkas, and Littman noticed that for a while the freshwater that was poured into the evaporation pans did dissolve the salt deposits, but that before long it became much less effective in doing so. What was happening, they realized, was that a layer of brine accumulated underneath the freshwater, serving as a kind of seal that the water could not penetrate. In order to wash the salt away, they saw that they would have to dig trenches by which this brine could be pumped out from underneath so that the freshwater could settle directly on the salt.

This new method proved to be a much improved way of washing the pans, but Bloch and his associates learned something else along the way. The brine that they were pumping out from the bottom of the pans was very hot, as much as 160° Fahrenheit when the air temperature was 80°. Bloch remembered that his father used to take him to a certain lake in Czechoslavakia where the water was noticeably warmer at some depth than at the surface, but that the warm water rose, eventually mixing with the cool. Here, however, that homogenizing process did not take place, because the brine at the bottom of the evaporation pans was so heavy with dissolved salts that it could not rise. It was an exciting discovery, that one could pump out the hot brine without disturbing the layer of freshwater above. Why waste all that hot water, they asked themselves in 1943, when it could perhaps be converted to electricity? They applied to the Mandate government for research funds, but never received a reply.

Other crucial projects at the Dead Sea potash industry kept Bloch occupied, and little was done in relation to what had already come to be called the solar pond. In 1959, because of his work with dyestuffs he was invited by the Ford Foundation to a conference in Arizona on solar energy, and there he gave his lecture on the solar pond. Hardly any interest was expressed, and Bloch turned to Harry (Zvi) Tabor, who had also been invited from Israel because of his invention of a solar absorption heater, and tried to persuade him to join him on the project. Tabor (now a leading figure in solar energy in Israel) was involved in other things, and again the development of the solar pond was delayed. Four years later, however, he was ready, and by 1966 a small test pond had been built at the potash plant.

Pools of water, even the ocean itself, had long been thought of as potential solar collectors. A body of water absorbs the greatest amount of the sun's radiation approximately five feet below its surface, but, as Bloch recalled of his boyhood lake, the heated water, like heated air, rises, and once it comes to the surface, the heat is diffused. That initial problem had been solved more than two decades before, when Bloch realized that salt-saturated hot water, because of its weight, did not behave in this way. The design that was worked out by Tabor, with Bloch (then head of research and development for the Dead Sea Works) serving as advisor, called for a shallow pool lined with black plastic to maximize absorption of the sun's radiation. Because the pool was not to be more than six feet deep, it would collect the radiation not at its surface, but near the bottom. A layer of lighter water (ordinary sea water could be used) would be spilled into the pool, where it would rest on top and serve as a kind of insulating gasket, a lid to keep the heated water from being exposed to the air. In this way, convection—the transference, or in effect loss, of heat by means of circulation of the heated liquid—could be prevented. The sun would continually penetrate the top layer, which would be replenished as it evaporated.

The next problem was how to maintain the distinction between the layers, an important matter because the greater the distinction the easier it would be to prevent convection. As Bloch recognized forty years ago, the layers would not of themselves mix, but they would be subject to stirring by wind and waves and would eventually be rendered homogeneous. The problem was dealt with in what now seems quite simple a manner. Strips of plastic netting would be laid on top of the pool; criss-crossed, they would act as a floating windbreak while at the same time minimizing the formation of waves. In this way the necessary stratification of the pool could be preserved. Thus the non-convecting solar pond came into existence.

Heat, however, even the near boiling point temperature that could be achieved in the pool, is not electricity. In 1968, Tabor approached Yehuda Bronitzki, an engineer long interested in solar energy, and asked him to design a low temperature turbine to convert the heat created by the pool into electricity. Bronitzki developed what would be the mate to the pond, a heat converter that operated with temperatures considerably lower than those required by conventional generators. Based on the two designs, the first experimental solar pond and power station were built on the shore of the Dead Sea in 1977. Because a liquid collector can hold heat for a relatively long period of time, electricity can be generated at night as well as during the day. To demonstrate the point, the switch was first thrown, in December of 1979, at night, lighting up the shore of the Dead Sea by means, one could say, of a sun that was then shining half a world away.

The power station works in a beautifully simple way. The sun's radiation is absorbed by the lower layer of water, which gets increasingly hot until a temperature near the boiling point is reached. The hot brine is transferred through insulated pipes to a chamber in which it heats a more volatile liquid which turns to vapor, expanding and turning the wheels of the turbine, producing

193

electricity. From there the vapor is forced into a condenser, where circulating water from the top layer of the pond cools it and returns it to a liquid state, after which it is conveyed back to the pond, where the cycle begins again.

The solar pond has several advantages over conventional glass collectors. Bodies of water offer the large flat surfaces required for solar collection; heavy brine has proved more effective than glass for long-term storage of radiation; and there are no glass surfaces to keep clean. But there are drawbacks, as well. The ponds cannot be tilted and are thus suitable only within a latitude of plus or minus forty degrees, and the immense area needed for production of electricity might be prohibitive. Further, one has to consider the price of salt, the availability of a water source, and the threat of contamination of freshwater aquifers. Many underdeveloped regions of the world do meet the requirements. So far, however, the only serious work conducted has been by Israel and the United States.

The 150 kilowatt test pond was so successful that plans for further development leapt forward. In the early 1980s the Israeli government invested in a new facility then under construction at the northern end of the Dead Sea; the sixty acre pond was to power a three megawatt plant, the electricity to be fed into the national grid. Experiments were also conducted with "floating ponds," which are twenty per cent more efficient than the ones now in use, and which could make the deep northern basin usable. Researchers were initially confident that by the turn of the century the ponds could supply around a fifth of Israel's energy needs. But broad application of the solar electric pond may not be feasible, for their ultimate viability is linked to water, whether fresh or brackish, with which to replenish the top layer of the pool as it evaporates. There is only enough water in the available wells and springs to convert about a fifth of the lake into a floating pond, and though fossil water sources could double that, they will have been exhausted after around twenty years. If work on the solar ponds is to proceed, water will have to be brought from elsewhere. Israel's only lake other than the Dead Sea is the Sea of Galilee, and that supply cannot be spared. For this reason, among others, sights turned, not surprisingly, to the Mediterranean.

In 1902, Theodore Herzl's utopian novel *Altneuland* (Old-New

194

Land) offered a vision of a reconstituted and revitalized Jewish people at home in Palestine. Jews would farm the land and run the mills, and the yoke of European oppression would be lifted. Central in his conception of this progressive society was its ability to provide for its own energy needs, which Herzl believed would be satisfied in large part by the Dead Sea. The key to all the industrial efforts which would be concentrated there was, according to this vision, a canal that would link the lake with the Mediterranean, forever replenishing it and supplying the country with unlimited hydroelectric power.

The idea of digging a canal from the Mediterranean to the Dead Sea did not originate with Herzl. Earlier proponents had military matters on their minds and saw a canal as part of a global strategy. William Allen's 1855 proposal came out of concern for England's continuance as a maritime power, and he viewed a canal as a shortcut to its Indian Ocean possessions. "Providence," he explained, "has here almost furnished industrious nations, at a time when growing intercourse is seeking for improved channels of communication, with the means of constructing a noble canal between the two seas." Allen was confident that his plan, which called for a canal to run inland to the Sea of Galilee, down the Jordan Valley, through the Dead Sea and south to the Red Sea, was, despite its greater length, better than the French plan to dig at Suez. One of his main reasons was that the slope from the Mediterranean to the Dead Sea would supposedly create a current that "would carry off all the earth (previously loosened by blasting), whereas the canal of the isthmus would have to be wholly dug out and carried away." (He was not wrong, though the procedure would have been somewhat messy.)

Allen conceded that there would be some sacrifices, but he insisted they would be trifling compared with the advantages of his scheme. One of the sacrifices would be the inundation of 2,000 square miles "of the territories belonging to our faithful and gallant ally, His Highness the Sultan." Another would be the submersion of some Arab villages, along with the city of Tiberias, which had been severely damaged in the earthquake of 1837 and had not been rebuilt. Without a historical feeling for the town, Allen saw no reason to preserve what he described as a "filthy heap of ruined buildings." His only slight misgiving was his consideration for Jewish reaction, but he was able to rationalize that: "The Jews would possibly object strongly to the loss of Tiberias, which is one of the four holy cities; but they are strangers, from Russia, Poland, & c., who have no property in it, and come there in the hope of seeing the Messiah rise out of the lake, which is a general expectation among them, though on what authority it is not known... If such is really the general belief of the Jews, they must consider it as a miracle, and of course it could not be impeded by a few fathoms more or less in the depth of the sea."

Little more was heard about a canal for the next few decades. Meanwhile, the French did open the Suez Canal, which took care of the West's communication and transportation needs. When Charles Gordon, of Khartoum fame, proposed his canal scheme in the early 1880s, he was motivated by something else. He feared Russian advances in the East and was certain the Russians had their eye on Afghanistan. A canal through Palestine would serve as an eastern defense line for the Suez, which by then had become vital to England as well as to France.

It was only later, when a similar plan was considered by the early Zionists, that the focus shifted. Far from conceiving of the canal as vital to international strategy, they were thinking in terms of the needs of their future state. In 1899, Max Bourcart, a Swiss engineer, proposed to Herzl a canal system that would address the dual needs of electricity and water. As he saw it, a waterway would run from the Sea of Galilee parallel to the Jordan River; that part of the proposal was more or less adopted in the Israeli National Water Carrier, though the fields it irrigates extend much further south than Bourcart imagined. The second part of the plan had a canal running from the Mediterranean inland to the Jordan River, on the way to which the difference in elevation would provide hydroelectric power.

Nothing was heard in relation to a Mediterranean–Dead Sea canal for a number of years. In the early 1940s, when Lowdermilk proposed a comprehensive program for meeting the problem of water resources in Palestine and Transjordan, he included in his plan a canal extending from the Mediterranean to the Jordan River to replace the water lost through the projected tapping of the river and to provide hydroelectric power to the region. His proposal generated a good deal of interest, but the Mandate Government made no effort to act on it. Only thirty years later, when the price of oil shot up after the 1973 October War, did Israeli engineers

196

resurrect the idea. Aside from the hydroelectric energy it would provide, the canal water could also be used to cool power plants and supply the solar ponds with the unlimited water which is essential to their operation. A further objective was the replenishment of the lake itself; water was to flow into the Dead Sea until the optimum level was reached, that level defined by the dikes and coinciding roughly with the 1950s shoreline. Afterwards the level was to be controlled so that the amount of inflow from the canal would counter evaporation.

The plan was approved in principle in 1980, and a steering committee chose a route which would go from the Gaza Strip to Ein Bokek. To the dismay of even some of those who favored the controversial project, a groundbreaking ceremony was held a year later. The motivation of the Likud government was obviously political, and many felt that the enmeshment of politics in a scientific endeavor of this magnitude did not bode well, for there were complicated issues still to be addressed. For one thing, the final cost would probably be a good deal higher than the one and a half billion dollars projected. Perhaps more important, there was disagreement about what energy advantages it would finally yield. The hydroelectric plant—the canal's raison d'etre—would provide, according to the canal committee, around twenty per cent of Israel's energy needs. But some scientists disagreed, asserting that if the canal were being done for the purpose of hydro power, it was not worth it.

The problems were not confined to the canal itself; there was the Dead Sea Works, for example, to consider, not to mention the Arab Potash Company. The water from the canal would not mix with the deep water of the Dead Sea because of their different densities, so neither company would be affected by the dilution of the lake's surface—at least not at first. After some years, however, the lake would become homogenized, with an overall decrease in its salinity. From then on, each step in the mineral-extracting process would be protracted.

The political issues were at least as complicated as the technical. The Dead Sea is a lake owned jointly by two countries who are in a formal state of war. If there are no international laws governing the use of a shared natural resource, there are international conventions, according to which unilateral tampering with the lake would be a violation. A 1981 United Nations conference on energy did call the project illegal, but one has to be careful in interpreting such pronouncements. At the same conference, Jordan submitted a report on various projects for development of energy sources. The report outlined Jordan's own plan for a canal similar to the Israelis', a Red Sea–Dead Sea waterway by which water would be conveyed from Akabah for the generation of hydroelectricity. Whether Jordan's plan would also be defined one day as illegal is debatable.

It is far beyond the range of probability that two canals would ever be constructed, for the lake can only accept a finite amount of water without both potash works being flooded. Furthermore, though some planners even from Israel favored a Red Sea connection over a Mediterranean one, the route appears to be less inviting, for the distance is greater and the descent much less dramatic, not to mention the risk for either country of sabotage, since the canals would be on the border. Nonetheless one can see the potential danger of prolonged unilateral activity. There are those in Israel who still hope that one day a canal will be constructed; among them, some who wish it only as a project that will serve both nations.

Eventual contact between the two countries may one day be dictated by that most compelling of political motivations, self-interest. Whether or not they like it, Israel and Jordan are linked by the natural forces of their shared region. The same process of evaporation on which their industries rely is raising the bottom of the Dead Sea's southern basin—because of the precipitated salts—by around three feet every ten years or so. To maintain a constant depth, the level of the lake has to be raised in accordance. In several more decades this might be a problem for the dikes, especially the Jordanian ones, which are not as massive as the Israeli ones. In addition, Jordan has a particular vulnerability that Israel does not have. There are two major wadis in the Aravah Valley that drain into the Dead Sea, and both extend at such an angle that should there be heavy flooding, the water could be dashed with damaging results against the Jordanian dikes. It happens that there haven't been severe floods for several years, but they could come any time, and the Jordanian dikes were not constructed to withstand them. The wadis lie in Israel, and Israeli diversion of the floods could be a relatively uncomplicated matter.

For a while, a project much less grandiose than a canal was being planned in Israel. A pumping station was being constructed on the southwest shore of the lake with the idea of running Dead Sea water through a tunnel and up the cliff at night, when electricity is least expensive, and allowing it to pour back down during the day, producing hydroelectricity at peak hours. But that too was abandoned early in 1986 out of financial considerations and amidst disagreement about Israel's energy future.

The postponement or cancelling of the canal means that the solar pond project cannot proceed much further. That is unfortunate, for the ponds might one day produce something like ten times the power that could be generated from the canal's hydroelectric stations. Yet despite the fact that Israel's distinct worldwide advantage in the development of liquid solar collectors could be lost for lack of water, certain researchers devoted to the ponds nevertheless applauded the shelving of the canal. Their reason was environmental; some feared the inadvertent poisoning with salt of Israel's coastal aquifer, and in general felt that far more study had to be conducted on the potential effects of major development.

The ecological system of the Dead Sea valley is fragile enough so that the consequences of the encroachment of the technological world cannot be fully predicted now. There is, for instance, the question of the region's fauna. The diverse and prolific wildlife which roamed the Judean Hills in Biblical days had been disappearing since the time of the Romans. Some species are gone forever, but others, under a careful program of conservation and restoration, have been placed under protection and even reintroduced into their ancient home. Israel has a very active and successful nature protection network, and one of its most remarkable achievements in the last decade has been the restoration of the leopard. Until the early 1970s, it was thought to have vanished, but rare sightings indicated otherwise, and an intense effort had already resulted by the turn of the decade in a slight but significant increase in its numbers. By the early 1980s as many as two dozen could be counted in various places, including Ein Gedi, and by 1985, with the maturation of the young, the population had spread out. The return of the leopard is a sign that the valley's ecosystem is healthy, for it means there is enough food to sustain it. Once too the magnificent ibex was rare; now it springs from rock to rock with all the alacrity of its ancestors, and in safe numbers once more. Because ibex is a target of the leopard, the herd is kept strong, since it is the weak that fall prey. As the valley's ecological system links these two animals, it joins them also with numerous other known and unknown factors. Any drastic changes in the environment could upset the delicate balance of nature which alone insures the survival of endangered species.

Tourism also is a mixed blessing at a time when more and more visitors are attracted to the valley. In the early 1980s, a tourist town was being considered for the vicinity of Masada, and environmentalists were gearing up to challenge the project. With Israel's relinquishment of the Sinai and the relocation of its air bases to the Negev Desert, the Israeli wilderness has dwindled. And while the vast majority of Israelis take their security needs with utmost seriousness, environmentalists fear that the country's empty desert regions will become filled in with concrete and studded with iron. To their relief, the tourist town seems to have died a natural death.

Tourism is expanding as news of the therapeutic qualities of the valley's mineral springs and of the lake itself spreads. As we have seen, such recognition is not new. Pliny recounted the habit of some rich men of Rome who had water from the Dead Sea conveyed to them for their baths. A thousand years later, the Arab geographer Mukaddasi related that the water of the Dead Sea is a cure for many disorders, so much so that "they have a feast-day for the purpose of thus taking the waters, and it occurs in the middle of the month of Ab (August), when the people with those who are afflicted with sickness assemble thereto." Among the Jews, bathing in the lake for therapeutic reasons was permitted even on the Sabbath, when water could also be drawn and carried off (a practice normally proscribed by law) for medical purposes.

Throughout most of his trip in 1835, John Stephens was either mildly or severely ill. Fearing for his health, he was hesitant to bathe in the Dead Sea. But curiosity was stronger than caution in the young American, and he gave in to his impulse. Afterwards, to his surprise and delight, he felt oddly and remarkably refreshed. Half a century later, Tristram was effusive: "What a sanatorium Engedi might be made, if it were only accessible, and some enterprising speculator were to set up a hydropathic establishment! Hot water, cold water, and decidedly saltwater baths, all supplied by nature on the spot, the hot sulphur springs only three miles off, and some of the grandest scenery man ever enjoyed, in an atmosphere where half a lung is sufficient for respiration!"—the last comment an exaggeration, but a reference to the increased air pressure at the Dead Sea, whereby the very sensitive hiker might feel less winded after a strenuous walk. And later he bid a reluctant... "Farewell for the present to the Dead Sea, and the balmy climate of its shores! A winter sanatorium at Engedi would surpass all that the Nile, Madeira, or Algiers can promise." Finally, near the turn of the century, a P.E.F. associate went a step further. Predicting that one day the value of the Dead Sea's water would make the lake a resort in the winter months for curative purposes, he went on to say that he himself found the water most invigorating: "I get a supply at my house [in Jerusalem] brought in old petroleum tins on donkey back, and use it somewhat diluted for my morning tub." One's morning tub is somewhat easier to prepare today, as Dead Sea salts may be found in Israeli pharmacies.

There are several hotels now situated on the Israeli side of the Dead Sea, clustered on the shore of the southern basin, and Jordan is enlarging a tourist center at Suweimeh, at the lake's northern end, while also developing a large tourist complex at the Zerka Ma'in, where there are over fifty hot springs. Many of the clientele are seeking a cure for skin and rheumatic diseases and respiratory ailments. Some European and Scandinavian doctors prescribe treatment at the Dead Sea for certain skin conditions, notably psoriasis; and in Denmark, for example, a stay at this modern-day magic mountain is considered for insurance purposes a form of hospitalization. (The most effective treatment for psoriasis is prolonged exposure to sunlight—generally a very dangerous practice. At the Dead Sea, most of the sun's harmful ultraviolet rays never reaches the valley's floor. Patients can sit outside for six or seven hours a day without burning, beyond which the lake's magnesium nourishes the skin.)

One is struck by the incongruity of modern hotels sitting on the barren shore where as little as half a century ago no building stood, or had stood, in well over a thousand years. There is something surreal about the scene. The air is still, even stiller it seems than on the northern shore; but looking out at the intensely turquoise water, one is startled, then puzzled, to see whitecaps, as if this motionless lake were a windswept sea. Is it hallucination? The effect of the relentless sun? But as one stares, wondering, one notices that these whitecaps are motionless, as inert as the desert air. Slowly the scene becomes real, as one's perceptions adjust—like shifting for a comfortable position in a lumpy chair—and one realizes that the snow white points, frozen on the aqua sea, are not whitecaps at all but mounds of salt exposed in the shallow water. For a moment one can stand outside time, then a bather paddling his or her body out to one of these salt islands, or another already lying on a small mound of white crystals, suddenly comes into view and draws one back. Every thread of geological and human history is gathered as perceptions millennia apart accumulate. And the fabric that is woven reveals a pattern of time and change, and challenge.

For finally we return to the Dead Sea itself. The popular view that its eventual disappearance is inevitable because of the loss of its historic lifeline, the Jordan River, is probably erroneous. It seems that in the last number of years it had more or less stabilized, even if at a level a good deal lower than many would have liked. While the southern basin had a disproportionately large surface area (it accounted for more than one quarter of the lake's total surface, though for only five per cent of its volume), the northern basin has a surface that is small relative to its great depth. The water lost through evaporation was experienced disproportionately by the two basins, so that when the southern basin dried up, the relative evaporation decreased substantially. The northern basin was not endangered as much as one might think by the loss of the Jordan River, for it no longer had to "share" whatever inflow it received. It reached a certain level (and may still be adjusting) and to some extent stabilized, a condition, interestingly enough, predicted by Lynch in 1848. Like animal life, a lake can exhibit adaptive tendencies to new circumstances; it seems that the Dead Sea has been successful in conforming to conditions imposed not like natural ones, over millennia, but in what is, in geo-historical terms, a handful of years.

Furthermore, most investigators agree that a fall in level of forty-five feet, such as the Dead Sea has experienced in this century, is neither anomalous nor in itself particular cause for concern. There seems after all to be some unanimity of opinion among the foremost investigators that climate, not human intervention, had at least until recently been the primary cause of the Dead Sea's fluctuations. That subject has been the thirty years' work of Cippora Klein, who first established the pattern of fluctuations over the last two centuries and then tried to determine the reasons for them. The lake is at the bottom of a drainage basin that extends north to Mt. Hermon and south into parts of the Sinai. While Klein did not discount the influence of the Jordan River, she became convinced that variations in the amount of rainfall in the catchment area, which reaches the Dead Sea also by subterranean channels, is the major factor in determining its level. If not, she asked, why was the level stable for six years after Israel's National Water Carrier opened, and why did the seven years of drought which followed see a parallel seven-year recession?

It is a difficult enough subject, but in the last few years it has been further complicated, to the extent that it is almost impossible to study the lake's level as it is related to climate. As we saw, Israel and now Jordan too are pumping water from the northern basin to the southern for their mineral works, and the Dead Sea has reacted with a loss of level that causes some to fear it may never be able to overcome these great and recently doubled demands. For the time being, it was observed, the Dead Sea seems to have given up. On the other hand, until the winter of 1986–87, the last several winters were dry, and when the rains return, not only does inflow increase, but irrigation needs diminish. The Dead Sea's rhythms may not be completely understood, but it seems to be quite a resilient body of water, capable of discovering an equilibrium level for nearly every climatic situation. Although the relationship of rainfall to level may be permanently disrupted, those who believe that climate is the most significant influence feel, and hope, that with a substantial wet period, the lake will at least partially recover.

The debate over the Mediterranean–Dead Sea canal has receded for the time being, but its echo resounds, for the issues it raised persist. There are the practical questions, which become increasingly more complex. There is the question of preserving the Dead Sea's unique environment, and there is the political issue of unilateral versus bilateral regional activity. In all, that echo comes as a reminder that development is a two-edged sword, that what may be good in one arena may be harmful in another, and that Israel's long-range vitality will at least in part be determined by how it addresses the political and environmental threats begotten by development.

There is also another view, one that sees the development of the valley not as something to fear, but as a cause for hope. The location of the Dead Sea between Israel and Jordan might one day turn it into an instrument of peace, as cooperation such as there once was under Novomeysky could be fostered by the two countries' reliance on and faith in the same lake. The Dead Sea has always been a border, first separating tribes, then nations, the groove in which it lies once described as extending like a fragile backbone between the mountains of Judea and Moab. But why divide? If a backbone, why not extend the metaphor and let the lake serve as a true backbone—of peace. As Jordan's industry develops, the interests of the two countries become identical. The incentives are very clear, and of a practical nature. There is already respect for one another, even if it is unpublicized; that becomes apparent when one talks with representatives of the two potash industries. Respect has a way of leading to cooperation under the right conditions. Clandestine associations have long marked affairs in the Middle East, and the silent relationship that already exists between the two industries could be the backdoor to more extensive discussions. As unlikely as this scenario may appear, that very thing might have come about in the early days of Israel's and Jordan's existence as independent states, before Abdullah's assassination. "I have often been a guest of his," recalled Novomeysky, "either at Amman or his winter residence at Shuni near the River Jordan, and he was more than once my guest at the Dead Sea. In welcome distinction from other Arab leaders, he was hostile neither to the Jews as a people nor to Zionism, that is, to the Jewish national idea... He often told me that he had inherited this attitude of friendliness from his father. It was clear to him that respect for Zionism was no derogation of Islam."

Their meetings continued even after Israel's War of Independence, and one cannot help but imagine that their relationship might serve as a paradigm for future ones. In November 1949, the war over, Novomeysky requested an interview with the king to discuss the acquisition of water for his beleaguered southern plant and was invited to Shuni for dinner. "The journey there was made with careful precautions. One of his adjutants met me at night with a car on the demarcation line between New and Old Jerusalem. The passage through hostile Jericho was particularly difficult. Our talk was a very long one, and it was only in the small hours that I returned home. The principal subject of Abdullah's interest had not been water, but the possibility of real peace and the conditions on which this might be concluded." Since then, strong feelings have congealed, and circumstances are less malleable than they were in those days; and it must also be borne in mind that Novomeysky was powerless and Abdullah was not a Palestinian. Nevertheless, with this precedent, there may be room for optimism. Sceptics might be startled by a report that in the summer of 1984 Israel and Jordan did in fact talk about a common concern—the infestation of mosquitoes in the Akabah–Eilat area. No joint project to control them was launched, and the meeting was between only low level officials; yet according to an Israeli source the talks extended beyond the mosquito problem and touched on the question of mineral extraction from the Dead Sea.

It is hard to resist the temptation of development when all the ingredients are there and the alternatives seem so meager—harder still when the potential gains are so great. But caution seems essential until the risks can be completely evaluated. What the ultimate correspondence will be between the benefits and detriments of development is a matter of widely divergent and adamantly held opinion. One thing, however, is clear: the Dead Sea valley has a purely physical limitation. The lake is small and its shores narrow, and there is simply not room enough for everything without causing some disturbance, whether to the lake, its coasts and springs, or the wadis. How much disturbance can be tolerated—and what "toleration" means—is a key question, and one which is constantly being debated. On both sides are people who have devoted years to the Dead Sea, whether studying it or guiding development. One can only hope that their devotion is not manifested in ways finally irreconcilable; that they can come together to formulate a program which will foster international cooperation and protect the Dead Sea environment, and in which the word sacrifice, as it pertains to the lake, is used minimally.

Centuries ago people began falling under the spell of what was considered an inscrutable and forbidding sea. Once they discovered that its uncongeniality was largely the product of over-indulged imaginations, they ventured nearer, asking questions, weighing, measuring, testing, learning to appreciate. Hardly the miasma it was made out to be, the Dead Sea was found not to contain much life, but to hold a store of information about life. Exploration led to research which branched out to include all fields of study, and as each new answer suggested another question, research possibilities seemed inexhaustible. By the first third of this century, investigation had turned more utilitarian, and those who were actively

205

involved at the lake were determined to prove false its western name.

By now, enough life has been derived from the Dead Sea to expose forever the fallacy of that name. But only human beings can insure that the lifecycle so recently discovered will be prolonged. Pinned like a helpless giant in its deep, closed basin, the Dead Sea is more subject to the vagaries of human activity than those lakes whose mere location—and ordinariness—frees them from human whim and gives them independence from human history.

The powerful sense of permanence that one has when standing in the Dead Sea basin and looking up at the surrounding cliffs does not extend to the lake itself. Perhaps it once did; but now, given civilization's encroachment, one is struck not by the sea's immutability but by its vulnerability. And it is not just an impression. As a natural phenomenon, the lake is fragile, and decisions made in the next years could determine, possibly once and for all, its fate. At stake is the Dead Sea as we know it and as it has been known through all recorded history. Will it continue to live, or will it follow its predecessors, receding, changing, and finally vanishing into the cracks of geological history?

Afterword & Chapter Notes

THERE IS an enormous body of work concerning both historical and scientific aspects of the Dead Sea and its environs. I hope this book will serve as an introduction for anyone interested in further exploration. Naturally the first thing one might want to do is visit the lake and its surroundings and experience for oneself the valley's beauty. I would also recommend becoming acquainted with the texts of the explorers. Frequently illustrated with beautiful drawings and paintings, with large maps folded into cover pockets, these narratives offer far more in their original editions than I can convey in mere excerpts.

The following is an arrangement of the many books and articles without which I could not have written this book.

CHAPTER ONE

The ancient world's encounter with the Dead Sea is chronicled in detail by Diodorus Siculus in the *History* (esp. vol. X, book 19; trans. Russel M. Geer, Cambridge, Mass., London, 1954); Strabo in his *Geography* (vol. 3, book 16; trans. H.C. Hamilton and W. Falconer, London, 1881); Pliny in his *Natural History* (vol. I, book 5; trans. John Bostook and H.T. Riley, London, 1893); Josephus in *The Jewish War* (trans. G.A. Williamson, Middlesex, 1959) and *Antiquities of the Jews* (based on trans. by William Whiston, Grand Rapids, Mich., 1960); and Cornelius Tacitus in *The History* (vol. 2, book V; trans. Albert W. Quill, London, 1896).

A useful overview of geography in the Middle Ages is provided by George H.T. Kimble's *Geography in the Middle Ages* (London, 1938). Robert Steele's *Medieval Lore from Bartholomæus Anglicus* (London,

1907) and H.F.M. Prescott's *Friar Felix at Large* (New Haven, 1950) are also instructive. Thomas Wright, editor of *Early Travels in Palestine* (London, 1848), made available an excellent selection from the works of medieval travellers; and Guy Le Strange, in translating and editing selections from medieval Arab geographers, provided an invaluable resource for the non-Arabic-reading: *Palestine Under the Moslems, A Description of Syria and the Holy Land from* C.E. *650 to 1500* (London, 1890).

Thirteen volumes of travellers' accounts were published by the Committee for the Palestine Exploration Fund in 1897. In this Library of the Palestine Pilgrims' Text Society, the reader interested in medieval encounters with the Dead Sea might want to read "The Pilgrimage of the Russian Abbot Daniel" (vol. 4), who travelled in the first decade of the twelfth century, a few years after the Crusaders conquered the Holy Land; also the account of the pilgrim Burchard (vol. 12), who spent ten years at Mt. Zion from roughly 1275, and the fifteenth-century Felix Fabri (vol. 7). Ludolph von Suchem's *A Description of the Holy Land, and of the Way Thither* (1350) includes a detailed description of his encounter with the lake, and John Maundeville's *Travels* is a curious and singular work.

Pre-nineteenth century accounts of journeys to the Dead Sea may be found in Thomas Fuller's *A Pisgah-sight of Palestine, and the confines thereof* (1650), Henry Maundrell's *A Journey from Aleppo to Jerusalem* (1697), and Richard Pococke's *A Description of the East, and Some Other Countries* (1740).

The reader interested in literary responses to the Dead Sea may want to read Sir Walter Scott's *The Talisman, A Tale of the Crusaders* (1825); Herman Melville's *Redburn* (1849), *Clarel* (1876), and *Journal of a Visit to Europe and the Levant, Oct. 11, 1856 to May 6, 1857*; Benjamin Disraeli's *Tancred; or, the New Crusade* (1853); and Mark Twain's *The Innocents Abroad; or The New Pilgrims' Progress* (1869).

CHAPTER TWO

The notable narratives of the early part of the nineteenth century include Ulrich Jasper Seetzen's *A Brief Account of the Countries Adjoining the Lake of Tiberias, the Jordan and the Dead Sea* (Palestine Association of London, 1810); John Lewis Burckhardt's *Travels in Syria and the Holy Land* (London, 1822); and *Travels in Egypt and Nubia, Syria, and the Holy Land During the Years 1817 & 1818* (London,

208

1823), by Charles Irby and James Mangles.

Other noteworthy accounts are François de Chateaubriand's *Travels in Greece, Palestine, Egypt and Barbary during the Years 1806 and 1807* (London, 1811); William MacMichael's *Journey from Moscow to Constantinople, in the Years 1817, 1818* (London, 1819); Thomas Jolliffe's *Letters from Palestine* (London, 1819); L.E. de Laborde's *Journey through Arabia Petræa to Mount Sinai* (London, 1836).

Highly recommended is John Lloyd Stephens' *Incidents of Travel in Egypt, Arabia Petræa and the Holy Land* (New York, 1837). Stephens never resumed a sedentary life after his journey to the East. He went on to Mexico and Central and South America, and is credited with the discovery of the ancient Mayan civilization. The interested reader will want to read Stephens' excellent books (he was described by the critic Van Wyck Brooks as "one of the few great writers of travels"). I would also recommend Victor W. Von Hagen's biography: *Maya Explorer, John Lloyd Stephens and The Lost Cities of Central America and Yucatan* (University of Oklahoma Press, 1947).

Also, Count Jules de Bertou's "Notes on a Journey from Jerusalem by Hebron, the Dead Sea, El Ghór, and Wádí 'Arabah to 'Akabah, and back by Petra, in April, 1838," *Journal of the Royal Geographic Society*, vol. IX, 1839; Edward Robinson and Eli Smith's *Biblical Researches in Palestine, Mount Sinai and Arabia Petræa*, esp. vol. 2 (Boston, 1841); Robinson and Smith's "Extracts from a Journal of Travels in Palestine, and c., in 1838," *Journal of the Royal Geographic Society*, vol. IX, 1839; and Eliot Warburton's *The Crescent and the Cross; or, Romance and Realities of Eastern Travel* (London, 1844).

One who wishes to follow the whole of the fascinating story of the discovery and definition of the depression of the level of the Dead Sea would go to several nearly consecutive issues of the *Journal of the Royal Geographic Society*. The first mention of the Dead Sea occurs six years after the Journal's founding; in vol. 7, 1837, we find the editorial note on the trip made by G.H. Moore and W.G. Beke. In volumes 9, 10, and 12 (1839, 1841, and 1842 respectively), the reader would take note of the anniversary addresses given to the Society's members by William R. Hamilton. In vol. 13 (1843–44), we read of the gold medal award presented to Lt. Sykes. Mr. Roderick Murchison delivered a noteworthy address in vol. 15 (1845). Finally, vol. 17–18 (1847–48) offers us Edward Robinson's "Depression of the Dead Sea and of the Jordan Valley," Augustus

Petermann's "On the Fall of the Jordan, and of the Principal Rivers in the United Kingdom," and Thomas Molyneux's posthumous account of his journey, "Expedition to the Jordan and the Dead Sea." One might also want to consult the following, also in the *Journal of the Royal Geographic Society*:

"On the Use of Common Thermometers to Determine Heights," by Lt. Col. W.H. Sykes, vol. 8, 1838.

"Remarks on the Use of the Aneroid Barometer," by Col. Philip Yorke, vol. 21, 1851.

"An Attempt to Account for Numerous Appearances of Sudden and Violent Drainage on the Sides of the Basin of the Dead Sea," and "On the Watershed of Wadi el Araba," both by Capt. William Allen, in vol. 23, 1853.

Finally, William Hamilton's address in vol. 19, 1849; and Roderick Murchison's talk in vol. 23, 1853.

Edward Masterman's lengthy piece, "Three Early Explorers to the Dead Sea Valley: Costigan, Molyneux, Lynch," may be found in the Palestine Exploration Fund's *Quarterly Statement* for 1911.

William Lynch's *Narrative of the United States Expedition to the River Jordan and the Dead Sea* (Philadelphia, 1849) is a lively and often impassioned account of his journey. His *Official Report of the United States Expedition to Explore the Dead Sea and the River Jordan* (Baltimore, 1852) is not intended as popular reading. It contains a condensed travel narrative, essays and notes on geological formations, analyses of Jordan River and Dead Sea water, ornithological and botanical reports, and comments pertaining to scientific questions of his day. Finally, the reader who becomes taken with Lynch might want to read his anecdotal, autobiographical *Naval Life, or Observations Afloat and on Shore* (1851).

Pioneers East, The Early American Experience in the Middle East, by David H. Finnie (Cambridge, Mass., 1967) chronicles the experiences of American missionaries and travelers in the Middle East through roughly the mid-nineteenth century. Though few of those visited the Dead Sea, the book is a most informative account of a little known chapter in American history—arranged, interestingly enough, according to the routes followed by John Lloyd Stephens.

The interested scientific reader might consult "Geophysical Investigations in the Dead Sea," by David Neev and John K. Hall, in Sedimentary Geology, 23 (1979), 209–238, © Elsevier Scientific Publishing Company, Amsterdam.

CHAPTER THREE

The centerpiece of the second half century is the work of Henry Baker Tristram: *The Land of Israel, A Journal of Travels in Palestine* (London, 1865); *The Land of Moab, Travels and Discoveries on the East Side of the Dead Sea and the Jordan* (London, 1873); and *The Fauna and Flora of Palestine* (London, 1884).

Other notable accounts of the second half century include Louis Félicien de Saulcy's *Narrative of a Journey Round the Dead Sea and in the Bible Lands, in 1850 and 1851, including an account of the discovery of the sites of Sodom and Gomorrah* (London, 1854); C.W.M. Van de Velde's *Narrative of a Journey through Syria and Palestine in 1851 and 1852* (London, 1854); Captain William Allen's *The Dead Sea, A New Route to India: with Other Fragments and Gleanings in the East* (London, 1855); Reverend Albert Augustus Isaacs' *The Dead Sea: Or Notes and Observations Made during a Journey to Palestine in 1856–1857* (London, 1857); Thomas Lewin's *The Siege of Jerusalem by Titus* (London, 1863); and Edward Hull's *Mt. Seir, Sinai and Western Palestine* (London, 1885). One might also want to look at *Murray's Handbook for Travellers in Syria and Palestine*, by John L. Porter, first published in 1858, or *Bædeker's Palestine and Syria* (1876).

In addition, the *Quarterly Statement* of the Palestine Exploration Fund offers a running commentary on the state of Dead Sea exploration from 1865 onwards.

Numerous references to the Dead Sea may be found in Yehoshua Ben-Arieh's *The Rediscovery of the Holy Land in the Nineteenth Century* (Wayne State University Press, 1979), a very useful resource for the reader about to plunge into the literature of the last century.

In recent years, Len Aronson devoted himself to studying the wildlife in the Ein Gedi region, and he is an authority particularly on the Nubian ibex. His major research is not yet published, but one may want to refer to his article, "The Ein Gedi Field Study Center of the Society for the Protection of Nature in Israel," which appeared in *Israel: Land and Nature* (vol. 2, no. 4, Summer 1977), while we await his longer work.

The reader interested in the subject of life in the Dead Sea might be curious to see the very first mention of it. Fifty years ago, the microbiologist Benyamin Elazari-Volcani (then Wilkanski) published a two-paragraph announcement: "Life in the Dead Sea," *Nature* (no. 138, 1936), 467. In 1970, I.R. Kaplan and A. Friedman published their paper, "Biological productivity in the Dead Sea.

Part 1: Microorganisms in the water column," *Israel Journal of Chemistry* 8: 513–528. In 1980, microbiologists Aharon Oren and Moshe Shilo began their extensive research. One might consult: "Population dynamics of *Dunaliella parva* in the Dead Sea," by Aharon Oren and Moshe Shilo, *Limnology and Oceanography* 27 (2), 1982, 201–211; also, "Population dynamics of halobacteria in the Dead Sea water column," by Aharon Oren, *Limnology and Oceanography* 28 (6), 1983,1094–1103. Dr. Oren's summary of his work at the Dead Sea—"The Microbial Ecology of the Dead Sea"—appears in the 1987 annual publication (vol. 10) *Advances in Microbial Ecology*, ed. K.C. Marshall (Plenum Press). Also of interest is a paper publised by the Israel Academy of Sciences and Humanities: "Life in the Dead Sea," by Margaret Ginzburg (Jerusalem, 1982, section of sciences, no. 20).

A most informative article on the adaptation of plant life to the desert is "Structure and Ecology of the Vegetation in the Dead Sea Region of Palestine," by Michael Zohary and G. Orshansky, *Palestine Journal of Botany* (vol. 4, no. 4, Jerusalem series, March 1949). In addition, Zohary's *Plants of the Bible* (Cambridge, 1982) was a key to unlocking the mystery of the balsam, and H.F.M. Prescott's *Once to Sinai* (London, 1957) was also an interesting aid.

The *Encyclopedia of Archaeological Excavation in the Holy Land*, edited by Michael Avi-Yonah (Jerusalem, 1976) provides an excellent history of settlement at Jericho, Qumran, Ein Gedi, and Masada, and of course numerous longer works are available on the particular excavations, as well as on the Dead Sea Scrolls.

There are several journals, ranging from technical to popular, that can be counted on to keep up with archaeological developments in the Dead Sea region. In the *Bulletin of the American Schools of Oriental Research*, the interested reader would find: "Another Settlement of the Judean Desert Sect at En el-Ghuweir on the Shores of the Dead Sea," by Pessah Bar-Adon (No. 227, Oct. 1977) 1–25 (first published in Hebrew in 1971 in *Eretz-Israel* 10:72–89). Also, "The Winter Palaces of the Judean Kings at Jericho at the End of the Second Temple Period," by Ehud Netzer (No. 228, Dec. 1977) 1–13.

In reconstructing twentieth century thought concerning the location and fate of the Cities of the Plain, I used the following sources:

Abright, William F., "The Archaeological Results of an Expedition to Moab and the Dead Sea," *Bulletin of the American Schools of Oriental Research*, vol. 14, 1924, 2–12.

––, "The Jordan Valley in the Bronze Age," *The Annual of the American Schools of Oriental Research*, vol. VI, 1924–25, 13–74.

Glueck, Nelson, "Explorations in Eastern Palestine, II," *The Annual of the American Schools of Oriental Research*, vol. XV, 1934–35, 1–202.

––, "Explorations in Eastern Palestine, III," *The Annual of the American Schools of Oriental Research*, vol. XVIII–XIX, 1937–39, 1–288.

––, "An Aerial Reconnaissance in Southern Transjordan," *The Bulletin of the American Schools of Oriental Research*, nos. 66 and 67, April 1937, pp. 27–28, and Oct. 1937, pp. 19–26.

The reader hoping for less technical but highly informed views might go to "The Site of Sodom and Gomorrah," by Frederick G. Clapp, *American Journal of Archaeology*, vol. 40, 1936, pp. 323–44; also two articles by J. Penrose Harland: "Sodom and Gomorrah, The Location of the Cities of the Plain," *Biblical Archaeologist*, vol. V, no. 2, May 1942, pp. 17–32; and "Sodom and Gomorrah, The Destruction of the Cities of the Plain," *Biblical Archaeologist*, vol. VI, no. 3, Sept. 1943, pp. 41–54.

Finally, for information about contemporary excavations at Bab edh-Dhra and vicinity, the reader should consult the reports of the participating archaeologists themselves:

Rast, Walter E. and R. Thomas Schaub, "Survey of the Southeastern Plain of the Dead Sea, 1973," *Annual of the Department of Antiquities of Jordan*, vol. 19, 1974, 5–54 and 175–85.

––, "Preliminary Report of the 1979 Expedition to the Dead Sea Plain, Jordan," *Bulletin of the American Schools of Oriental Research*, No. 240, Fall 1980, 21–61.

––, "Preliminary Report of the 1981 Expedition to the Dead Sea Plain, Jordan," *BASOR*, No. 254, Spring 1984, 35–61.

As we saw, Rast and Schaub did not mention the Cities of the Plain but opened the door to conjecture for others. The *Biblical Archaeology Review* published an article (no author) entitled "Have Sodom and Gomorrah Been Found?" (vol. VI, no. 5, Sept./Oct. 1980, 27–36); and the *Biblical Archaeologist* followed with "Once Again: Sodom and Gomorrah," by Willem C. van Hattem, vol. 44, no. 2, Spring 1981, 87–92.

Jacob Bronowski's *The Ascent of Man* (Boston, 1974) offers an interesting picture of the early settlement of Jericho, and *Lives of the Fathers of the Desert*, by Countess Ida Hahn-Hahn (1867) offers a glimpse into monastic life in the region until the Arab conquest.

To suggest the range of topics in the Palestine Exploration Fund's *Quarterly Statement*, I include here a list of some of those articles which pertain to subjects discussed in this chapter:

Captain R.E. Warren was one of the first contributors to the new P.E.F. *Quarterly Statement*, with his "Remarks on a Visit to 'Ain Jidy and the Southern Shore of the Dead Sea in Mid-Summer of 1867," *Quarterly Statement*, vol. 1 of that year.

Lt. Claude R. Conder, looking for the cave in which David hid from Saul, submitted "The Survey of the Dead Sea Desert and a Visit to Masada," *Quarterly Statement*, 1875.

The naturalist H. Chichester Hart submitted a book chapter about the flora and fauna of the Dead Sea region: "South End of the Dead Sea," *Quarterly Statement*, 1885.

Beginning in 1874 with Tyrwhitt Drake's "Report," numerous travellers conveyed their observations about the level of the Dead Sea. Between 1900 and 1901, Gray Hill, Charles Wilson, and R.A. Stewart MacAlister all submitted reports, and Edward Masterman's findings were published annually. Masterman's brief but important summary of more than a decade of observations appeared in the *Quarterly Statement* of 1913: "Summary of the Observations on the Rise and Fall of the Level of the Dead Sea, 1900–1913." (Masterman's interest was not confined to the lake's level; in 1908 he contributed "Notes on a Visit to Engedy, Masada, and Jebel Usdum.")

After Masterman, the next important article on the Dead Sea's level to appear in the *Quarterly Statement* was in 1936: "The Level and Cartography of the Dead Sea," by T.J. Salmon and G.T. McCaw.

In 1961, Cippora Klein published her important paper, "On the Fluctuations of the Level of the Dead Sea Since the Beginning of the Nineteenth Century," Jerusalem, Ministry of Agriculture/Hydrological Service, (Hydrological Paper no. 7), 1961.

By the late 1960s, the Palestine Exploration Fund's *Quarterly Statement* had turned into the *Palestine Exploration Quarterly*, and in 1967 we find H.W. Underhill's "Dead Sea Levels and the P.E.F. Mark."

214

My reliance on the work that others have carried out in writing this chapter may be best expressed by a simple bibliography:

Ackroyd, W., "On a Principal Cause of Saltness in the Dead Sea," *Palestine Exploration Fund Quarterly Statement*, 1906, 64–66.

Arad, V., M. Beyth, Y. Bartov, *The Dead Sea and its Surroundings, Bibliography of Geological Research*, Geological Survey of Israel, special publication no. 3 (Jerusalem, 1984).

Assaf, Gad and Arie Nissenbaum, "The Evolution of the Upper Water Mass of the Dead Sea, 1819–1976," *Desertic Terminal Lakes*, ed. D.C. Greer (Utah Water Research Laboratory, University of Utah, 1977), 61–72.

Begin, Z.B., A. Ehrlich, Y. Nathan, "Lake Lisan: The Pleistocene Precursor of the Dead Sea," Ministry of Commerce and Industry/Geological Survey Bulletin no. 63, Jerusalem, November 1974.

Ben-Arieh, Yehoshua, "The Geographical Exploration of the Holy Land," *Palestine Exploration Quarterly*, July–Dec., 1972, 81–92.

Bentor, Y.K., "Some Geochemical Aspects of the Dead Sea and the Question of Its Age," *Geochimica and Cosmochimica Acta*, 25 (1961), 239–260.

Bloch, M.R., "Dead Sea Whiteness and its Origin," published by the Israel Academy of Sciences and Humanities (Jerusalem, 1980, section of sciences, no. 19).

Bloch, M.R., and Leo Picard, "The Dead Sea—a Sinkhole?" Z. deutsch. geol. Ges. Sonderh. Hydrogeol. Hydrogeochem, Hannover (1970), 119–128.

Cady, Reverend Putnam, "Exploration of the Wady Mojib from the Dead Sea," *Palestine Exploration Fund Quarterly Statement*, 1901, 44–45.

Freund, R. et. al., "The Shear Along the Dead Sea Rift," *Philosophical Transactions of the Royal Society of London*, series A, vol. 267 (1970), 107–130.

Hammond, Philip C., "The Nabataean Bitumen Industry at the Dead Sea," *The Biblical Archaeologist*, vol. 22 (1959), 2, 40–48.

Hull, Edward, *The Geology of Palestine and Arabia Petræa*, London, 1886.

Neumann, J., "Tentative Energy and Water Balances of the Dead Sea," *Bulletin*, Research Council of Israel, 7 (1958), 137–163.

Neev, David and K.O. Emery, "The Dead Sea," *Science Journal*,

Dec. 1966 (published monthly by Associated Iliffe Press Ltd., London.)

Neev, David and K.O. Emery, *The Dead Sea: Depositional Processes and Environments of Evaporites*, State of Israel, Ministry of Development, Geological Survey Bulletin no. 41, Jerusalem, 1967.

Neev, David, and John K. Hall, "Climatic Fluctuations during the Holocene as Reflected by the Dead Sea Levels," paper presented at the International Conference on Terminal Lakes, Weber State College, Ogden, Utah, May 2–5, 1977.

Nir, Y., "Some Observations on the Morphology of the Dead Sea Wadis," *Israel Journal of Earth Sciences* 16 (1967), 97–103.

Nissenbaum, Arie, *Studies in the Geochemistry of the Jordan River-Dead Sea System*, Dissertation, UCLA, 1969.

Orni, Efraim, and Elisha Efrat, *Geography of Israel*, Israel Program for Scientific Translation, Jerusalem, 1964.

Picard, Leo, "Structure and Evolution of Palestine," Geology Department of the Hebrew University, publication no. 84, 1943.

Poole, Henry, "Report of a Journey in Palestine," *Journal of the Royal Geographic Society*, 26 (1856), 55–70.

Quennel, A., "The Structure and Geomorphic Evolution of the Dead Sea Rift," *Quarterly Journal of the Geographic Society of London*, 115 (1958), 1–24.

Raz, Eli, "The World's Lowest Sea-Coast," *Israel – Land and Nature*, Quarterly Journal of the Society for the Protection of Nature in Israel, vol. 5, no. 2, Winter 1979–80.

Steinhorn, Ilana, and Joel R. Gat, "The Dead Sea," *Scientific American*, vol. 249, no. 4 (Oct. 1983), 102–109.

Vroman, A.J., "Is a Compromise Between the Theories of Tension and of Shear for the Jordan–Dead Sea Trench Possible?" *Israel Journal of Earth Sciences* 22 (1973), 141–156.

Zak, I., and R. Freund, "Recent Strike Slip Movements Along the Dead Sea Rift," *Israel Journal of Earth Sciences* 16 (1966), 33–37.

CHAPTER FIVE

Like the man himself, Moshe Novomeysky's books deserve a wider audience. They are: *My Siberian Life* (1956), and *Given to Salt: The Struggle for the Dead Sea Concession* (1958). One might also find of interest the pamphlet, "The Truth About The Dead Sea Conces-

216

sion" (1950). A brief insight into Novomeysky's political life in Palestine may be had from Susan Lee Hattis' *The Bi-National Idea in Palestine During Mandate Times* (Haifa, 1970).

The reader wishing to consult the British record would refer to the pertinent years of the *Index to the General Correspondence of the Great Britain Foreign Office*.

CHAPTER SIX

Jordan: A Country Study, edited by Richard F. Nyrop (Washington, D.C., 1980) and Rami Khouri's *The Jordan Valley: Life and Society Below Sea Level*, published in association with the Jordan Valley Authority by Longman (London & N.Y., 1981), provided me with views from the eastern side of the lake. I would also recommend Walter C. Lowdermilk's *Palestine, Land of Promise* (New York, 1944), a very interesting book about land reclamation and water resources in Palestine in the 1930s and '40s.

David Neev and K.O. Emery's publication, *The Dead Sea: Depositional Processes and Environments of Evaporites* (Jerusalem, 1967) continued to be valuable, as was David Anati's paper, "The Top 50 Meters of the Dead Sea, 1980–1984: A descriptive account of four years of measurements for Solmat Systems Ltd." (Jerusalem, 1984).

Cippora Klein made available to me her important studies: "The Influence of Rainfall over the Catchment Area on the Fluctuations of the Dead Sea since the 12th Century" (Meteorological Service, Bet Dagan, Israel Meteorological Research papers, vol. 3, 1981).

Klein, Cippora, "Morphological Evidence of Lake Level Changes, Western Shore of the Dead Sea," *Israel Journal of Earth Sciences*, vol. 31, (1982), 67–94.

——, "Fluctuations of the Level of the Dead Sea and Climatic Fluctuations in the Country During Historical Times," International Association of Hydrological Sciences; International Symposium on Scientific Basis for Water Resources Management, Jerusalem, Sept. 1985.

A paper by Harry Tabor entitled "Solar Ponds (Non-Convecting)" and delivered at a UNITAR conference on long-term energy sources in Montreal in 1979 (published by the Scientific Research Foundation), gave me an overview of the solar pond. An article entitled "The Leopards of the Judean Desert," by Giora Ilani, published in *Israel – Land and Nature* (vol. VI, no. 2, Winter 1980–81), discusses the conservation efforts made in Israel on

217

behalf of the threatened leopard, and a brief update may be found in vol. X, no. 4 (Summer 1985).

Other twentieth century works of general interest are: Sir George Adam Smith's *The Historical Geography of the Holy Land* (1902); Jacob E. Spafford's "Around the Dead Sea by Motor Boat," *The Geographic Journal* 39, 1912; *Down the Jordan in a Canoe*, by R.J.E. Boggis (London, 1939); and "Canoeing Down the River Jordan," by John D. Whiting, *The National Geographic Magazine* (vol. lxxviii, December, 1940).

Also, *The Dead Sea Region*, by Ben-Zion Eshel (Jerusalem, 1958); *The Dead Sea*, by Menachem Talmi (Tel Aviv, 1966); and Ze'ev Vilnay's *Legends of Judea and Samaria* (Philadelphia, 1975).

Nelson Glueck's books are immensely readable and make accessible to a non-scholarly audience his work on both sides of the Jordan River and in the Negev Desert: *The Other Side of the Jordan* (1940), *The River Jordan* (1946), and *Rivers in the Desert* (1959).

List of Illustrations

1. Cover: Map of the Dead Sea, with its various names, showing the Cities of the Plain in flames. From *A Pisgah-sight of Palestine,* by Thomas Fuller, 1650. From the Laor Cartographic Collection, Jewish National and University Library, Jerusalem.
2. Map of the Dead Sea region, p. 18.
3. The conquest of Jericho. From *Yosifon,* 1743, a Yiddish translation of *Josippon,* tenth century. From the collection of the Jewish National and University Library, Jerusalem, p. 30.
4. A view of the monastery Mar Saba and the Dead Sea, by David Roberts. From *The Holy Land,* vol. II, 1843. From the Laor Cartographic Collection, Jewish National and University Library, Jerusalem, p. 32.
5. Map of the Dead Sea, showing four of the Cities of the Plain submerged beneath its water, and the spared town of Zoar (upper left). From an 1867 facsimile of the original map (located at the Bodleian Library) which accompanied *The Itineraries of William Wey,* 1458 and 1462. From the Laor Cartographic Collection, Jewish National and University Library, Jerusalem, p. 42.
6. Section of the sixth-century Madaba map, the earliest known of the Dead Sea, showing the Dead Sea, with two boats, and a fish fleeing up the Jordan River. Map reproduced by the Survey of Israel and the Israel Exploration Society, from Palmer and Guthe's reproduction, 1906. From the Laor Cartographic Collection, Jewish National and University Library, Jerusalem, p. 45.
7. View of the Dead Sea. From *Picturesque Palestine*, vol. 2, edited by Charles Wilson, 1881. From the Laor Cartographic Collection, Jewish National and University Library, Jerusalem, p. 56.

8.   Map of the Dead Sea, showing Costigan's route, as drawn by John L. Stephens, based on the account of Costigan's servant and originally appearing in Stephens' *Incidents of Travel in Egypt, Arabia Petræa and the Holy Land,* by John Lloyd Stephens, Edited with an Introduction by Victor Wolfgang von Hagen. Copyright New edition ©1970 by the University of Oklahoma Press, p. 58.

9.   Pilgrims at the Jordan River. From *Landscape Illustrations of the Bible,* by T.H. Horne, 1836. From the Laor Cartographic Collection, Jewish National and University Library, Jerusalem, p. 65.

10.   William F. Lynch's caravan to the Sea of Galilee. From Lynch's *Narrative of the United States Expedition to the River Jordan and the Dead Sea,* 1849. From the Laor Cartographic Collection, Jewish National and University Library, Jerusalem, p. 79.

11.   The town of Tiberias and the Sea of Galilee, drawn after the earthquake of 1837, by David Roberts. From *The Holy Land,* vol. I, 1842. From the Laor Cartographic Collection, Jewish National and University Library, Jerusalem, p. 81.

12.   The immersion of the pilgrims, by David Roberts. From *The Holy Land,* vol. II, 1843. From the Laor Cartographic Collection, Jewish National and University Library, Jerusalem, p. 85.

13.   William F. Lynch's Camp Washington, at Ein Gedi, named in honor of "the greatest man the world has yet produced." From Lynch's *Narrative of the United States Expedition to the River Jordan and the Dead Sea,* 1849. From the Laor Cartographic Collection, Jewish National and University Library, Jerusalem, p. 88.

14.   William F. Lynch's guide, Sheikh 'Akīl Aga el Hasseé. From Lynch's *Narrative of the United States Expedition to the River Jordan and the Dead Sea,* 1849. From the Laor Cartographic Collection, Jewish National and University Library, Jerusalem, p. 91.

15.   Palestine Exploration Fund logo, as it appeared on the title page of *Tent Work in Palestine,* vol. 1, by Claude Conder, 1878. From the Laor Cartographic Collection, Jewish National and University Library, Jerusalem, p. 96.

16.   Ein es-Sultan, or Elisha's Spring, at Jericho. From *Landscape Illustrations of the Bible,* by T.H. Horne, 1836. From the Laor Cartographic Collection, Jewish National and University Library, Jerusalem, p. 99.

17.   Jericho. From *Liber cronicarum,* by Hartmann Schedel, Nürnberg, 1493 (published by Anton Koberger). From the Laor Cartographic Collection, Jewish National and University Library, Jerusalem, p. 102.

18.   Ein Gedi. From *Picturesque Palestine*, vol. 2, edited by Charles Wilson, 1881. From the Laor Cartographic Collection, Jewish National and University Library, Jerusalem, p. 108.

19.   View of Masada. From *Narrative of the United States Expedition to the River Jordan and the Dead Sea*, by William F. Lynch, 1849. From the Laor Cartographic Collection, Jewish National and University Library, Jerusalem, p. 117.

20.   Lot's Wife, with view towards the Dead Sea. From the colored frontispiece to *Desert of the Exodus*, part 1, by E.H. Palmer, 1871. From the Laor Cartographic Collection, Jewish National and University Library, Jerusalem, p. 120.

21.   Lot's Wife, with view from the Dead Sea. From *Narrative of the United States Expedition to the River Jordan and the Dead Sea*, by William F. Lynch, 1849. From the Laor Cartographic Collection, Jewish National and University Library, Jerusalem, p. 121.

22.   The Destruction of Sodom. From *Liber cronicarum*, by Hartmann Schedel, Nürnberg, 1493 (published by Anton Koberger). From the Laor Cartographic Collection, Jewish National and University Library, Jerusalem, p. 124.

23.   Wadi Mojib. From *Narrative of the United States Expedition to the River Jordan and the Dead Sea*, by William F. Lynch, 1849. From the Laor Cartographic Collection, Jewish National and University Library, Jerusalem, p. 143.

24.   The eastern shore of the Dead Sea. From *The Land of Moab*, by Henry Baker Tristram, 1874. From the Laor Cartographic Collection, Jewish National and University Library, Jerusalem, p. 146.

25.   View of the Dead Sea. From *Picturesque Palestine*, vol. 3, edited by Charles Wilson, 1881. From the Laor Cartographic Collection, Jewish National and University Library, Jerusalem, p. 155.

Photograph gallery follows p. 128.

Index